BLOOD RIVER

BLOOD RIVER

The Passionate Saga of South Africa's Afrikaners
and of Life in their Embattled Land

by
BARBARA VILLET
photographs by Grey Villet

NEW YORK EVEREST HOUSE PUBLISHERS

Library of Congress Cataloging in Publication Data:

Villet, Barbara.
  Blood river.

  Includes index.
  1. Afrikaners—History.   2. South Africa—Race
  relations.   3. South Africa—History.—1. Villet, Grey.
II. Title.
DT888.V54   1982   968'.0043936   81-22077
ISBN 0-89696-034-X   AACR2

Published by Everest House
33 West 60th Street, New York, New York 10023
Published simultaneously in Canada by
Beaverbooks, Don Mills, Ontario
Manufactured in the United States of America
Designed by Judith Lerner
First Edition   RRD782

CONTENTS

BOOK ONE

—◆◆—

South Africa:
The Paradoxical Present

CONTRASTS AND CONTRADICTIONS

A SUBTLE SIGNAL of jet engines indicated that the Pan Am flight out of Rio had begun its long glide down out of the South Atlantic night toward the coast of Africa. Below, the Black Sea, where Diaz and da Gama had once sailed their mothlike ships toward unknown destinations, rolled salt mists up over the deserts of Namibia, feeding its microlife, shrouding its emptiness. Somewhere to the north lay Angola and Zaire, stretching beyond the arid reaches of the Kalahari "thirstland." There the last surviving remnants of the Bushmen, who had once commanded all of this land, had hidden from the onslaughts of black men and white, of time and change, only to find themselves caught in this century in crosscurrents of a new struggle for the hidden riches of a subcontinent on which the modern alchemists of high technology depended to work their powerful magic. Chrome, manganese, cobalt, platinum, vanadium—more than half of the known supply of the stuff upon which the West depended to alloy its stainless steel, refine its oil, build its power plants, jet engines, computers, nuclear warheads, run its cars, trains, planes, its communications networks, its defense plants—all were down there in the African night. And ahead, astride its vein of treasure miles long and deep lay the city of gold, "Egoli," Johannesburg, our destination.

As the cabin lights went up and John Denver's disembodied voice twanged "Country roads, take me home, back to the place where I belong . . ." I had the sensation of coming back to a land almost as familiar to me as the corner of the American Northeast where I lived. South Africa. "Two and a half times the size of Texas. Larger than the combined areas of West Germany, France, Italy, the Netherlands and Belgium," so the fact book in my purse read, "South Africa can be divided into four major geographical regions: the narrow coastal belt . . . the Little Karoo, a narrow tableland . . . separated from the coastal belt by the Langeberg and Outeniqua mountain ranges . . . The Great Karoo . . . with altitudes varying between 1,900 and 2,700 feet . . . The high veld . . ." I could conjure visions from each. Elegant old Cape Town, climbing up toward Table Mountain beneath its cloud "tablecloth," reflected more than three centuries of history not only in the solid curves of its Cape Dutch architecture but in the faces of its people. It was a city of blends, done in pastels. Its faces were varicolored: European whites, pale coffee Coloreds, golden Malay, Xhosa brown, a rare Zulu black. One even saw the cast of Bushmen eyes in the street and followed the rump of a Hottentot through its crowds. A city of flowers and the sad sound of penny whistles, Cape Town was surrounded by ruled vineyards that terraced northward toward an upthrust of mountains that ran eastward, cutting the Cape's gentle coastal plain off from the hard semideserts beyond, and reaching to the sea just south of Port Elizabeth. Beyond that city's industrial sprawl lay the green Transkei, home to 5 million Xhosa. The Transkei had been declared an independent black republic in the sixties. We had been there, covering the elections as a reporter-photographer team, when its orange-blanketed tribal people had voted for their first all black government in 1963, and afterwards had spent months traveling through South Africa, my husband's homeland, to document its life for a Time-Life book.

Inland lay the Karoos, great and small. White with heat on a summer's day, populated by aloes standing like dessicated soldiers on moonscape "koppies" and by desert-hardened Afrikaners and Coloreds, both deserts were places of primordial power that reminded one of Greece and godly forces. Farther north, where Johannesburg glittered on its "ridge of white waters," lay the high veld. Lion colored, but now a land of cattle, it seemed to long for the multitudes of buck, wildebeest, and zebra that now ran only in the great Kruger game reserve, which claimed the northern corner of the Transvaal. Crowded out by the black man and the white, the animals had taken refuge in its "feverlands," hard by Mozambique, which the southward migrating Nguni tribes, the forebears of today's Xhosa, Swazi, and Zulu, had disdained when they had come to the region sometime around 1500. The Zulu are now South Africa's largest ethnic group. Over 6 million strong, they account for a third of its 19.8 million blacks and by themselves outnumber its 4.5 million whites. Roughly half still live in a tribal twilight in Qwa Zulu. A patchwork of eleven pieces of territory, scattered through Natal,

South Africa's Indian Ocean province, Qwa Zulu was one of ten such "homelands" which had been set aside for its tribal groups under its policy of "separate development." And therein lay the root of much of modern South Africa's grief. For while roughly 9.5 million blacks subsisted in the "homelands," and another 9.5 million blacks, 2.6 million Coloreds of mixed ancestry, and 800,000 Asians scrambled to dig their way out of poverty in South Africa's cities, the country's ruling minority of 4.5 million whites had waxed wealthy on the profits from South Africa's advanced economy and abundant cheap labor.

In most accounts of South Africa, blame for this unhappy state of affairs was laid at the doorstep of the country's white Afrikaner minority. A fractional percentage of South Africa's total population of 27.7 million, the 2.7 million Afrikaners who claimed descent from its early Dutch, German, and French settlers, nevertheless represent a majority of its 4.5 million whites and they had used this narrow margin to dominate South African politics ever since their unified vote had brought the ruling National Party to power in 1948. In the ensuing decades, the Afrikaners had not only consistently condoned the Nationalists' refusal to grant South Africa's non-white majority any say in its political life but until recently had unswervingly supported the grandiose schemes of "separate development" hatched by their late Prime Minister, Hendrik Verwoerd.

Theoretically meant to defuse the potential for racial conflict in South Africa by creating separate ethnic homelands and Group Areas for its blacks, Coloreds, Asians, and whites, "separate development" and "apartheid" were regarded instead by most of South Africa's critics as a cynical attempt to block eventual majority rule and save white privilege by forcing the blacks to "hive off" into a series of dependent "national states" and requiring them to forfeit their citizenship in the republic. As migrant workers from these satellite states, it was reasoned, they could neither claim the privileges of citizenship nor demand fair labor practices of its government but would remain available as a "labor pool" to be exploited in its white-owned industry. Consequently, in most analyses, not only were the Afrikaners cast as the villains in the strange morality play of South African politics, but because "apartheid" left the disenfranchised majority with no means other than violent ones to protest their economic and political dispossession, the Afrikaners were also commonly blamed for the rising wave of black unrest inside the country. Yet as persuasive as this argument seemed, the better one knew South Africa and the Afrikaners, the less plausible it became. Simplistic, it not only disregarded the awesome complexity of South African life but the ironic truth that in the last twenty years the land of "apartheid" had done more to advance the cause of black development than any other nation on the continent.

In the nineteen fifties and sixties, South Africa had been caught in one of the maelstroms of history. The old colonial order that had ruled Africa for centuries was dying, a series of new black states were being born of its travail and the Afrikaners had faced a daunting prospect as the winds of change had carried the cries of "Uhuru" (Freedom) throughout the continent. For unlike the British, French, German, Belgian, and Portuguese colonials who had packed their bags, one by one, and abandoned Africa to its fate, the Afrikaners had no place else to go. Cut off from Europe three hundred years before, formed blood and sinew in Africa, it was their only home. As a consequence, the Afrikaners had been required to confront problems within South Africa that derived from the vast cultural and economic distances between the so-called First and Third Worlds which the rest of the West had quietly walked away from and their answer to them had been to propose the "separate development" of South Africa's whites, Coloreds, Asians, and blacks.

Hendrik Verwoerd, who became Prime Minister of South Africa in 1958, had been the principal architect of this racial policy. Aware of the hunger of Africa's impoverished masses to obtain through the use of revolutionary politics and expropriation economics the powers and privileges their white rulers had flaunted, Verwoerd had met the rise of black nationalism inside South Africa by proposing to give blacks and other non-whites precisely what the Afrikaners had always wanted for themselves: political independence and racial isolation. Under a "blueprint for the future" which called for the subdivision of South Africa into a series of "Group Areas" and "Black Homelands" whose economic development was to be guided and largely funded by the wealthy white core state, Verwoerd's plan was expected to bring the latter to full political independence by the 1980's.

Already persuaded that God had set them apart in Africa to serve some special purpose, most Afrikaners accepted Verwoerd's schemes in the belief that they represented a return to the God-given tribal order of a millennial past and would consequently check the incipient chaos that threatened South Africa's peace. Moreover, as I had moved among them in 1963, I had realized that no matter how contrary to my own liberal predilections the politics of "apartheid" might be, the Arikaners were not a nation of brutal cynics, wholly concerned with the preservation of their economic privilege, but zealots, committed to what they believed to be a just if not holy cause. Persuaded that order must prevail if black as well as white South Africans were to be saved from the kind of regressive chaos that had begun to overtake much of the rest of Africa, and cognizant of the special risk they faced as the last "white tribe" on the continent, they had worn their convictions like an armor against both their fears for South Africa's future and the world's condemnation of their policies. In doing so, they were fully aware that time could run out for them before their radically reactionary reforms might bear fruit and prove their "virtue" to the world. For even then South Africa and the Afrikaners had been afforded little understanding and less tolerance than that allowed by the world's liberal press to equally repressive oligarchies possessed of the singular 20th-century virtue of being racially homogeneous. And in the decade and a half since Verwoerd's death, little reporting on the country had been without bias. Revolted by the Afrikaners' racial repressiveness, the press had continued to side with the "black majority" even after much of the rest of Africa had begun to slide into a political quagmire and it had become apparent that though "expropriation economics" and revolution had served the interests of a new black power elite in many African states, neither had done much to ameliorate the poverty of the masses.

By the end of the seventies, however, the question of "order" versus "chaos" and of conservative versus liberal values in South Africa had taken on a new urgency as one after another state in southern Africa had declared itself a "People's Republic" with Soviet and Cuban help. The moral questions represented by the Afrikaners' racial policies had become critical to the West. The last bastion of "white rule" on the continent, South Africa was also the most powerful and developed state south of the Sahara. Sitting athwart the route of the oil supertankers on their way from the Indian Ocean to Europe and America, it also held a position pivotal to the control of southern Africa's trove of critical resources. Whatever else it was, South Africa had emerged as one of the turning points of world politics since we had last traveled there, and for this reason we had been drawn back as journalists for another long look at the paradoxical Afrikaners who ruled it.

The plane, wheeling low over the spider web of lights delineating Johannesburg by night, made a smooth landing. In a few minutes we were through customs and on our way by cab into the city on a new "fly-over" freeway. Suddenly the towers of Johannesburg loomed against a velvet sky in which the Southern Cross hung low, seeming to drip fire. The city had become worldly and opulent since we had last seen it, and as we commented on its growth, our black driver, a Sotho from the tiny black enclave of Lesotho, high in the Drakensberg mountains, turned his head and beamed as if accepting a personal compliment. "Yah," he breathed, gesturing possessively toward the shining city, "this is the greatest country in the world. The greatest."

2

AFRIKANER ENCOUNTERS

Morning came early. From the hotel windows I looked down on Johannesburg. One could still find a few of the low sand-colored buildings with tin-roofed verandas that had given the city a wild-west-cum-colonial look in the sixties, but the overall impression was one of newness. Glass towers reflected the cloud-clotted veld sky. Freeways segmented the city's center. But for the hill-high heaps of yellow tailings from the gold mines, which perforated the ridge on which the city stood, Johannesburg might have been Houston. That it worshipped the same capitalist deities as its American architectural cousin also seemed evident. Above many of its most impressive buildings, the logos of great corporations had been raised heavenward to give witness that this was a city devoted to money and power and was South Africa's financial mecca. Shell, BP, IBM, Volkswagen, Datsun, Toyota, GM, Barclays Bank, Peugeot—all discreetly acknowledged their presence and with it the fact that, over the past twenty years, thriving Western investment in South Africa had accounted for 40 percent of its growth. With abounding affluence, moreover, Johannesburg seemed to have mellowed in mood. As we strolled its streets later in the day, searching out the familiar to get a grip on the new, from the fusty financial district where the Chamber of Mines and Anglo-American ruled to the "swinging" district of Hillbrow, it seemed that despite a spate of racial violence over the last several years, Johannesburg was more tolerant racially after thirty years of "apartheid" than it had been after fifteen. In its squares, blacks and whites shared the same urban patches of greenery. Black students studied in the reading rooms of its libraries. Blacks, Indians, Coloreds, and whites played the same electronic games in Hillbrow's amusement halls and even illegally shared flats in that "liberated" district. Many restaurants were mixed and most of the restrictive signs prohibiting blacks from areas once designated for "whites only" had disappeared. If one avoided Sauer Street, where tatterdemalion crowds of blacks and Coloreds by the thousands congregated in the evenings to catch the battered buses for Soweto, the outward signs that Johannesburg might be actively cultivating integration were everywhere and many whites with whom we spoke in the days immediately following our arrival were anxious to reinforce the impression.

On our first Sunday we met a brace of Afrikaners active in the cause of improved racial relations at a "braaivleis," a traditional Afrikaner cookout of lamb chops and boerewors, a savory sausage, given at their country hideaway by Johannesburg journalist Martie Meiring and her architect husband. The party had originally been laid on for the benefit of a black journalist and his wife from Washington, D.C., who were visiting South Africa on a whirlwind two-week tour organized by the South Africa Foundation, and though unsponsored, we had apparently seemed a serendipitous addition to the guest list.

Given the party's purpose, the conversation had had a certain predictability. Naas Steenkamp, a prominent young economist, talked urgently and at an astonishing pace about the pressures within the South African economy militating toward its integration and of the simultaneous need to create a new black middle class to fill middle management jobs. Sarie Steenkamp, his wife, an ethereal elfin creature with a distinct resemblance to the youthful Audrey Hepburn, and

Freida van Rooyen, a large blonde with a fluting voice, spoke of their organization Kontak, an Afrikaner woman's group that was attempting to bring whites, Colored, and Indian women together in the cause of interracial understanding. It had all had the surreal familiarity of a New York civil rights cocktail party, circa 1956, until the guest of honor asked Martie Meiring why her house was surrounded by an electrified fence. "To keep out the animals," she responded mildly, gazing down across the empty meadows in front of the cottage. "They trample the gardens." Dissatisfied with the explanation, the man asked the same question of Naas Steenkamp a few minutes later, implying that he thought the fence might be a protective device meant to keep out more than animals. "It's to keep out the cows," Steenkamp answered firmly. "There are some about, after all."

"The animals belong to the family that lives here full time," Martie Meiring offered in a soothing tone. "Shall we go back and see them?"

Following at her heels we walked a short distance through a grove of wattles to a sunny clearing in which a low, gray-brown adobe house, painted in geometric patterns of pale sky blue and white stood. "This is a traditional Pedi house," she explained cheerfully. "This was Pedi country before we Afrikaners got here. Some joined with us because the Matabele had been slaughtering them. This family has lived here for as long as this farm has existed." A golden-brown man, his body corded by age, greeted us with a gap-toothed smile. "Good day, Josef," Mrs. Meiring said easily. "We've come to say hello."

"Middag," he responded in Afrikaans, nodding slightly as the two took up a conversation in that softly guttural tongue, each asking the health of the other's family.

"His granddaughter had a bad accident," she told us as we turned away toward her cottage. "Her leg was shattered and she had dreadful surgery. But she'll walk." We learned later from another Afrikaner at the party that the Meirings had paid for her hospitalization. "It's in the tradition. We take care of our own," was the comment, which summarized a rural ethic as old as the Afrikaners' relationship with the black man. "It'll take a while for *that* to change." Back at the Meirings's cottage, our black compatriots began to talk of the pressing travel schedule they faced and Naas Steenkamp offered to return them to their integrated "international class" hotel.

When they were gone, leaving an impression of deep uneasiness behind them, Freida van Rooyen approached. "I hope he knows we are sincere in our efforts," she fluted, "and I hope you'll agree that our racial problems in this country are of a wholly different order from yours in America." A breeze moved in the blue gum trees as she spoke. Their sharp scent brought an incongruous recollection to my mind of the funeral of a Quechua boy I had once attended, high in the impoverished Andean interior. It seemed suddenly that immense distances separated all of us, and though I had no idea what emotions might have passed through the mind of the urbane man from Washington when he had met the old man in the wattle grove, I knew that, for me at least, the afternoon's strange encounters had suggested a racial cat's cradle whose complexities extended well beyond South Africa.

The next day I made two appointments, one with Tom Vosloo, editor of the Afrikaans newspaper, *Beeld,* who was reputed to be an astute and enlightened observer of Afrikaner politics, and the second with Piet van der Merwe, then chief economist in the Prime Minister's office. His vested suit notwithstanding, Tom Vosloo turned out to be one of those straightforward, rolled-up-sleeves sort of journalists with whom I'd come of age, and as he waded into his analysis of the political situation in South Africa, I found myself liking him. He accepted my unspoken skepticism. He seemed ambivalent about the Afrikaners' penchant for political repressiveness, even as he sought to explain it by giving me a thumbnail sketch of recent Afrikaner history, and he badly wanted to believe his own argument that the trend toward economic integration in South Africa would lead inevitably to political integration as well.

He had begun his analysis of the present political situation in South Africa by drawing a lesson from his own life. The son of working class parents who had been driven off the land during what he called the "mud and dung years of the depression," Tom Vosloo represented his own background as typical of most "rank and file" Afrikaners who supported the Nationalist party. Men of his father's generation, born on drought-ravaged farms of the great tablelands of the Free State and Transvaal, had become railway workers, policemen, and factory hands. "The low men," he called them, explaining that it had been their resentments of the city-bred English South Africans, who then controlled most of South Africa's wealth, that had given birth to modern Afrikaner nationalism. "We were afraid of the English," he admitted, "and when the Nationalist party finally came to power in 1948 by a margin of five seats in Parliament, it was our fear of English dominance that made us wary of moving toward integration because we'd seen them use the black man to further their own interests too many times before. Our compulsion to legalisms," he explained, "was based on insecurity."

But such fears were now behind the Afrikaners, Tom Vosloo insisted. Two generations removed from the platteland, better educated and better informed, these "new men" were increasingly in control of the National party and increasingly open to change and experiment. "The new technocrat is not what his father was," he reassured me. "He has a dichotomy of soul. He clings to the old tribal identity of his people, a minority identity like that of the Basques and Walloons or the French in Quebec. He cherishes his heritage and wishes to safeguard it against both absorption in the English-speaking world and in black Africa. But he's also aware that the urban blacks, in particular, must be accommodated. So our problem is how *do* you provide safeguards? Insure the Afrikaners tenure in Africa? You plan odd groupings. You redraw the map. You give away portions of the country to black homelands, and you're still left with a multiracial state that must be run on some confederated basis that will protect every group's interests. . . . So we are looking at power-sharing models, Cantons, Turnhalles, Federalist models. It's going politics at cabinet level, and Parliament is full of 35- and 40-year-old Afrikaners who are working in on the old line."

Vosloo offered as evidence of their effectiveness the progressive relaxation of the "hardline," which had begun with the racial integration of South Africa's playing fields and theaters in the 70's and progressed to official recognition of the right of black labor unions to strike and the creation of a racially mixed President's Council to advise on political reforms. He also noted the increasing presence of Coloreds and blacks in jobs once considered by Afrikaners to be strictly reserved for whites. "You can't educate them and not give them jobs, and economic integration now leads inevitably to political integration later," he told me confidently. "If you forget the grandies—the old folks who say we must keep the blacks down—you'll find that most Afrikaners today are prepared to live pretty normally with blacks and accept new configurations in our society. We know that to survive we must adapt. We've no Masada complex. We'd like to stay around, and this means it is up to us to devise a system in which people of particular nationalisms based on color can live together in peace—a system that will protect our interests as a minority as well as serve the needs of the black majority. It's our survival that is at stake, after all, and though we're past the days of thinking we can run the country for everyone, we've still got a helluva problem here—a brutal clash of numbers and cultures that could destroy us if we moved too fast."

From Tom Vosloo's point of view as an Afrikaner, the assessment he had given me was realistic, but as I groped my way across Johannesburg in the white light of midday to keep my next appointment, it occurred to me that there was a queer similarity between his statement that it was "up to" the Afrikaners to "devise" a new political model that would shape the future of South Africa's black majority and the Meirings's automatic acceptance of their responsibility for the well-being of their Pedi farmhand's granddaughter. Both smacked of "noblesse oblige" and seemed to rest on a set of peculiarly anachronistic assumptions, given what Vosloo himself had described as "the brutal clash of numbers and cultures" in South Africa, and as Piet van der Merwe documented that clash of numbers for me in the next hour, they were to appear no less so.

A slim, silvery man, haggard with years of attempting to rationalize the complexity of South African life in economic terms, Piet van der Merwe sat in an office cluttered with papers and charts projecting the shape of the country's future, and during our conversation he gestured vaguely in their direction several times with the distracted air of a man ascending quietly toward madness. "Some of the most pressing problems we face over the next twenty years are those associated with population growth," he began softly. "Tribal overruns that beg the question of how we are going to create sufficient employment for blacks before they fall prey to Marxism and rage."

He began to lay out facts like a man playing the Tarot pack, and I found his reading of them sobering. Numbers were attached to words like "regression," "unacceptable unemployment," and "subsistence," as he spoke of the need for "labor intensive schemes" in the "homelands" to prevent blacks from "flocking" into the cities. Charts were presented to illustrate the inability of the core economy to provide sufficient jobs to meet the needs of an ever-growing black population without stringent "influx controls." One chart indicated black population curves exploding upward in the funnel shape of a tornado, squeezing all of the other population lines aside. I knew that I was looking at the shape of the "Black Peril," a specter often raised by the Afrikaners to justify their political schemes of "apartheid" in the sixties but that fact did not make van der Merwe's assessment of the eighties any less dismaying, considering that every earlier prediction of black population growth had been outrun by reality in the seventies. He was clearly persuaded that his bleak scenario was true and that without carefully rationalized management of South Africa's oversupply of black labor, which subordinated black interests to the cause of economic order, chaos awaited. "We believe influx controls are preferable to anarchy," he said wearily about halfway through the interview. "The world asks 'Why are influx controls limited to blacks?' The answer lies in the demographic fact that only 33 percent of 19 million blacks in this country are urbanized. The potential for their further urbanization is enormous, and that means that we face all the problems of transforming a Third World people into a First World people in a generation! How do you cope? How do you plan?" he asked, with a sigh that verged on a shudder. "How do you persuade the Afrikaners who are reactive and afraid of all that this implies to try to live on *positive* terms with the blacks, to establish cooperation, to give up their fears and their fundamentalist faith for the kinds of uncertainty we deal with here in this office every day?"

Back at the hotel the black room clerk who had been on duty since six that morning and would go off at midnight handed me my room key. Upstairs, one of his Zulu compatriots, who had slipped through "influx controls" to find employment at the hotel, polished the already gleaming floors. Paid less than the legal wage by the Portuguese Angolan refugees who ran the hotel, he sent all that he earned back to his wife and children in the impoverished tribal "homeland" from which he had come. The Colored maid, Doris, had told me his story "He has to stick to this job," she said, "because the employer won't give him the paper form to take to the pass office so he can get a 'pass.' That means he must work for less and when he gets caught by the police, he must either pay a twenty-rand bribe or go to court and be fined twenty-five rand and be sent home. So he makes himself invisible, never leaves the hotel, and sends all he can home. I'm sorry for him," she added, "but not for the young black 'tsotsies' in Soweto. They have no jobs. They are black animals. We are afraid all the time, afraid they will come at night to kill and rob us. When I was growing up in Sophiatown, it wasn't like this," she said. "It makes me sick to my heart to remember. We had Zulu on this side, Xhosa on that, Shangaan and Sotho the other way. We all knew each other. We all ate together and played together. Now we hate each other. We are afraid of each other. It's 'apartheid.' We have to hate and fear each other because we live apart and cannot know each other."

3
THE VIEW FROM QWA ZULU

We drove country roads down to Qwa Zulu, the homeland of the "invisible" man who polished the floors in our Johannesburg hotel. We went southeast from Johannesburg through the cloud-patterned reaches of the high veld. Wild cosmos streamed rosy stars shoulder high along the roadside but the land beyond was buck-colored, a subtle blend of brown, tan, shadow gray, and blue. On the way I searched for a ghost—a ubiquitous lone figure whom I had seen along every byway on my previous visit. Black, ragged, and barefoot, he had come to represent South Africa to me. He was not there. In his stead I saw blacks driving battered Toyota vans and new Fords and at the roadsides black children wearing school pinafores and carrying their shoes, evidently waiting for a lift to school.

The road cut through rich grasslands. The farms, all Afrikaans, were often named for women, as if the farmers here wanted to give the earth itself the name of someone familiar and beloved. To the southeast, we could see the clouds piling up over the Drakensberg range, which marked the great fault where the earth sheared away into Natal. At a town called Winburg, where we should have turned east, we mistakenly continued south to come upon a soaring monument to the Voortrekkers, the Afrikaner pioneers who had opened this land to white settlement in 1838. A self-conscious plinth with wagon wheels worked into the base, the monument told less about the bold men and women who had come this way in their covered wagons a century and a half before than about the valley surrounding it. The fields were ruled. The white houses were unpretentious but set slightly apart from the painted adobe dwellings, decorated in the sky's blue, earth's reds, and sorghum's golds, where the native farmhands lived. Called "Edenville," the place seemed to deserve its name, although the region had been fought over for centuries and successively claimed by the Bushmen, Barolong, Batlokua, Zulu, Matabele, Sotho, Boer, and Briton. As we wended our way eastward into Natal, other place names—Bethlehem, Harrismith, van Reenen, Tugela, Vryheid, Rorke's Drift, Ulundi—spoke of history and of the prayers, heroes, hopes, and anguish of those who had fought over this land.

Ulundi, the Zulu capital, was our destination, and as our objective was to take a firsthand look at homeland "development," we chose to reach it by using a cross-country route that carried us across two of the largest of Qwa Zulu's eleven segmented sections. The land was naked, devastated by years of overgrazing and burnt brown by sun and drought. In a back-country Zulu kraal, a nubile bare-breasted girl stared at us wide-eyed while a boy dressed in a loin cloth cavorted past, improbably playing a rather fine fiddle. Goats grazed on nothing. Old men, too indifferent to brush away the flies, squatted in the doorways of huts. Farther on we saw women turning the earth where a scrabble crop of maize had been harvested. Ulundi itself, however, was modern, proud with government buildings and a legislative assembly hall. The Afrikaner whose name we'd been given as the development officer attached to the transitional homeland govern-

ment made it abundantly clear he wished we had not come. Several
Mercedes Benz parked outside the buildings seemed in part to explain
why. The creation of an "infrastructure" and a governing black elite,
whom we had heard referred to as the "Wabenzi" elsewhere, coupled
with the costs of acquiring and consolidating lands and building
roads into the Zulu territories, had, he explained, consumed most of
its precious development budget. Those ground-level development
projects that did exist, he indicated, were in any case run by separate
development groups, among them the C.E.D.—the Council for Economic Development—a quasi-government agency that used private
as well as public funds in its work.

It took another half day to track down the senior C.E.D. man in
Qwa Zulu, but when we found Louis van den Aardweg he proved
to be another of those Afrikaner enthusiasts who believed South
Africa was on the "verge of great things." "It's all preparatory work
now," he admitted easily. "Just beginnings. But wonderful ones, and
when we have the homelands set and running, there will be one
South Africa, a federation of many states, white and black. We as
whites must accept that. And if the blacks will give us a bit of time,
it will come. It's all a matter of changing attitudes," he added cheerfully, "white and black alike and that does take time. Right here in
Qwa Zulu, for instance, Chief Buthelezi recognizes that he must have
sufficient trained blacks to assume leadership jobs before Qwa Zulu is
independent. So he wants to wait for his own people to be ready and
he's happy, meanwhile, to have us here doing the leadership jobs in
development until enough blacks are trained . . ." As I had heard
other young Afrikaners speak just as optimistically of homeland development many years before, van den Aardweg's enthusiasm seemed
rather too familiar and I asked how many on-going development
projects C.E.D. actually had. "Not as many as we need," he admitted, "but C.E.D. has doubled its investment in agriculture in the
last few years, will treble it in the next five, and is slated to spend
some 20 million rand on agricultural development this year. Our
objective is profit motive farming, commercial farming in the homelands. Here in Qwa Zulu, we've been buying land from whites, keeping it productive or making it so, and training the blacks as we go.
When they are ready we hand the farms over to them, and what

profits we've made meanwhile go back into new C.E.D. projects. We are even venturing on old tribal lands up in Tugela . . ."

Charles du Plessis, the man in charge of C.E.D.'s venture at Tugela estates, was 45, tough-minded, plainspoken and an "old Africa hand." He had joined C.E.D. in 1976 after black terrorists in Rhodesia had driven him off a farm he'd bought there. Before that, he'd been employed as the white foreman of a large tobacco plantation in Malawi, owned by that state's black President, Hastings Banda. His chief problems in Malawi, du Plessis recalled, had stemmed from the fact that Banda had paid his field workers R3 ($2.70) a month and had not provided them with food. "As those farms were fifty miles from nowhere and there were no stores," he said, "the men were quite simply starving and unable to work. I convinced Dr. Banda that if he wanted his tobacco, he had to feed his workers. When I left, they were being fed but still got three rand a month."

Tugela Estates had been purchased by C.E.D. in 1976. It had been a functioning citrus farm at the time, but soon after the local Zulu sub-tribes, the Majola and the Madondo, learned it was eventually to go to Qwa Zulu they had begun cutting down the ten-year-old citrus groves for firewood. "I could barely believe it," du Plessis said. "I'd come down here from the Transvaal, where I'd been working with blacks who were settled agriculturalists, to take over the estate, and I walked into an awful mess. These Zulu, you see, are a fighting tribe. They count their wealth in cattle, disdain to work the land, and in the past always answered their problems by raiding neighboring tribes and taking their beasts. The groves meant nothing to them, except something to fight over for firewood, and when I got here, my predecessor warned me there was trouble brewing. 'The impis [regiments] are gathering,' he told me. My driver, a Majola, said the same thing, said he couldn't work for me because the Madondo were getting ready to go on a rampage. I persuaded him to stay, but by January, in the full heat of summer, even I knew the factions were getting ready to attack each other. And one afternoon it came. They ambushed my driver and six others and killed them all. I went to retrieve the bodies. They'd been slashed to pieces by the young ones, 'wetting their spears' and I was back 200 years in time. No one would come to work after that. The men stayed under the trees near their huts for fear of being burned up by night. They'd talk all night, and the witch doctor would give them medicine. Then when the spirit was right, they'd go out and kill. On and on it went. The police came out, but they couldn't stop it. One evening I was just closing the gates here when I heard it, 'Uffa, Uffa, Uffa'—a weird breathing sound and there they were: an impi in full war colors, running in tight formation, inches apart, so that if one man misstepped they'd all fall. But they didn't. They streamed past like a machine with their spears gleaming and eyes all red and, I can tell you, the hairs raised on my neck. That night two Madondo and twenty Majola were killed. And it goes on and on, all over Zululand. Why, over at Tugela Ferry, C.E.D. got *given* a farm because the Matemba and the Qamu, their enemies, had been fighting for so many years that *nobody* could farm. It's been going on for a donkey's age. I tried to find out why and learned that maybe a century ago someone did something to a woman, but no one can entirely remember why, because this year they'll be back at it, then lick their wounds and lick 'em until they're up again next year. Can you imagine it? They roll down here from Johannesburg in their Toyotas and Datsuns when the impis are up. They take off their city clothes and put on their skins and revert 200 years! That night when I saw them I said, look here, these aren't an apparition! These are *men. Men!* It chills you. Here you are trying to teach modern farming methods in a place where they keep reverting to a fighting society. Ulundi tried to stop them. Buthelezi ordered that they stop building a school here as a punishment. It's still unbuilt. The kids go to school next to its foundation. The factions go on fighting. And in between we get some farming done, persuade one or two to try sorghum, which is drought-resistant, in the place of maize which isn't. And we try to show them how to raise cotton as a cash crop. Ach, man, it's a crazy business. But I like it. I like to study their customs. And besides, you have to work with people as they are. They are strict people, used to strict disciplines of their own, so that's the way I treat them—and it seems to work."

We walked over Tugela Estate with Charles du Plessis that afternoon, visiting the cotton fields, which were being harvested by mixed groups of Majola and Madondo women. A few older men sat outside their adobe houses, while other women, dressed in beads and cowhide kilts tanned a dark chocolate color that matched their shining skins, tended children and goats. In the middle of the village, school was improbably in session al fresco, taught by a young Zulu woman in Western clothes wearing a beret as if she were in Johannesburg. The children worked on slates and wrote in English as well as Zulu.

Back at du Plessis' home—the original plantation house set atop a knoll where soft breezes played in the evening—we surveyed his domain: the patches of cotton fields on both sides of the river, the remaining citrus trees, the ribbon of road linking the Madondo and Majola kraals, and felt curiously out of touch with time. "Our planning here goes only so far as trying to teach them to be better farmers," Charles du Plessis said, as we prepared to take our leave in the dusk. "Eventually we'll cut up these lands of mine into two and three hectare plots for those who will come forward and be permanent farmers. We'll plow and disc and plant and irrigate for them, but they'll have to keep it clean of water weed and pick the cotton. And then we'll buy it and transport it and begin to develop a cash crop economy down here. Right now, though, they are hanging back. It's the women who do all the work. They work the fields, carry the wood, carry the water, everything. They are immensely strong and can carry thirty liters of water on their heads straight up a hill with a kid on one arm and another gallon of water on the other. But the men won't work, except when they fulfill the Zulu prophecy and go on a 'journey' up to Johannesburg. Still, we've a few learning to drive lorries and tractors. And we've the women. They earn 70 to 80 cents in a day picking cotton, and we've moved 3,300 bales out of here, so I'm encouraged. I guess I like the challenge. Like to see things happen. But I'd like them to come along out of the past now too."

We stayed the night at Weenen, a village just over the edge of Qwa Zulu in Natal territory. Its name in Afrikaans meant "The Weeping," for in 1838, the remnants of a Voortrekker column, which had been attacked by Zulu impis along the Tugela and lost some five hundred men, women, and children, had gathered here to grieve their dead. It was a tiny town, with a single main street of shops, many of which were run by Indians, a scattering of houses, and a pink hotel. There were Zulu women of several clans about, dressed in costumes like birds of paradise, but we were to discover that in some ways they were no more exotic than the regular patrons of the Weenen hotel. These counted among them a man who had made his living milking cobras and other poisonous snakes and whose hands had become so scarred that they were little more than crippled clubs; an elderly Englishman who sang through dinner; a clutch of demented old folks who had been deposited at the hotel by families who had never returned but sent checks monthly; the innkeeper proprietor who was building a fifty-foot boat of concrete in the hotel's backyard—a ghost ship of silver gray, marooned a hundred miles from the sea. It was his dream one day to sail it around the world. "But I don't expect that will happen," he said matter-of-factly, "because most ports are closed to South African vessels, and one can't just go sailing on and on and on and never call in anywhere, now can one?" Cuckoos called in the dusk. I felt as if I had stumbled on stage midway in a play by Samuel Beckett and wondered if Weenen's dottiness didn't come from living on a cultural fault line that might rupture any day, bringing the world crashing down about it.

4
THE VOICE OF TRADITION

Social seismology is an inexact business. Even the most highly reputed interpreters of those social rumblings said to presage revolutions can misread the signs, which may account for the fact that there have been warnings of an imminent "Fire to come to South Africa" for at least twenty years. Nevertheless, to live in a land where social tremors, presaging that the end is near, recur with the same regularity as those seismic upsets indicating that the west coast of America is about to cleave off into the Pacific, *can* produce cultural peculiarities of the same order as one finds in California. And about a week after we had returned from Qwa Zulu to Johannesburg we realized that the cultural fault line that ran through Weenan apparently extended all the way up to the Witwatersrand.

We had been invited by Freida Van Rooyen to a dinner party, arranged so that we might meet a neighbor of hers, an elderly woman who had been incarcerated by the British during the Anglo-Boer War at the turn of the century. The other guests were all to be Afrikaners of the professional classes, some of whom were active in Kontak's cause of "interracial understanding." Intrigued by what the guest of honor might have to tell us, we had accepted the invitation, but almost as soon as we had arrived at the van Rooyen's house, an unorthodox structure laid out in what seemed to be the form of a wagon wheel, I began to experience a peculiar sense of mental slippage that indicated I was back on uneasy psychological ground, and as the evening wore on the sensation grew more acute.

As promised, the company was varied. The doctor son of the elderly guest of honor, deferred entirely to his mother at the outset, but after Mrs. van Rooyen's superior wines had begun to loosen his tongue, he had taken to imitating American accents, badly. A lawyer, wearing a cashmere jacket in "racing checks," made a number of references to his political connections in high places but otherwise talked only of the rugby game he had seen that afternoon. As neither his wife nor the doctor's ventured any comments, other than on the excellence of Mrs. van Rooyen's beef Wellington, the conversation had moved naturally from rugby to religion, another Afrikaner national passion. One of two young ministers of the Nederduits Gereformeerde Kerk, the most powerful denomination of the Dutch Reformed Church in South Africa, among the guests, had begun to tell us about "Koinonia," an ecumenical organization working for racial reforms. But as he was describing one of its offshoots, a movement to "Learn Together," which brought together whites and blacks—the latter largely the live-in house servants of the former—on week-nights in church halls, he was interrupted suddenly by the other minister. This thickset young man, wearing an electric-blue suit, asked me abruptly, "What do you think of the Declaration of Independence?"

"Why do you ask?" I had blurted, more startled by the hostility of his tone than by his question, which did not seem out of order in the context of the conversation. "Because," he had rasped back in a voice hard with tension, "it is one of the most corrupt documents ever written and I will tell you why."

Launching forthwith into a withering attack on Jefferson's eloquent evocation of "truths" most Americans "hold to be self-evident," the angry young "dominee" had proceeded to condemn the Declaration for its corrupt "humanism," its "impious notions" of equality, and

its godless goals. "How," he had demanded to know, his black eyes glittering, "could anyone consider all men to be created equal when some were tall, some short, some brilliant and too many fools?" God, he had insisted, had made all and made them unequal in accordance to His inscrutable Will—some to be saved, some to be damned. God has preordained the spheres of human endeavor and the spheres of human society from before all time, marking some men for mastery and others for servitude in accordance with His own divine plan, and to question His Order was as blasphemous as to claim that the "pursuit of life, liberty and happiness" in this world was of any consequence whatsoever.

With amazement, I had realized I was listeing to thinking that was centuries old, which recalled the preachings of Cotton Mather at Massachusetts Bay and of John Calvin, who had conceived in 1534 the creed on which it was based; the arguments of a man whose mind apparently was untouched by the ideas that had set all of Europe and America ablaze during the 18th-century Enlightenment. But even as I had pondered the anachronism of his thought, I had realized with astonishment that, as the young man in the electric-blue suit had spoken, lapsing at times into an impassioned Afrikaans, no one else at the table but my husband and I had found anything bizarre in his argument. On the contrary, not a few of the other guests had seemed to regard my defense of this document, whose nobility had heretofore seemed to me to require no defense, to be as demented as his ravings seemed to me. And at that moment of furious confrontation, as I felt my mind begin to tilt and spin into another realm, I realized suddenly that heretofore I had been looking at South African life from an angle of vision so utterly foreign to that of my dinner companions that my perceptions of its realities and theirs existed on a different plane. Like Alice-down-the-rabbit-hole, I had landed, half bewildered, in Afrikanerland, right between the main course and dessert, to realize that, for all the deceptive similarities between their society and that of present-day America and Europe, the Afrikaners were a unique people whose thinking could be as alien to most Americans as that of the mullahs of Iran. For not only did South Africa sit athwart a cultural fault line that ran between the First and Third Worlds, which threatened perennially to open up and swallow the country whole, but the Afrikaners themselves brought a

substantially different set of perceptions to their precarious situation. Time, it seemed, had unwound itself differently in South Africa. And because the 16th, 17th, and 20th centuries were intimately intertwined there, the intellectual and emotional references that many Afrikaners brought to their present dilemma had, until very recently, belonged almost exclusively to an age that had been all but forgotten elsewhere in the Western world. To make them comprehensible, therefore, it was going to be necessary for me, as a journalist, to go back to the beginning of their evolution as a nation and, by bringing past and present to bear upon each other, to reconstruct the peculiar patchwork of historic experience that made them what they are.

BOOK TWO

---◆·◆---

A People Set Apart

5
CAPE BEGINNINGS

THERE ARE untouched coves along the Cape coasts where one can still see primordial southern Africa as it once was—coves in which the elephant-footed mountains, clothed only in brush and mist, rise gray out of the sea, and the wind speaks of enormous emptinesses. In them, it is possible to imagine how the curved shore of the bay, lying at the foot of Table Mountain, must have looked to the two hundred men and scattering of women and children who arrived there in April of 1652 aboard three small Dutch ships. These Netherlanders and Germans, commanded by 32-year-old Jan van Riebeeck, were under orders to develop a small plantation and trading station at the very tip of Africa for the Dutch East India Company.

This spot on the Cape peninsula had been well-reconnoitered. In 1648 a Dutch ship called the *Haarlem* had been wrecked at Table Bay. Wintering ashore, its crew had found much that was promising in the Cape. The climate was Mediterranean, the soil sufficiently fertile to invite cultivation, and the inhabitants—the pale Koikoi and the small, elusive San, whom later settlers would call the "Hottentots" and "Bushmen"—had shown no hostility to the white seamen. When they had returned to Holland, the *Haarlem*'s officers had, therefore, urged the Company to develop a plantation and "refreshment station" at Table Bay from which to reprovision the scurvy-ridden crews of its East Indiamen on their long voyages to Holland's profitable outposts in Indonesia, along the straits of Malacca, in the Moluccas and Ceylon.

When van Riebeeck's men—scurvied and weak from a three and a half months' voyage—landed at the Cape they faced an arduous task. Storms battered their small shelters and washed out the new gardens. Baboons and other wild animals harassed the workers. Bartering with the cattle-keeping Hottentots proved difficult, and illness overtook the underfed and overworked whites. But van Riebeeck persevered and within a year, a small wooden fort was built, two hun-

dred cattle had been acquired from the Hottentots, and the gardens were beginning to take hold. Soon the little station was flourishing, along with its trade. But as more and more ships began to call at Table Bay to be reprovisioned, van Riebeeck realized he would have to enlarge his operations to supply them. Therefore, he decided to release nine of his men from their contracts at the station and to grant them twenty-one-year concessions from the Company to begin farming independently on lands just east of Table Mountain, formerly used by the Hottentots for grazing. A year later, to meet the needs of his own enlarged plantations, he had also begun importing Malay and West African slaves to the Cape, no blacks being indigenous to the region. Practical in the context of van Riebeeck's immediate situation, both decisions were to have far-reaching effects; for the first had created a semipermanent class of independent farmers at the Cape by permitting their usurpation of native lands, and the second had created a racially stratified social order in the little white settlement in which the most menial tasks were assigned to slaves.

There was, of course, nothing unusual in any of this in the context of the 17th century. Taking lands by what van Riebeeck described as "the sword and the rights of war" was commonplace among the European conquerors of empire, and slavery was widespread at the time in the colonial holdings of Spain, Portugal, France, Britain, and Holland. Nor did the white adventurers who raised the flags of these nations over much of the non-white world by the end of the 1600's question for a moment the rightness of their conquests. Christians all, they accepted as intrinsic their superiority to pagans. But there was a degree of difference in the attitude of Dutchmen like those at the Cape toward these "others" that had its origins in their particular Protestant creed. Followers of Calvin, they accepted the subjugation of "heathens," such as the Cape's Hottentots, as proof of his central doctrine that God had condemned Adam's unregenerate sons to eternal damnation and chosen only a few for salvation. In the divine order of things, Calvin had written, "lordship and servitude" were therefore foreordained and "God doth arm with sword and power whom He will have to be excellent in the world." The white man's worldwide subordination of the non-white consequently seemed to the Calvinist Dutch no more or less than an expression of God's will at work in the world, and though this unhappy view of the human condition would

be called violently into question in Europe in the 1700's, it was to be reinforced at the Cape at a critical point in that settlement's development by the arrival of some two hundred French Huguenots at Table Bay in 1688.

6
THE CALVINIST PAST

The Calvinist faith that the hardy Dutch, German, and French settlers brought with them to the Cape in the 17th century was the product of one of the most tumultuous ages in Western history. A religion forged in a period of unremitting anxiety in Europe, it was to prove well matched to the needs of a people who were to lose themselves in the African wilderness in the next century and to remain fundamentally unchanged to the present day. To examine the origins and development of Calvinism, therefore, is to illuminate, at least in part, the otherwise seemingly inscrutable workings of the Afrikaner mind.

One of several "heretical creeds" that sparked the century-long wars of the Reformation in Europe, Calvinism was conceived by a dour young Frenchman named John Calvin. A law student at the Sorbonne in the 1530's, Calvin had come of age in an era in which the very foundations of European society seemed to be crumbling. Once a mighty edifice, the Holy Roman Empire, which had kept Europe safe for centuries, was falling into decay, weakened by dissension from within and mortally threatened from without by the armies of the Ottoman Emperor Sulieman, who had overrun Hungary and was threatening all of Europe.

It was a time when neither men nor nations felt secure, and in Germany the audacious Martin Luther had translated its fearfulness into a rage with Rome by charging that the Vatican's flirtations with the "corruptions" of Renaissance "humanism" had directly contributed to the dissolution of the Empire and the Satanic disorders of the age. Intrigued and finally convinced by Luther's fiery protest, Calvin had become associated with the Lutheran cause in Paris and was soon branded a heretic. Driven from the city in 1533, with a price on his head, he had taken refuge at Angouleme and there, at the age of 26,

had produced his masterwork, the *Institutes of Christian Religion.* In it, he had expounded a doctrine that was less a theology than an ideology and destined to raise armies in its cause.

The sternest of the Reformation creeds, Calvinism offered no explanation of the divine nature but instead demanded absolute obedience to an unknowable God. Nevertheless, it had a potent appeal for Europe's fearful masses because it combined the appearance of accessibility with a great mystery, that of Election and Predestination.

Rejecting the humanism of Rome as devilish, Calvin restated his own belief in the medieval concepts of Heaven and Hell, the Last Judgment, and the omnipresence of evil in this world and insisted upon the the literal truth of the Bible as God's revealed Word. In demanding the absolute submission of his followers to that Word, Calvin seemed to imply that those who embraced any other creed were probably not among God's chosen and went on to elaborate the tasks of God's Elect as that of magistracy in this world. Those who submitted to the absolute authority of Calvin's church and its ministers, therefore, gained, in the promise of Election, release from what was for them the very real terror of eternal damnation at the very moment that they also submerged their own identities in the larger community of Calvin's church. And it was in this that Calvinism gained the power of an ideology with profound political implications; for Calvin's church not only offered its faithful an explanation of the uncertainty and evil of human life but a way to escape from its anxieties and rectify its wrongs through service to its holy cause. Since Satan had produced the ungodly disorder of the world, it followed that God willed His Chosen to stand against Him, whether He appeared in the robes of kings or priests. Theologically reactionary, Calvin, at 26, had produced a doctrine that was nevertheless politically radical in its implications and the militant societies it produced in 16th- and 17th-century Europe were to have far-flung influence in the world and produce a vigorous progeny in South Africa.

The Calvinists of the 16th century who raised a theocracy at Geneva became the "Christian soldiers" who brought the Cromwellian Revolution to England and waged almost a century of war for religious independence in the Netherlands and France. At Geneva, where church and state were unified under Calvin's personal leader-

ship, the populace unquestioningly accepted the governing authority of the clergy. In exchange for their obedience to church rule, they gained both the promise of salvation in the next world and security in this. Similarly, in England, where Cromwell's Puritan armies had cast down a king, regicide was justified and repressions of a reactionary revolution were condoned for the sake of His order and in the Netherlands and France the militant Calvinists, in the name of reform, waged wars that spanned a century.

Flourishing in adversity, Calvinism rapidly emerged as the most important political force in Holland during its struggle to free itself from Catholic Spain, and even before the Dutch had gained a final victory over Spain's King Philip, they had convened a Synod at Dordrecht in 1618 to fix the Canons of the Dutch Reformed Church for "all time" and to declare Calvinism the official religion of the newly formed United Provinces.

The sessions at "Dort" had been stormy, reflecting a much wider spectrum of religious opinion among the Protestant Dutch than the reactionary Calvinist leaders were willing to tolerate, and when one of the country's most revered patriots, 71-year-old Johan Oldenbarneveldt, had dared to question whether Predestination might be conditional and atonement possible, he had been officially charged with heresy and was later executed for his "crimes." Discouraged from dissent, the Dutch had thereafter become resigned to religious conformity, and the unity and militancy of the Reformed Church had not only strengthened the Netherlands during its continuing struggle with Spain but enhanced Dutch aggressiveness so that even before their war with Philip ended in 1648, Holland had acquired a vast world empire. And as Dutch piety had given way to the pursuit of world power and profits, Calvinism's secular stepchild, capitalism, had been born to flourish as the Netherlands entered its "golden age."

In France, however, from whence the Huguenots were to arrive at the Dutch enclave in Africa in 1688, the Reform movement was unsuccessful politically. From the outset, the French Calvinists had been hampered by an essential ambivalence about their own cause. Unlike the Dutch, the Huguenot "saints" who followed Calvin were not commoners, bent on ejecting a "foreign despot" from their homeland, but French nobles seeking only to protect their religion and their political rights. Far from being radicals, bent on tearing

down the old order, the Huguenots were conservatives who dreamed of reform without revolution, and when these noble "saints" took up arms against their king in 1568, they failed to carry their struggle to its logical conclusion. Victorious in the field, they did not demand the king's abdication and, in failing to do so, sealed their own fate. For in spite of a royal edict, issued at Nantes in 1598, guaranteeing their religious and political freedoms as Protestants, the Huguenots became the object of a campaign of terror that continued until the entire Huguenot population had either been slaughtered or driven from French soil. Moderates in rebellion, the Huguenots who fled France after 1685 were to become zealots in exile. Their belief that God Himself had willed their diaspora to the four corners of the earth became an important element in their will to survive, and the two hundred Huguenot refugees who arrived at the Cape in 1688 brought with them a fervid Calvinism that was to reinvigorate the religious spirit of the little Dutch outpost at a pivotal moment in its development.

7

VAN DER STEL AND THE HUGUENOTS

The Europe that the Huguenots left behind when they sailed for the Cape in 1688 was already moving headlong toward a new age. In the Protestant north, the taste for conformity, thrift, and hard work that Calvinism had encouraged among its adherents had created a climate in which capitalism and imperialism flourished. Waxing rich and powerful, the English and the Dutch had vied for control of the East Indies, and their commercial rivalry had soon ripened into a war. Fought intermittently on the high seas from 1672 onward, it was this conflict that had finally convinced the directors of the Dutch East India Company of the Cape's strategic value and led them to open it to colonization. By 1679 they had sent a vigorous new governor named Simon van der Stel to Cape Town, and it had been at his urging that the Huguenots had been recruited for the new colony.

Van der Stel, portly and periwigged, with a shrewd eye and canny

smile, was a representative man of his times, as much interested in power and profit as in Calvinist piety. Captivated by the beauty of the Cape, he dreamed of turning it into a New Holland whose splendors might rival those of its parent state, and he had given expression to his ambitions for the colony not only in the grand house called Groot Constantia, which he had built for himself just east of Table Mountain, but by founding a new village he called Stellenbosch, some 30 miles north of Cape Town, to accommodate new colonists. But van der Stel's worldly ambitions for the Cape placed him on a collision course with the unworldly Huguenots who had come to Africa with little more than a Bible in one hand and a grapevine root in the other. Within a year of the latter's arrival the governor and his new charges were quarreling bitterly over the Huguenots' insistence on maintaining their own separate schools and churches. Unwilling to bend to van der Stel's demands that they accept assimilation in the Cape's predominantly Dutch society, the French had petitioned his superiors in Holland for their "religious rights and freedoms" and had won a favorable compromise. But in doing so the Huguenots had also set a precedent of defiance to the governor's authority that was to have an extraordinary impact on the Cape in the next decade.

Trouble between the Company's officials and the Cape's independent farmers had been brewing for some time before the Huguenots landed in 1688. Since 1657, when Jan van Riebeeck had released nine of his men from the Company contracts to farm independently at the Cape, the numbers of "free burghers" there had proliferated while the market for their produce—the shipping trade—had not kept pace. As a result, the Company, which maintained its monopoly on reprovisioning all ships that called in at Table Bay, had been able to force farm prices lower and lower while increasing its own margin of profit at the expense of the "free burghers." By the time the Huguenots arrived, therefore, there was already friction between the Company and the Cape's independent farmers, and when Adriaan van der Stel, who succeeded his father as governor in 1699, began to misuse his office to further enrich himself and a circle of well-placed friends, an outraged group of Stellenbosch farmers, half of them Huguenots, had protested his conduct and won his recall as governor. But their actions had also produced an unlooked-for consequence by

focusing the attention of the Dutch East India Company's seventeen directors on the Cape's growing unrest since the arrival of the Huguenots. Dismayed by what seemed to them the increasing rebelliousness of the Cape colonists, the "Seventeen" put an end to all recruitment for the colony. As a result, for the next ninety years there were to be almost no new arrivals at the Cape, and the only additions to its white population of just under 2,000 were to be those that accrued from births, the retirement of Company officials, and a trickle of immigrants who made their way to the African outpost by their own means. Tied to Europe by the winds that carried the great fleets around the Cape of Good Hope, only Cape Town remained in contact with the outer world. And because it was what it was, a "Tavern of the Seas," catering to a roistering cross section of the world's sailors, it, too, remained almost as insensitive to the intellectual upheavals that were to change the way men thought about themselves in the 18th century as the Cape's upcountry farmers. Isolated in their green-gold valleys, these so-called "Cape Dutch" were to marry and intermarry, reinforcing with blood ties the bonds of a religious faith that already bound them together as Calvinists of the old order until they became a single grand clan, unique unto itself, and a new people who would call themselves Afrikaners had begun to emerge under Africa's white sun.

8

IMPRINT OF THE 18TH CENTURY

In the 18th century, the reordering of Europe's political and economic life which had begun with the Protestant rebellions would be continued in ways that the dour John Calvin could not have conceived. By mid-century, Holland and Britain had emerged as powers equal to France, Portugal, and Spain and all had become engaged in a worldwide contest for empire which had enriched them, put an end to the pessimism that had characterized the previous century and paved the way for an intellectual revolution that was to reshape man's perceptions of himself and the world in which he lived.

By 1750, the Enlightenment had come to all of Europe, and on

both sides of the Atlantic a new faith in man's ability to govern his own affairs and control his world through science had been born. Word of Ben Franklin's experiments with a kite and of Volta and Galvani's discoveries in Italy had excited Europe. Priestley and Cavendish had isolated hydrogen and oxygen. The invention of the flying shuttle, power loom, and steam engine had ushered in the industrial age, and in France, Jean Jacques Rousseau had set men's minds afire with ideas that would not only contribute to explosive political revolutions in America and France in 1776 and 1789 but change the way much of humanity thought about itself.

Though born at Geneva and raised a strict Calvinist, Rousseau had turned Calvin's ideas upside down and transformed the Enlightenment's belief in human rationality into a new faith in man's intrinsic value. To Rousseau, a romantic by temperament, man in his natural state was not depraved, but innocent, and civilization alone had corrupted him.

Published in 1749, Rousseau's *Contrat Social,* in which he developed his concepts of man's "natural rights" and "freedom," had been widely read and received with particular enthusiasm by the American colonists and emergent French bourgeoisie, both of whom hungered for political powers being hoarded by their overbearing monarchs. But Rousseau's message had little impact at the Cape, in part because of its isolation and in part because that isolation had intensified the concern of its "free burghers" with their own affairs.

At Cape Town in the 1700's, a commercial society dominated by the Company's officials had continued to hold sway. Though aloof from the rough life of Cape Town's harborside, where a motley of the world's varicolored races mixed freely in the taverns and brothels and a Colored people of mixed blood who proudly called themselves the "Bastaards" had begun to emerge, the well-to-do-classes displayed the same easy attitude toward the sexual behavior of the commoner classes and their own Malay and black slaves as they did toward business, and despite laws against both, miscegenation and smuggling were commonly tolerated. But upcountry where the "freeburghers," unable to break the Company's iron monopoly on the shipping trade, had given themselves wholly to the land in an attempt to build an independent life, a separate and more strictly ordered society had be-

gun to emerge. Dutch in its penchant for political republicanism but Huguenot in its religious ardor, conservatism, and respect for order, tradition, and the authority, it cast each farmer in his own isolated valley in the role of a Biblical patriarch and made him the absolute master not only of his own family, but of the Hottentots, Coloreds, and black slaves who worked the land. It was this society that was destined to leave the most lasting imprint on South African life.

In the 1600's, there had been very few black slaves at the Cape and those there were had been largely registered to the Company. But as the skills that the Huguenots had brought with them from France had begun to turn the valleys around Stellenbosch into vineyards capable of producing excellent wines, its farmers had grown prosperous and the numbers of slaves they owned had increased steadily. By 1716, there was roughly one slave for every two whites in the colony. Alarmed by the extraordinary growth in their numbers, the Company had queried the Cape's governor as to whether it might not be time to put an end to the slave trade altogether. But when he had demurred, the trade had continued. As a result, the Cape's farm economy had, by the quarter century, become almost entirely dependent upon black labor, and many of the more prosperous wine and wheat farms of the western Cape had been turned into quasi-feudal fiefdoms in which pious Afrikaners lived, almost as the feudal overlords of old Europe had done, in separate, self-sustaining little worlds in which black slaves had replaced the serfs. Magistrate and master of their own little community of whites, browns, and blacks, these Afrikaner patriarchs assumed their authority to be God ordained, and by the rules of primogeniture the patriarchs' responsibilities were passed from father to eldest son along with the land itself. What had been a pious assumption on the part of the earliest Cape farmers had, over the years, become a tradition so deeply imbedded in Afrikaner life that, to this day, most white farmers in South Africa construe their relationship with the black and brown men and women who work their farms to be that of master, benefactor, teacher, guide, and "Ou Baas" (old boss). Entrenched in the 18th century, this patriarchal tradition served as a bulwark against the liberalizing influence of the Enlightenment when it belatedly reached the Cape at the end of the 1700's, and one needs only to drive in a

radius of forty miles from Cape Town to find oneself in a world that time seems to have bypassed.

At Vergenoeg, a wine farm in the Eerste River Valley east of Cape Town, one has the illusion of stepping backward into the dreaming past. Steeped in the peace of centuries, Vergenoeg, which in old Dutch means "Contented," seems at first like some Afrikaner Brigadoon—a place half illusion, utterly serene, and entirely out of place in the troubled South Africa of world headlines. The farm's present owner, Jacob Faure, 47, is a gentle, cultured man, opposed to "apartheid" for its own sake but nevertheless imbued with the traditions of Vergenoeg and quite willing to accept his responsibilities as its "master" with all that this implies.

Faure and his wife, Betty, and their two sons live in a house that has been changed little since 1773, when an ancestral cousin named Johannes Colyn, who "sometime, somewhere married a Faure" added a "new" gabled façade to the original 1696 structure. Vergenoeg's vineyards are generations old, planted and replanted by Faures who have held the farm in direct descent since 1820. Ruled by the round of the seasons and the slow demands of the wine maker's art, its secrets also passed down to him over generations, Jac Faure's life at Vergenoeg bears the imprint of times past.

Faure runs his 2,000-acre farm as his forefathers did, with the help of some twenty-five Colored families and a scattering of blacks who have lived at Vergenoeg "from before memory." Provided with housing, food, some clothing and wine as well as a small wage, most of these workers are tied to Vergenoeg and to the Faure family by a subtle web of personal relationships of the sort that have traditionally bound peasants to the land where they were born and the families they have served for generations. An anachronism that betrays its origins in the feudal societies of Europe, where it also persists into the present day, the arrangement plainly owes much to the legacy the Huguenots passed on to their Afrikaner descendants along with their reverence for the past and its traditions.

Jac Faure makes no apologies for the semifeudal quality of life at Vergenoeg. Like most white farmers of his background, Faure is convinced that farms like his have not only been kept viable and

humane over the centuries by what he calls "the old ways," but that
the customs and traditions that have prevailed at Vergenoeg and
throughout much of rural South Africa have also fulfilled an important function for the country's tribal peoples by providing "halfway stations" on the road to modernity as their own traditional
societies have slowly disintegrated under the impact of the white
man's culture.

But Jac Faure has no illusions that the protected and anachronistic
little world that is Vergenoeg can remain unaltered for much
longer. In the past decade, the sons and daughters of the Colored
families living on his farm have begun to drift away in increasing
numbers, drawn to the cities, as are the majority of South Africa's
blacks, by a desire to break with the past and to take advantage of
new opportunities that now exist for them, "apartheid" notwithstanding. And the drain of these formerly rural folk from the countryside has created a vacuum on Cape farms like Vergenoeg that has
been increasingly filled by migrant workers, recruited from among
the Xhosa tribes, whose Transkei "homeland," northeast of the Cape,
became an independent republic in 1976. Formerly citizens of the
Republic of South Africa, the Xhosa are now classed as "foreigners"
by its government and are therefore subjected to a variety of rigid
influx controls and other regulations that have undermined the traditional order of things on farms like Vergenoeg. Prohibited from
bringing their families with them, they may be recruited for Jac
Faure's vineyards only under limited labor contracts that seem explicitly designed to discourage them from forming any ties either
with him or with the land, and Jac Faure finds that the impact of
the present system is often inhumane.

"I have a neighbor who had two good boys working for him on
his farm last year," Faure explains to illustrate his views, "and after
they'd been with him the better part of a year they came and asked
for permission to build two little shacks in some uncultivated fields,
out away from the permanent houses where the Colored families
lived. Asked why, they explained that when they went back to the
Transkei on the month's break in their contract, there wasn't time to
make a baby and as both were in their middle twenties they felt the
need to begin a family urgently. Now the boys who were not allowed
to bring families with them under their labor contracts, couldn't

afford to give up their jobs to go back to the Transkei where there was no work. So the girls had to come down illegally and take up life in these shanties, just as they were doing at that time all over the Cape; wives drifting down to join their husbands as illegal immigrants and living in shanty towns. But after the Soweto riots in '76, the government clamped down on these 'illegal immigrants' and sent thousands of the poor wretches packing back to the Transkei where there was no work and no hope for them. Even on the neighbor's farm, they found the two shacks, made the boys take them down and shipped the wives back home. The farmer, of course, had done something illegal in allowing the wives to come live on his farm, but when he was asked about it, he just said he didn't know they were there. And, of course, there's nothing to prevent him looking the other way again should the girls return, now is there?"

Opposed to "apartheid" because he feels it has produced unnecessary economic and social dislocations within the country and created unnatural barriers among South Africa's several races, Jac Faure believes that one day a multiracial society must emerge in South Africa because its heritage—like Vergenoeg's—is essentially a multiracial one.

"Change is coming in South Africa because it has to," he says flatly, "but it must grow naturally out of our own traditions and cannot be forced before its time; because you simply cannot force civilization on people. Race, after all, is not the real problem in this country. How could it be? We've lived with race all our lives. It's the many levels of civilization that coexist here, from that of the tribal peoples, some of whom are truly primitive, to that of the most sophisticated and modern Europeans—all living cheek by jowl in one country. And because the least developed are in the greatest majority, it does not follow that it would benefit all to hand the country over to them before they are ready to take responsibility for it. Because to do that, you see, would not simply destroy white privilege in South Africa but the black man's own best hope for the future along with it."

Because he does not believe in forcing changes "before their time" and must deal with the present reality that many of his own workers at Vergenoeg are neither willing nor able to cope with the complexities of the 20th century, Jac Faure has consequently continued

to accept a paternalistic responsibility for them and for their families with the same attitude of noblesse oblige with which he has accepted his obligation to preserve Vergenoeg. Born to the role of its hereditary patriarch, Faure's life still bears the imprint of the 18th century when his own Huguenot ancestors first farmed at the Cape, and one glimpses at Vergenoegd the shape of times past from which—for better or for worse—present-day South Africa evolved.

9
TREKKING AWAY FROM TIME

Sleepy, serene, seemingly out of touch with time, Vergenoeg is nevertheless real, and the influence of such patriarchies on South African life has been pervasive. Entrenched on farms like it, the ideas of "white mastery" or "baas kap" spread from the Cape to the rest of the country as it grew, and because the memory of these well-ordered little worlds also went with those who were forced to leave them behind, like the recollection of some paradise lost, generations of Afrikaners were to idealize the benign life they seemed to represent and seek to regain it without examining its flaws. But the flaws were there and the costs of the old order were high, not only to the thousands of blacks whom the plantation system enslaved but to the whites whom it "dispossessed." For as the numbers of slaves on the great Cape plantations had increased annually in the 1700's, it had also become necessary that these farms be enlarged simply to remain economically viable. The result, by 1725, was that the once empty valleys of Simon van der Stel's original Cape colony were almost entirely under cultivation, there was little land available for those who wanted it, and the Company markets for farm produce were glutted. Furthermore, as usually only an eldest son could expect to inherit his father's farm, there had been a slow but steady displacement of whites from the Cape's farming society and a new "landless" class was beginning to form in the colony whose plight was worsened by its deepening economic malaise. Enticed to the hinterlands by a Company offer to rent "loan places" to would-be cattle farmers in regions to the north once claimed by the Hottentot (Koikoi) tribes—

who had been all but annihilated by repeated epidemics of the white man's smallpox—these emigrant farmers who were called "trek-boers" had begun moving into the interior in the 1720's in search of grazing lands, all unaware that they had embarked on an epic adventure of great historic consequence.

Assembling in small family groups, they had driven their ox wagons through passes populated by leopard and baboon that wound upward over the heights of the first dizzying escarpment, which separates the narrow Cape coastal belt from the veld, into a new world. Those who moved northwest, beyond the "trembling lands" where earth shocks were frequent, found themselves in a vast light-tormented plain of immense horizons where sky and earth seemed to fuse. Those who moved eastward, over the Hottentots' Holland mountains, through a pass where one can still discern the scars their metal-rimmed wheels left upon the sheer rock faces as they winched their wagons upward, found themselves in cloud-shadowed grasslands whose dappled flanks lay beneath the blue rock faces of still more mountain ranges beyond which lay the arid plateaus of the Great and Little Karoo.

Two of God's botanical playgrounds, both of these semideserts were carpeted with plants and bushes of fantastic form and variety and inhabited by wild ostrich, strange buck, and the seldom-seen but always dangerous Bushman. Remnants of a people who had once reigned over most of Africa and perhaps portions of Europe, the Bushmen, who called themselves the San, were small in stature, had yellow skins, flat-panned faces, and an oriental cast to their eyes. Stone Age huntsmen, they had been driven out of their hunting grounds to the north by the slow, ponderous southward migrations of tribes of black men who had apparently arrived in the regions now known as the Transvaal, Free State, and Natal in three great waves somewhere between the 11th and 15th centuries. Caught between the blacks in the north and east, and the remaining Koikoi and whites who claimed the western Cape, the San greeted the approach of the trek-boers with a fierceness born of desperation that grew more intense as they were pushed steadily northward along a frontier that by 1775 extended to the Swartberg, the Nuweveld, and Sneeuberg ranges in an enormous crescent just to the north and east of the present town of Graaff-Reinet. Fighting for their survival as a race,

the Bushmen had attacked the trek-boers' wagons and isolated farm-steads with stealth and ferocity, and the whites had retaliated by hunting the San mercilessly, as if they were animals, until they were driven back into the far Kalahari desert, and the trek-boers found themselves in possession of an enormous solitude.

There is, to this day, a fierce beauty about the Karoo regions. The earth is lion-colored, the sky cobalt, and the sunlight of such a merciless clarity that it seems to burn the brain. Here, nothing seems familiar—not the plants that masquerade as stones, nor the grasshop-pers that grow to be the length of a man's hand, nor the tiny buck, no bigger than a hare (called the klipspringer) that evades the merci-less gray cobra by its dauntless acrobatics. Shaped as the protocon-tinent of Gondwanaland parted and Africa floated free of Australia, India, South America, and Antarctica some 350 million years ago, the Karoo region still seems to breathe with the fire of the young earth. A land for poets, visionaries, and madmen, it was here that Africa began to take possession of the Afrikaners in spirit as it had claimed them, heart and hand, in the Cape.

Settling in isolated family units wherever they could find water, often at vast distances from one another, they measured their claims to the land by mounting a horse and riding it at a walk for half an hour to the four points of the compass and gave their farms names like Soebatsfontein, Riviersonderend, Bitter-puts and Buffelsvlei—Begged for Spring, Rivers-without-end, Bitter well, and Buffalo's Pond. Where there was enough water to maintain the grazing for their cattle and sheep, they stayed put, turning the land with archaic plows of wood and iron, seldom planting more than three of their six- to ten-thousand-acre claims in crops, and building houses with walls thick enough to withstand the charge of elephants in the remote oases that are today the "dorps" of the Little Karoo. But where the water was insufficient, they usually remained only long enough to exhaust the grazing and then moved on in their covered wagons to a new claim, always more remote than the first and always at a greater remove from the civil authority of the Dutch East India Company at Cape Town.

Strangers in a strange land, the trek-boers were forced to learn much they needed to know to survive from Hottentots and Bushmen whom they had impressed into their service and so had begun a

process of adaptation to primordial Africa that would transform them slowly from Europeans into a new breed of white Africans. Reduced to a life of essentials, what mattered to them were their families, their stock, the larger community of kinship they shared with their fellow Boers, and their simple faith in God.

The Calvinism of the frontier was a bare-bones sort, reminiscent of Dort in its narrow interpretation of the doctrines of Predestination, Election, and Grace. But it also incorporated much of the Huguenots preoccupation with the past in a reverence for tradition and Biblical precedent. To explain the mysteries of the strange world in which they found themselves, these Afrikaner pioneers turned to Genesis in the Good Book and found in its pages accounts of the plagues of locusts comparable to those that devastated the veld, and godly answers for the wild migrations of millions of springbok that at times came thundering across the land to seek death in the far-off western seas. And they also found an analogue for their own hard lives in the Old Testament accounts of the tribulations of Abraham's sons that encouraged them to believe—as their Huguenot forebears had—that God had chosen them for some high destiny in Africa. So literal in fact did their belief become that they were a Chosen People sent to follow in the footsteps of the ancient Jews, that when some stone cairns, perhaps marking the graves of long dead Koikoi chiefs, were discovered along the Fish River in the 1770's, the frontiersmen took them to be monuments left behind by the Israelites and so named the place Israelites Kloof.

Reinforced by the clan ties that already bound them and by the universal difficulty of their lives, they came to feel a sense of spiritual community with one another in spite of their individual isolation. As a result, the society that grew up on the frontier was a paradoxical one in that it placed great emphasis on freedom and self-reliance but was at the same time religiously conformist and strangely similar to the theocratic societies that had grown up among the beleaguered Calvinists in the early years of the Reformation. Having left civil authority behind in the Cape, its governing force was religion, its ultimate magistrate was God, and its laws were those of the Decalogue. Survival centered, it placed a high value on clan and kinship, the land, stock, water, and the trek-boers' ancestral religion and, in this, resembled the grazier societies of the tribal blacks whom these wan-

dering whites had finally begun to encounter en masse along the Great Fish River by the 1770's far more than it did that of their own European forebears who had abandoned the nomadic life thousands of years before.

10

THE KAROO: THEN AND NOW

The years have no meaning in the Little Karoo. Though the land is fenced now and roads cut their way through the veld, these great brown expanses have never been entirely subdued. Hard-scrabble country, it makes the same demands on those who would farm it today as it did on the trek-boers two hundred years ago, so that something of their self-reliant spirit seems to linger still in its isolated villages.

Calitzdorp, a town of a few thousand souls, stands athwart one of the original routes the trek-boers used as they drove their wagons eastward in the 18th century in search of better grazing. Huddled along the banks of the Gamka and Nel rivers, two of the rare streams that sustain life in this skeletal land, it seems to cling precariously to its existence on the very edge of nowhere and despite its age has about it still the raw, half-finished quality of a frontier town that grew up suddenly and not long ago.

First claimed as a "loan place" in 1755 by a soldier of the Dutch East India Company named Matthys Galitz, the oasis where Calitzdorp clusters was not settled by whites until his son Frederick brought his family to live there in the 1770's on a farm he called "Buffesvlei." As its name implied, Buffalo's Pond was a wild place, visited not only by herds of buffalo, eland, wildebeest, and ostrich, but by the leopard, lion, Bushmen, and Hottentots who hunted them. But as in most years the grazing was good along the rivers, two other families of trek-boers named Nels and Stassen eventually also claimed loan places in the valley and many of the present farmers of Calitzdorp are descended from these three families.

Life at "Buffelsvlei," "Half-an-Hour," and "Daniel's Kraal" as the original Galitz, Nel, and Stassen farms were called, bore little re-

semblance to that of the settled Cape in the same era. While Jac Faure's ancestral cousin was busy refurbishing Vergenoeg with its graceful gabled facade, the pioneers of Calitzdorp sheltered in their covered wagons or crowded their families and few Colored servants into temporary cottages of clay and wattle not unlike those still in use at Calitzdorp to house farm laborers. Lacking permanent titles to the lands they claimed, they were to let many years pass before they built the sturdy, unadorned dwellings that still stand beside their poorly marked graves as monuments to their perseverance. For the one thing that was certain about frontier life, as the 18th century waned, was its uncertainty. Three weeks removed from Cape Town by ox-wagon these farmers had little reason to plow or plant more than a few acres of crops for their own use and instead eked out a tenuous existence as pastoralists.

In years when the rains came to their semidesert home, even the stones of the Little Karoo seemed to bloom and it flowered forth in a myriad of colors and forms that left no doubt of God's glory. But there were years when no rains came at all, and when the rivers ran to sand and the veld turned to stone under the unyielding sun these simple folk could not but wonder why God chastened them. For in this fierce place, where men and women marked in family Bibles the passage of the years by notations of births, deaths, droughts, floods, and pestilence the hand of the Creator seemed to hover very near and, perceiving His mighty presence in all things, the early Afrikaners became as intensely mystic and fatalistic in their faith as an ancient Biblical tribe.

But if it wanted the faith of an Old Testament mystic to endure life in the Little Karoo at the end of the 18th century, it also wanted physical hardiness, stubborn courage, and a high degree of adaptability and all of these characteristics as well as a profound feeling for the encompassing force of the Creation, are marked in a man like Sam Brink, a present-day Calitzdorp farmer descended from the trek-boer Nel family.

A short, compact individual, as gnarled and as tough as one of the massive vine roots in his well-tended vineyard and just as deeply attached to his land, Sam Brink is a fruit, stock, and ostrich farmer reputed to be among the best in his desert district. The strip of 125 acres of irrigated lands elbowing the river's twists that he and his

eldest son, Dirk, farm at Calitzdorp was part of the original Galitz claim at Buffelsvlei, and he also owns some 6,000 acres of grazing lands for sheep in the unwatered veld near the old Stassen homestead at Daniel's Kraal. Wise in the ways of earth and animals, Sam Brink can boast truthfully of producing peaches that weigh two and a half pounds each, raisins as big as a man's thumb, and some of the best breeding stock for the ostrich trade, centered in nearby Outdshoorn, where these indigenous birds are raised principally for their feathers and the fine leather that is made from their hides.

Like most Little Karoo farmers, Brink has no illusions about man's ability to control nature. In his sixty-some years, he has known periods in which not a drop of rain has fallen on Calitzdorp for seven years at a stretch and the veld has been desiccated by the merciless sun. In other years, he has seen torrential rains fall on the mountains that surround the town and come cascading down into the valley to raise the Gamka and Nel in floods that have ripped the earth apart and carried away everything that stood in the way—people, houses, animals, crops, and the carefully tended topsoil of his fields. When he talks of these events, his speech has a Biblical ring to it that brings his trek-boer ancestors to mind, for he marks the epochs of his own lifetime by "the years of the drought," "the day of the locusts," and the "time of the flood" and his respect for the awesome power that resides in Nature is infused with a religious quality that owes much to his Afrikaner heritage. For to Sam Brink, the earth and all the creation from stones to stars are one and, like Jan Smuts and Eugene Marais, two celebrated Afrikaner political activists who were also prophets of the philosophy of "holism," his faith in that "oneness" had made him into what he calls "a natural democrat."

"God put us all on this earth to live together," he says fiercely, "and that means we'll have to learn to do it or perish. 'Apartheid' is an evil because it sets men against men, builds barriers where there were none and gets in the way of natural processes of change and growth that, prior to 1948, were well on their way to creating a new kind of society in this country. Now I don't delude myself that I have to love the black man or the Colored. Liking him will do. Because if I want respect for myself and my own kind then I must give it to others. It's that simple. During the Second World War, I fought in North Africa before being captured by the Germans. I learned up

there that men of all kinds *can* live and be together, regardless, and like each other. Death taught us a lot about valuing life and its variety, you see, so to come home from a war like that to find hate and separation preached in my own country disgusted me. And to see a country as gifted as this turned into a fortress of race sickens me. No—it's wrong, this business of 'apartheid.' Wrong because it's unnatural. And unless we take down within the next few years the whole ugly structure it has taken thirty years to build up, it will destroy everything we have managed to create here and with it, South Africa."

Sam Brink's distaste for "apartheid" is shared by his son Dirk, who would also eliminate such vestiges of the Afrikaners' patriarchal tradition as the daily distribution of a wine ration to Colored farmhands, on the grounds that it enhances their dependency on whites. Based on religious convictions wholly in keeping with their Afrikaner heritage, both regard "separate development" as unnatural and hence wrong. But the same sense of God's all-encompassing power that induced a mystic strain in the Brinks and some of their trek-boer ancestors, engendered a fanatic Calvinism in others. And it was the narrow faith of those who perceived the world's order as forever fixed that was destined early in this century to become the dominant element of the cultural legacy the early Afrikaners left to their descendents, for as the 18th century drew to a close, the trekboers who had pushed eastward across the Little Karoo found themselves for the first time confronting the massed strength of the black man.

II

CLASHES WITH THE XHOSA

A little over a century and a quarter after Jan van Riebeeck had landed at Table Bay to claim the Cape for the Dutch East India Company, descendants of its original settlers finally encountered the black man en masse some 500 miles northeast of Cape Town along the Great Fish River. Honed and hardened by years of wilderness living, the trek-boers had already been transformed by their African

experience into a new pioneer breed, clannish, strangely mystic, and as deeply attached to the land as any of Africa's native tribes. Their encounter with the Xhosa, who occupied the grasslands that marked the end of the arid reaches of the Karoo deserts in the east, was therefore laden with significance. In the black man these emergent Afrikaners saw a rival for the land on which both sides believed their survival and their future in Africa depended.

Settled along the eastern slope of the Fish River's watershed, their neat, circular adobe huts dotting the green hills, the Xhosa were members of the Nguni people. The advance guard of the Nguni, which also included the present-day Zulu, Swazi, and Ndebele tribes, the Xhosa had followed their cattle steadily southward over the centuries to reach the regions between the Drakensberg mountains and the Indian Ocean, presently called Natal, some time before the 16th century.

A sturdy, brown-skinned people, the Xhosa were a clannish collection of ten sub-tribes who lived in extended family units under hereditary chiefs, who were in turn ruled by a single paramount chief. Like the trek-boers, they were stock farmers, and it was therefore inevitable that when the trek-boers and Xhosa met, their conflicting claims to the same grazing land would lead to hostility.

To the Xhosa, what was at stake on the frontier was not only their freedom to graze their cattle where the grass grew the greenest but, ultimately, their existence as a nation, for these tribes had been pushed steadily southward in search of new grazing lands by their own increasing population, drought, and the presence of fierce rival tribes of blacks farther north. To the trek-boers the issues were much the same: the good lands behind them were occupied, the semideserts of the Karoo did not provide safe grazing for their cattle, and their economic survival as herdsmen depended on moving on to new grazing lands.

Faced with imminent warfare between the trek-boers and Xhosa along the Cape colony's ill-defined eastern frontier, the Dutch East India Company attempted to forestall it by restraining the trek-boers, fixing the colony's borders at the Fish and obtaining a treaty to this effect with several Xhosa chiefs. But the Xhosa and the Bushmen had continued their attacks on the Boers and skirmishing had become general from the Bamboesberg to the Fish River by 1779 when a

frontiersman named Adriaan van Jaarsveld had launched a retaliatory attack in defiance of the company's treaty that touched off a two-year border war.

Lawless and inconclusive, in that it did little more than restore the status quo along the eastern frontier when it ended in 1781, van Jaarsveld's little war was nevertheless significant for several reasons. It brought into focus for the first time issues that were to plague South Africa for the next two hundred years as Boer and Bantu sought to possess a country to which each claimed an "inalienable" right. Fought in defiance of the Company's authority, it had also congealed the upcountry Afrikaners into a political entity and stirred a spirit of rebellion among them that would not be defused even after Britain seized the Cape, putting an end to Dutch rule in Africa.

12

THE ENLIGHTENMENT AND THE ENGLISH IN AFRICA

It was inevitable that the tumult which had engulfed America and Europe in the final decades of the 18th century would be felt even at the remote Cape. By 1776, fired by the ideas of Locke, Hume, Rousseau, and Jefferson, the American colonists had rebelled against their British king. By 1780, as the doughty Adriaan van Jaarsveld had led his commandos roughshod into Xhosa territory, Britain had become engaged in a worldwide power struggle, which evolved from the American revolution, that had pitted her against the forces of rampant republicanism in general and France in particular. When the Netherlands—itself divided by republican and monarchist factions—had proposed to join in a League of Armed Neutrality with France, the British had declared war on the Dutch and the Cape had been placed in jeopardy. In 1781, a French fleet had landed troops at Table Bay who were to remain there three years.

Caught in the crosscurrents of a much larger conflict, the Dutch East India Company had sought to strengthen its grip on the Cape Colony by putting its own house there in order and in 1786 a new legislative district had been established at Graaff-Reinet, where re-

newed border fighting again threatened the peace. But the young man whom the Company chose in 1787 to bring order out of the chaos of the lawless frontier—Honoratus Christiaan Maynier—was a poor choice for the assignment of landdrost (district administrator). A child of the Enlightenment, young Maynier brought a liberal spirit to the far frontier that men like Adriaan van Jaarsveld found completely foreign. When he sought to keep the peace by placating the Xhosa and preaching to the trek-boers about the "natural rights" of these "noble savages," Maynier only succeeded in alienating them further. After the Xhosa had been permitted by Maynier to overrun some 120 farms in a district west of the Great Fish River called the Zuurveld, an incensed van Jaarsveld led an armed commando into Graaff-Reinet to eject the young landdrost from his fine new "Drosty" house.

Driven out of Graaff-Reinet, the hapless Maynier had arrived back in Cape Town in March of 1795 to report a revolution in progress in the eastern Cape. His report, and a second one brought from the district of Swellendam, which had declared its own independence from the Company in April, were still under consideration at the Castle when a British fleet rounded the Cape of Good Hope. By September British troops had landed and taken Cape Town.

The British said they had come to Africa to protect the interests of Holland's hereditary ruler, the Prince of Orange, from his republican enemies. But they also did not want the Cape, which commanded the route to India and the East, to fall into the hands of the French revolutionary government. Shortly after the French revolutionists had beheaded King Louis XVI, in January of 1793, Britain went to war with France, plunging all Europe into a conflict that would last twenty years, see the maps of the world redrawn, and sow the dragons' teeth of future conflict even at the faraway Cape.

Britain had entered the French war divided. Republican sentiment had grown strong in England following the loss of her American colonies in 1783, and not a few of the country's leading writers favored the cause of revolution. Trumpeting their own versions of Rousseau's doctrines, they extolled the natural rights and virtues of simple folk who were, they said, exploited shamefully by the rising new barons of industry and the old lords of hereditary wealth. But as the French Revolution degenerated into the Reign of Terror in

1793–94, Britons of all classes reacted against the excesses of the bloodthirsty mobs in Paris, and the impulse to revolution in England had been deflected into a zeal for reform at home and religious missions abroad. Finding its voice in the Anglican Church and the newly formed London Missionary Society, the Evangelical movement in Britain united liberals, radicals, and non-conformists of every social rank into a political force that was to influence the domestic and foreign policies of successive British governments for decades to come.

Meanwhile the war with France had not gone well for Britain as a young military genius named Napoleon Bonaparte reinvigorated the French armies and made the first of several political moves that were soon to give him dictatorial power. Plagued by economic setbacks at home and worried by Napoleon's mounting influence in Europe, Britain had sued for peace and under the terms of the Treaty of Amiens, signed in 1803, had returned the Cape Colony to a new government in the Netherlands—the Batavian Republic—which had been organized with French help.

Jacob de Mist, the new Dutch commissioner-general at the Cape, set out to improve the colony's government by taking closer control of its civil affairs and codifying the functions of its landdrosts and heemraden (district council). A liberal, humane individual, deMist sought to aid the Hottentots by supervising their labor contracts with the Cape's farmers and by allowing the Rev. Johannes van der Kemp, a representative of the London Missionary Society (LMS), to establish a mission among them not far from present-day Port Elizabeth at a place called Bethelsdorp and he also permitted the Griqua, a people of mixed Hottentot, Malay, Colored, and European extraction, to establish themselves under their leader, Andries Waterboer, beyond the Orange River with LMS help. But Dutch rule at the Cape was ended for all time only three years after deMist's arrival there, for in 1804, the war in Europe had been resumed, Britain had met Napoleon's threat of invasion by sinking his fleet at Trafalgar, and by 1806—while the British Navy danced across the high seas with impunity, adding the territories of her enemies to the Empire—the Cape had been retaken by British troops and the claim, which would give Britain permanent control of the colony under the London Convention, after Napoleon's defeat in 1814, had been established.

The missionaries and colonial servants who embodied the British

presence at the Cape in the early decades of the 19th century were representative of contrary elements in British society. The missionaries belonged to that breed of Englishmen whose ideas had brought a liberal government to power in England long enough, in 1806, to abolish the slave trade throughout the Empire. Disciples of Rousseau, they were to be the primary conduit through which that French philosopher's revolutionary ideas, costumed in the clothing of ardent Christianity, reached the Cape, and their impact on Boer and black man alike was to prove profound. The first six governors appointed to the Cape, on the other hand, were all representatives of the conservative ruling classes whose reactionary government had been returned to power as social disorder had erupted in Britain during the Napoleonic Wars. Tories to a man, they all regarded the Cape as a backwater of civilization, chose to govern it by edict rather than consultation, and were as likely to look askance at the activities of the LMS as the Afrikaners, who were increasingly outraged by the missionaries' defense of natives whom they believed, quite literally, to be the Sons of Ham, condemned by God Himself to their lowly station for the ancient sins of Cain. But the governors were, after all, also Englishmen, sensitive to the political climate in Britain where the liberal Evangelical movement remained a powerful force. Consequently, they could not afford to disregard the missionaries' complaints or run the risk of backing the Afrikaners against them, for fear of being criticized at home.

Lord Caledon was the first Governor of the Cape to attempt to deal directly with the problems raised by the LMS. Britain's abolition of the slave trade in 1807 had created some resentment among the Afrikaners but no major economic upset for the large farmers of the western Cape who were well supplied with slaves. But on the eastern frontier, it had left the poorer farmers with no recourse but to rely entirely on Hottentot labor, and as the Hottentots had no reputation either for honesty or earnestness among the trek-boers, complaints of their vagrancy, thieving, and unpredictability had begun to reach British authorities almost as regularly as the missionaries' complaints that the farmers were using strong-arm methods to keep these laborers in line. A fair-minded man, for all the haughtiness of his manner, Lord Caledon tried to resolve the dispute between the missionaries and the frontiersmen over the Hottentots by a compromise. In 1809,

he issued a decree that the Hottentots must be given labor contracts and a fair wage by the Afrikaner farmers who employed them, but that in exchange they must be bound to "fixed abodes" on the colony's farms and carry passes whenever they left them. However significant Caledon's decree may have been in setting a precedent for present-day South African pass laws, his actions at the time pleased no one. To the Afrikaners, the decree represented government interference in private affairs, while to the LMS it seemed to place intolerable restrictions on the Hottentots' freedoms. Far from defusing the hostility between the LMS and the upcountry Afrikaners, Caledon's actions intensified it and he soon found himself replaced as Governor of the Cape by Sir John Cradock.

Cradock was to fare no better when he sought to resolve the native question by establishing a new Circuit Court in 1812, explicitly to hear claims filed by the LMS on behalf of non-white farm workers against their employers. Fair enough by British standards, Cradock's "Black Circuit" outraged the Calvinist Afrikaners. Insulted by being required to answer charges brought against them on behalf of heathens by clerics who made a mockery of what they believed to be God's own order in the world, their resentment of British rule was only deepened by Cradock's "Black Circuit" and was to be further inflamed during the tenure of the Cape's next Governor, Lord Charles Somerset, by his own policies and by the actions of a new LMS spokesman at Bethelsdorp, Dr. John Philip.

Somerset and Philip were the quintessential "ruler" and "missionary." Somerset explained the Afrikaner's quarrelsomeness as due to Dutch influences at the Cape, and his answer to it was to anglicize the colony by flooding it with British immigrants and revamping its institutions along British lines. Philip, on the other hand, insisted that only by extending full civil rights to the Hottentots and preventing any further Afrikaner encroachment into native lands could the quarrel be resolved fairly. Neither, however, seemed to care much about the impact of their proposals upon the Afrikaners, who now found themselves facing the proposition of being turned into a powerless minority in the land they had thought to be their own, and the equivalent arrogance of both the Governor and Dr. Philip was not lost upon the frontier.

Somerset, 46, who arrived at the Cape in 1814, was the wealthy

scion of one of England's most illustrious families and is said to have likened his official residence at Cape Town to a "dog kennel." Born to splendor, Somerset found little to be desired in the provincial capital of a colony populated by Boers, half-castes, and Hottentots and was at first disposed to regard the Afrikaners as lawless rabble, to be dealt with harshly. He had therefore made a legal decision in 1815, meant to underscore his intention to *rule* these quarrelsome folk, that was to have a major impact on the frontier.

The case had evolved from a charge of maltreatment brought by a Hottentot against a trek-boer named Bezuidenhout. Called to appear in court in 1815, Bezuidenhout had refused the summons and later defied a platoon of Hottentot soldiery, led by two British officers. When he was shot dead in the ensuing fracas, Bezuidenhout's brother had vowed to avenge him and gathered a band of fellow frontiersmen to plot a rebellion against British rule in which they hoped to enlist the help of the Xhosa. At the last, however, the group had thought better of the scheme and surrendered to British authorities. Charged with treason nevertheless, they had been found guilty and five of the thirty-nine sentenced to death, much to the astonishment of their neighbors who had sent a plea for reprieve to the Castle. It was refused, and Somerset, meaning to make an example of the five, had ordered them executed. The hangings, held in public at a place thereafter called Slachtens Nek, were botched, with cruel results.

John Philip was sent out to Africa to take charge of the LMS mission at Bethelsdorp in 1819. The son of a Scottish weaver, Philip had been engaged for much of his young life in the struggles of those crofters to survive the impact of British industrialization on their livelihood. He had watched them lose the struggle, and as a preacher in Aberdeen had also seen first hand the devastation of rural life as a result of the draconian policies of an unreformed Tory Parliament dominated by men of Somerset's ilk.

Persuaded to an ardent liberalism by this experience, Philip had come to Africa determined that Africa's innocent "noble savages" would not be victimized by the colony's privileged whites as the good folk of Aberdeen had been. He arrived at Bethelsdorp in the same year that Lord Charles Somerset, who was still being reviled on the frontier for what had happened at Slachters Nek, announced his plan to bring a large number of new British settlers into the colony. Ex-

pecting support for his own efforts from these newcomers, Philip
had laid aside his suspicion of the Governor to applaud his decision.

The 1820 settlers were to disappoint both Somerset and Philip.
Settled by the Governor's orders in the much-contested Zuurveld,
they found it much less inviting than the Huguenots had found
Stellenbosch. Though half were crop farmers and a third artisans,
they were wholly unprepared for the harsh realities of life in the
southeastern Karoo. They had few skills for coping with an extended
drought that reduced them to near starvation and brought the restless
and hungry Hottentot and Xhosa cattle raiders into the region.
Feeling duped by the Castle and as outraged by the LMS's protesta-
tions in favor of the "natives" as were the local Afrikaners, the
Zuurveld English were drawn into a natural alliance with their fellow
frontiersmen that rankled Somerset almost as much as it did Philip.
But as the latter began to outline a new program of "separate development" for the Cape's natives, aimed at protecting them from all
white influence, and so became "apartheid's" earliest advocate,
Somerset, his irritation with the Zuurveld English notwithstanding,
went forward with his own plan to resolve the Cape's difficulties by
making it governable as a *British* outpost.

Using the presence of so many Englishmen in the colony to justify
his decisions, he began to promulgate a series of decrees aimed at eradi-
cating Dutch influence in the colony once and for all. The first, issued
in 1822, declared that by 1828 English alone would be the official language. The next decree substituted British coinage for the Cape's chaotic Dutch currency but also devaluated the Dutch Rix dollar against
the pound by two thirds, suddenly impoverishing the Afrikaners. A
third decree dissolved the old Burgher Senate that had long represented
Afrikaner interests, and revamped the Cape's entire system of justice
by adopting English practices and rules of court. At the same time
Somerset also replaced the landdrosts and heemraaden with civil com-
missioners and magistrates.

Delivered in an unrelenting procession by the haughty Governor,
Somerset's decrees had made his country's intentions for the Cape
plain. Henceforward it was to be a British colony, governed by Englishmen for Englishmen without regard for the language, traditions,
or attitudes of its original Afrikaner settlers, many of whom were
soon to decide that the only way to cope with the threatened destruc-

tion of their identity as a people and with the abrogation of rights they considered both traditional and inviolate was to quit the Cape altogether and to seek their fortunes in the wild high veld to the north. Called the Great Trek, this extraordinary exodus, which carried some 14,000 people into the African wilderness, all but emptying the frontier districts, was to become the central epic of Afrikaner history and to leave an indelible mark on the Afrikaner national psyche.

13
THE RISE OF AN AFRICAN EMPEROR: CHAKA ZULU

Somerset and Philip were ambitious men—the former in the service of Queen and country, the latter in the service of religion—and both have left their marks on history. But while these two Britons labored for their reputations at the Cape, colossal events were taking place some 1,200 miles to the north compared to which the colony's internal difficulties seem minor. For in the same year that Philip arrived at Bethelsdorp and Somerset won Parliament's support for his plan to anglicize the Cape, a military genius named Chaka had become chief of a minor Nguni tribe called the Zulu. Within ten years, he was to become a legendary figure throughout southern Africa and to bring about a bloody diaspora of its black tribes that was to turn vast sections of the great central veld into a human wasteland.

The oral sagas of the Nguni, from which most of what is known about Chaka's early rise to power has been drawn, indicate that there had been intermittent strife among the northern Nguni for more than a decade before he became chief of the Zulu. During these quarrelsome years, two tribes had emerged as pre-eminent in the region, the Ndwande under Zwide and the Mtetewa under Dingiswayo, and though it was Zwide who began the bloodletting called the Difaqane, which was to ravage the lives and lands of millions of blacks, it was Chaka, a protege of Dingiswayo of the Mtetewa, who finished it.

The illegitimate son of Chief Senzangakona of the Zulu, Chaka had come to Dingiswayo as an outcast from his father's tribe. Power-

fully built and intelligent, he had found favor with the Mtetewa chief who had begun to treat the young man as a foster son and when Chaka's own father had died, Dingiswayo had been instrumental in having him installed as chief of the Zulu.

As a general under Dingiswayo's command, Chaka had perfected his military tactics with his own Zulu warriors before extending them to all the army. Organizing his men in regiments, which were called "impis," he trained them in "age-groups" and drilled them with a Spartan intensity. Required to run barefoot through the thorn-veld for as much as fifty miles a day in tight formations, his impis were hardened in body by the rigors of constant exercise and in will by Chaka's rigid rule that no man might marry until he had "washed his spear" in the blood of an enemy.

Running in tight formation, in a lock-step trot that calls to mind the equally disciplined goose step of the Nazis, they came to breathe as one, feel as one, and be as one. Enlarged in spirit and at the same time diminished in person by their incorporation into the mass of his army, which numbered 500 at the outset of his career and 50,000 when he died, they became truly its "members"—the arms that threw its spears, the legs that advanced in a rhythmic trot toward an enemy, the voice that broke a perfect silence in the moment immediately before the Zulus rushed howling into battle with a terrifying single whisper, "Si ji di!" . . . "One thousand!"

Drawn up in a formation shaped like the head and tusks of a bull elephant, hardened warriors at the center and inexperienced fighters forming the tusks, they attacked the enemy in waves. Armed with crescent-shaped ox-hide shields, spears and knives called "assegais," which Chaka may have invented, their unity enhanced by their uniform costumes of animal-skin kilts, leg ringlets, and headdresses of undulating varicolored ostrich plumes, the great head "consumed" the enemy's center while the fleet younger warriors encircled and slashed from the sides and behind. An incomparable killing machine, Chaka's Zulus, who knew no word for "retreat," conquered the Mtetewa's enemies one by one during Dingiswayo's lifetime, and when the Mtetewa chief was killed by the Ndwande, Chaka took his patron's place as paramount chief.

He was a brilliant leader of his people and the sagas indicate that more than once he followed Dingiswayo's example and sought peace

rather than war with his adversaries. But the pride of other chiefs made it impossible for them to acknowledge Chaka's superior strength and so conquest followed conquest until Chaka held sway over territories that stretched from the Kei to the Zambezi.

But as his power grew, so also did Chaka's fame and with them his appetite for both. Theatrical by nature, he took pleasure in flaunting himself before his subjects, often required thousands to witness his morning bath, boasted of his own sexual prowess, and gave himself august and megalomanic names like the "Great Elephant," "The Enormous One," and "Si ji di," which he justified by being the personification of his army's courage in battle. But as with many tyrants, Chaka's blood lust grew proportionately with his power. Murder for the sake of murder eventually became a game for him and he devised grotesque tortures for anyone suspected of disobeying or opposing him, burning his concubines alive for the slightest hint of infidelity, impaling and slowly dismembering seditious warriors and treasonous lieutenants. When his mother, Nandi, to whom he appears to have been inordinately attached all of his life, died, he ordered that an estimated 7,000 of his men be clubbed to death because he did not feel they mourned her sufficiently.

But Chaka did not reserve his sadism only for his own people. To avenge Dingiswayo's death at the hands of Zwide of the Ndwande, he not only systematically annihilated most of that once more powerful tribe, but put Zwide's mother to death by letting a starved hyena eat her alive.

A scourge to all who opposed him, he drove his Nguni enemies out of their lands in the territory now called "Qwa Zulu" and onto the high veld where they in turn ravaged the peaceful tribes living there. The "Difaqane" did not end until Chaka himself was murdered in 1828 by his own half brother, Dingaan. When it was done not one of the populous tribes who had claimed the central veld and much of present-day Natal had been left unaffected, and fugitives from Chaka's Zulu were dispersed over a vast, semi-circular region. Along the Indian Ocean coast in the southeast, the Xhosa, Fingo, Tembu, and the Pondo held the lands north of the Kei River. Northwest of them, a wise leader named Moshesh had led his own South Sotho and a number of smaller veld tribes to safety in the recesses of the Drakensberg in what is present-day Lesotho while the Swazi had

established themselves in a more northernly mountain climate. Farther north a deserter from Chaka's own armies, Mizilikazi, had welded another warrior nation out of legions of rebellious Zulu and remnants of other tribes. Called the Matabele, this fierce new nation, which later became a deadly foe of the Boers, held much of the high plateau between the Vaal and Limpopo rivers in its iron grip. But at the very heart of this enormous semicircle of land a great tract of the high veld lay almost empty, inhabited by the remnants of a few defeated tribes, vast herds of game, and a wind that played over the bleaching bones of upwards of two million victims of the Difaqane. And it was into this haunted land that the first of the northward trekking Afrikaners came in 1836.

14
BRITAIN IN CONTROL

There had been reports reaching the Cape of awful slaughter in the north for over ten years. But by the 1830's, the frontier Afrikaners felt less directly threatened by the distant Zulu than by the efforts of Lord Somerset and his successor, Maj. Gen. Richard Bourke, to reorganize and anglicize the Cape Colony.

By 1828, Somerset's currency reforms had become fact, damaging the Afrikaners economically. The Cape's schools, courts, and churches had all been required to conduct business in English only. The familiar landdrosts and heemraaden that had once governed its districts had all been replaced by British magistrates, and to compound the resentments accompanying all this change, Governor Bourke had no sooner replaced Lord Somerset, who had been called "home" as the result of another quarrel with the LMS, than he had announced the promulgation of a new ordinance that seemed to the Afrikaners to countenance mayhem.

Widely credited to the efforts of Dr. John Philip, who had extended his association with South Africa's natives to embrace the Griqua tribes in a region beyond the Orange River, the Fiftieth Ordinance swept away the Hottentot pass laws instituted by Caledon and gave "all persons of colour" permission to move about the Cape

Colony freely, to hold land, and to abstain from work if they wished. Becoming law in a period in which an extended drought had once again brought vagrant Hottentots and displaced hungry refugees from Chaka's depredations into the frontier regions, the new law seemed not only to sanction native vagrancy and the thievery that accompanied it but to weaken the white man's authority to deal with both. Worrisome in its immediate impact on the lonely frontier farms, the ordinance became even more suspicious in its implications in 1832 when a group of farmers, unable to cope with the impact of drought and increased cattle theft in the Zuurveld region applied to the government to remove themselves permanently to lands beyond the Orange River where they had for years been allowed to graze their herds. They were refused and, with this refusal, it seemed plain to many Afrikaners that the British had formed an alliance with "all persons of colour" inside and outside the colony. A year later their suspicions were confirmed when Britain's Parliament decreed an end to slavery in all British territories. By 1834, all slaves at the Cape were to be released from bondage, and by 1838, they were to be entitled to the same rights as the Fiftieth Ordinance had given the Hottentots and Coloreds. Compensation was, of course, to be paid to their owners but at half value.

The new law, which had been passed without any consultation with the Cape's citizenry, threatened to devastate its economy, and represented the "final straw" for the Afrikaners. Britain had come to a Dutch colony, taken it by force, belittled its citizenry, changed its laws, its language, and its customs, put Scots preachers into its pulpits, and even given its lands freely to "natives." Now, it seemed, they not only proposed to cut its settlers off from what they believed to be their birthright—the freedom to take new lands as they wanted and needed them—but to flout God's own order in this world and submerge the Afrikaners in a sea of color while retaining for themselves absolute political control of the country by raising some 36,000 slaves and countless other non-whites to equality before the law with Christians. To the Calvinist Afrikaners, there seemed something diabolical in all this, and they were quick to find proof of a devilish influence in British policy wherever they chose to examine it. In England, they knew, people respected blasphemous men like Dr. Philip, who had defamed the Boers and their Dutch Reformed Church

in print in his book, *Researches in Africa,* and in the newspaper *Spectator.* Closer to home, evil was afoot everywhere. The borderlands were full of vagrants of every skin shade and alive with deviltry. There was no true rule of law left in a land where men more and more distrusted the English courts and took to their guns for protection. Better by far to draw apart from all this confusion and corruption than to stay in a place ruled by ungodly men. "The shameful and unjust proceedings with reference to our slaves," wrote Anna Steenkamp, one of the female leaders of the Great Trek and a niece of its most important figure, Piet Retief, was the central cause of the exodus of thousands of Afrikaners from the Cape in 1836. "And yet it is not so much their freedom which drove us to such lengths," she continued, "as their being placed on an equal footing with Christians, contrary to the laws of God and the natural distinction of race and colour, so that it was intolerable for any decent Christian to bow down beneath such a yoke wherefore we rather withdrew in order thus to preserve our doctrines in purity. . . ."

And so the Great Trek began to take shape.

The land was there—mysterious, beckoning, and reportedly beautiful. Hunting parties that had ventured far beyond the Orange River had brought back news of good country, empty of men, to the northeast of the Griqua. Another road that ran eastward into "Kaffirland" all the way to a trading station at Port Natal on the Indian Ocean Coast reportedly also led to empty regions, cleared of people by Chaka's Zulu, where the grass was green and water plentiful. The time had come to go, to trek away from trouble and the condescension of the British. To find a place "to live in quiet, free, and to be exempt from taxation."

15
AN AFRIKANER REBELLION: THE GREAT TREK

The importance of the Great Trek to that substrate of the collective Afrikaner mind which has produced their fierce nationalism cannot

be underestimated. The Afrikaner language—Afrikaans—is permeated with "trek" terminology. Even the most educated Afrikaner
editor will talk, without the slightest embarrassment, of a "new trek"
of the spirit now under way in his country, of "in-spanning" and
going "up and out" of the country's present malaise, of leaving the
"laager" of the present garrison state behind by fulfilling the "mission" that began with the Great Trek. And the symbolism of the
"trek," as a journey aimed at the survival of the Afrikaner nation
in spirit as well as fact, is to be found throughout the country. There
are monuments, marking the way of the Trek like Stations of the
Cross, along the route the wagons took from Graaff-Reinet, now
a well-restored town, to the Drakensberg mountains in the north, and
the reverence that most Afrikaners seem to feel for the "Voortrekkers" is so essentially religious that it often obscures the reality
of the rough and courageous folk they were. But the Trek was a real
event, nevertheless, often commonplace in its difficulties and burdensome in its dullness but, ultimately, heroic because it was so stupidly
daring.

It began in 1836, after the Xhosa had once again surged over the
frontiers of the Cape Colony to pillage Afrikaner farms along the
Winterberg. As recompense, the new British Governor, Sir Benjamin
D'Urban, had offered the Boers new lands in territories beyond the
Fish, from which the Xhosa had been forced to retreat, but his magnanimity was swiftly cancelled by Lord Glenelg, Secretary of State
for the Colonies in London, when the LMS vehemently protested the
grant. "The Kaffirs had ample justification for the war into which
they rushed," D'Urban was instructed by Glenelg, "in the conduct
which was pursued (toward them) by the colonists and public authorities. . . ." As it happened, word of Glenelg's dispatch reached
the frontier districts within a few days of the news that the long
awaited compensation the British had promised for freed slaves could
be collected only in London.

And so embittered Boers loaded their wagons. Feather beds, and
chickens, a blue dish, plows, picks and spades, the root of an apple
tree and grape vines, seeds and tools, the family Bible—these were
the bits and pieces of lives dismantled and hard-won farms given up
that were piled onto the narrow trek-wagons, three feet wide and
fourteen feet long, as the Great Trek got underway. Within two years,

six thousand Afrikaners had headed north into the unknown wilderness. Left behind were elderly parents, old friends, brothers, sisters, cousins, and all that was familiar to eye and hand as one in every five of the Cape's white settlers abandoned the colony in the years between 1836 and 1838.

The men and women who gathered their children, flocks, and small belongings for the arduous journey knew what they were about. This was a rebellion against British despotism not unlike the American Revolution. Their mass exodus and all the sacrifices it entailed were required to throw off "the yoke" of British tyranny and found a new, God-fearing nation in Africa. But here the similarity between the American and the Afrikaner rebellions ended, for the former had embraced an optimistic new faith based on Locke's and Rousseau's theories of the "natural rights of man," while the latter represented a recoiling from the practical applications of these same Enlightenment ideas, and a withdrawal into a wilderness Africa to preserve an older and far more pessimistic view of human nature that accepted man's awful dependence upon God for salvation in this world and the next.

The fearful spirit of Calvinism haunted a manifesto, published by Piet Retief in the *Grahamstown Journal* on the eve of his own departure from the Cape Colony in February, 1837, listing the reasons for the Great Trek. Though Retief took note of the economic injury done to the emigrants by the emancipation of the slaves he expressed first their "despair of saving the colony from those evils which threaten it." Enumerating among "those evils," "the turbulent and dishonest conduct of vagrants," "plunder" by "Caffres," and the "unjustifiable odium" cast upon his fellow trekkers by "dishonest persons under the cloak of religion," Retief direly predicted "nothing but the total ruin of the country" could result from the British government's liberal policies.

"We are resolved wherever we go," he wrote, "that we will uphold the just principles of liberty; but whilst we will take care that no one shall be held in a state of slavery, it is our determination to maintain such regulations as may suppress crime and preserve proper relations between master and servant. . . . We will not molest any people, nor deprive them of the smallest property; but if attacked we shall consider ourselves fully justified in defending our persons and ef-

fects. . . . We are entering a wild and dangerous territory; but we go with a firm reliance on an all-seeing, just, and merciful Being Whom it will be our endeavor to fear and humbly to obey. . . ."

There was little revolutionary optimism in Retief's manifesto and no declaration of a new and inspired faith in mankind. Evil was afoot in the Cape Colony. The frontier was full of uneasiness and continually threatened with unrest by dark-skinned savages. Crime needed to be suppressed. A proper relationship between master and servant, which reflected the mystic relationships God had ordained on earth, must be preserved if "total ruin" was to be avoided. In conditions emotionally similar to those which had prevailed in war-torn 16th-century Europe, a reactionary Calvinist spirit stalked the frontier. Though Retief declared the trekkers willing to "live in peace and friendly intercourse" with the natives, he left no doubt of their equal willingness to defend themselves if attacked. Practical and prayerful, his manifesto espoused a belief in the principle of liberty but made no mention of "equality" or "fraternity." Reverting to an archaic attitude of absolute reliance upon divine will, the Voortrekkers kept their psalm books and shotguns close to hand as they drove their freighted wagons north. In the "wild and dangerous territory" where they were going they knew they would have need of both.

16
CONFRONTATION AT VEGKOP

The laden wagons and sturdy oxen of almost two thousand emigrants had already cut clear trails north through the purple and brown landscape of the Great Karoo by the time Piet Retief left Grahamstown in February 1837 at the head of a train of 100 wagons. The treks had grown steadily in size and number since 1835, when Louis Trigardt and Janse van Rensburg had led the way through this barren desert where little seems to live save the man-shaped aloes that stand in silent legions on the conically shaped hills. In 1836 two much larger treks under Andreis Potgieter and Sarel Cilliers set out to follow them north.

Potgieter's party consisted of some 40 armed men and their families

in 50 wagons while Cilliers had 28 fighting men and almost as many families with him. Among them were the Krugers, whose ten-year-old son Paul was destined to become the president of an ill-fated South African Republic and lead the Afrikaners in a tragic war against the British some 50 years later.

The two treks left the Cape Colony independently, but once across the Orange River joined for safety's sake, for both believed the "Promised Land" lay beyond the Vaal where scouts had reported good grazing in a country apparently empty of black men.

Though markedly different personalities, Potgieter and Cilliers were well matched. Tall, taciturn, and strong willed, Potgieter, who belonged to an extremely strict Calvinist sect called the Doppers, was a man of iron faith. Cilliers, short, ruddy, and talkative, was also mightily religious. Both willing to place their trust in God, they had few quarrels with each other, and the simple numerical preponderance of Potgieter's party gave him the leadership of the combined trek as it drifted slowly northward. Moving at the faltering six-mile-a-day pace of their grazing herds of sheep and cattle, they made slow progress through the empty bush land of the Great Karoo and it was several months before they emerged onto the true high veld.

Part of the great central African plateau that stretches away in a series of steppes all the way to Kenya, this vast plain opened out before them in an undulating sea of green and gold grass as far as the eye could see. Scrubby in the west, the land grew lusher as they pushed northward until the distant curve of the Drakensberg became visible on the eastern horizon under an upswept billow of cloud. It was better land by far than many of the trekkers had left behind in the southern Karoo and seemed empty of men. But the promise of even richer grazing farther north drew the trekkers steadily onward until the tumbled brown foothills of the Drakensberg began to rise about them in the valley of a river later to be called the Caledon.

Here, where water was sweet and the game sleek and plentiful, they found the Barolong tribe, the once dreaded Batlokua and the Batuang, living peacefully under the watchful eye of the great Sotho chief Moshesh who ruled the Drakensberg highlands from his "fortress of the night" at Thaba Bosigo. The presence of these friendly tribes had been noted by the Great Trek's organizers—Retief, Potgieter, and others—and as part of their plan for founding a new nation

somewhere in the north they had appointed a rendezvous for the various treks and "trekkies" at a place called Blesberg, near the kraal of the Barolong chief, Moroko, at Thaba Nchu.

First to arrive at this rendezvous, Potgieter had made a treaty of friendship with Moroko in May of 1836 and then camped north of Blesberg on the Sand River. There, after negotiating another treaty with Makwana, chief of the Batuang, who agreed to "give" the trekkers lands for grazing up to the Vaal River, Potgieter and Cilliers had left the main body of their party behind and set out with a few men to explore beyond the Vaal where earlier scouts had reported excellent land.

Riding north, they were to be gone three months in search of a "promised land." Informed by earlier scouts of the presence of a warrior tribe called the Matabele in the northern regions, they went warily. They knew that during the Difaqane this tribe had wreaked havoc in the high veld and only been turned back as it roved southward by a Griqua horse commando armed with guns. But from the Sand River to the Vaal, and for some 200 miles beyond it, they found no signs of human habitation save abandoned kraals and the bleaching bones of dead men, until they finally came upon tribes skilled in the use of iron and tin, living well to the north, where they also found Louis Trigardt's little encampment in the far hills of the Zoutpansberg. And along the rising ridges of what they called the Gatsrand, Suikersborand, and Witwatersrand, which hid in their depths all unsuspected the world's richest deposits of gold, land good both for grazing and growing crops went apparently unclaimed.

It was with high hopes of persuading their followers to settle in this promising region that the scouting party under Potgieter and Cilliers was returning south when it was met on the Vaal in September with news of disaster. For the seemingly empty country through which they had just passed was not entirely without claimants. Mizilikazi, the errant Zulu king of the Matabele, was master of its westerly reaches, and with his army of 20,000 ruled over a territory of some 30,000 square miles that stretched from the Vaal northwest of present-day Kimberley all the way to present-day Botswana and beyond.

In Potgieter's and Cillier's absence, some of their party had strayed with their herds from the Sand River encampment and unknowingly

invaded Matabele territory. Sweeping down on them in September, Matabele war parties had killed several members of two small "trek-kies" and annihilated a third. Fearful that these raids might be the harbinger of a full-scale assault, Potgieter ordered the men and their families to entrench their wagons on a hilltop south of the Vaal. Lashing the wagons end-to-end to form a circle, with four "safe" wagons at the center for the children and thornbush barricades encir-cling their makeshift fort, the little "laager" at Vegkop, or "Battle Hill," did not have long to wait for the massed Matabele attack.

It was a classic encounter, the first of many that would follow, which pitted the stubborn courage of a small number of desperate white men and women, armed with muzzle-loading flintlocks called "snaphans," against the equally stubborn courage of an overwhelming number of blacks armed with spears and stabbing assegais. At Veg-kop, 40 armed white men stood against an army of 5,000 Matabele.

The whites prepared for battle by praying and pouring tiny lead shot, each one carefully nicked to shatter when fired, which the women sewed into little buckskin bags for swift loading. The snaphan's range was 100 paces; that of the Matabele's throwing spear roughly 50. In the difference lay the critical edge on which the sur-vival of the Vegkop laager depended.

At dawn on October 19, a Batuang who had joined the trekkers gave the alarm. Savage and splendid in its regalia of ox-hide shields and animal-skin kilts, a vast army of Matabele blackened the plain at the foot of the hill. Drawing together inside the laager, Sarel Cilliers led the whites in prayer before Potgieter and a handful of men rode out to parley. They were greeted with a terrible hissing as the black army began to form its horns for the attack. Potgieter and his group fell back firing, hoping to draw the Matabele into range. The strategy failed. Just out of reach of the snaphans, the Matabele abruptly stopped their slow dance forward and squatted in perfect silence. Hours passed. Inside the laager, tension mounted to the breaking point. Potgieter's brother begged to ride out to lure the Matabele on. Three other whites bolted and got away. Those who remained could smell the Matabele's acrid sweat and hear their breath-ing blend with the wind's whisper across the grass. Finally, as the women and children wept and prayed, Potgieter raised a red rag on a whip and snapped it over the wagons. With a rush, the Matabele

came on, hissing, to hurl their weapons against the lashed wagons and swarm over the thornbush barriers surrounding them until the double canvas coverings of the wagons bristled with spears and the thorn-bush became mounded with black flesh. Unable to break into the laager after two more terrible charges, in which every third white was wounded and two of Potgieter's family were killed, the Matabele finally fell back, leaving Vegkop littered with their unnumbered dead but taking with them all of the trekkers' sheep and cattle and, worst of all, their draught oxen. Immobilized on their hilltop, with many wounded in their midst and low on ammunition, the trekkers dispatched a messenger on one of the few remaining horses to ask aid of Moroko and the Barolong at Thaba Nchu, 200 miles to the south-east, and waited for rescue, keeping watch on a plain whose quiet seemed now to mask a terrible threat. Rescue finally came many days later when a group of sky-blue wagons appeared.

17

PIET RETIEF
AND THE UNITED TREKS

Even after Potgieter's party was rescued by a newcomer, Gerrit Maritz, a wagon maker from Graaff-Reinet who had recently come north with a party of wagons, the story of what had happened at Vegkop was told and retold and rumors drifted among the several assemblages at Sand River like smoke in the wind. It was remembered that just before the trek had begun, the British had signed a treaty with Mizilikazi, a fact that seemed to gain ominous significance in the light of news from the south that under a recently proclaimed Punishments Act, the British had also declared the trek to be "illegal" and the trekkers to be "errant subjects," punishable by law.

Suddenly aware of their vulnerability as "outlaws" and exiles from civilization, the anxious trekkers drew together for safety, clamored for leadership, and took courage in an assertion of God's special inter-est in them as a "Chosen People."

In December, a rudimentary government was formed. Potgieter

was given command of the combined trek and made chairman of its war council and Gerrit Maritz was appointed "landdrost" and "voorsitter" of its legislative assembly, the Volksraad. Soon, a party of 107 armed Boers, 40 Griqua and Koranna, and 60 Barolong had been dispatched to raid the Matabele at Mosego. In January the raiders returned not only with the wagons and stock lost at Vegkop, but with several thousand head of plundered Matabele cattle and three American missionaries who had been living in Mizilikazi's camp. Reassured of the muzzle-loader's superiority to the assegai by this success, the trekkers took heart, but there was still no decision about what their ultimate destination should be. Potgieter still argued for the lands beyond the Vaal despite the Matabele attack. But Maritz had talked to Piet Uys, the man who had scouted the coastal lands for the trekkers in 1834, and had been persuaded by his rapturous descriptions that the Promised Land lay there. Stalemated, the trek remained where it was throughout the summer. By April, when Piet Retief's wagons at last came rolling into Thaba Nchu, there were more than 2,000 people scattered in several encampments across the veld and still no agreement among them as to where the Promised Land lay.

In publishing his manifesto in the *Grahamstown Journal,* Retief had not only succinctly stated the reasons for the trek but his intention to found an Afrikaner nation in the wilderness. Consequently, when he was urged at a mass meeting of men to assume leadership of the combined trek, he had readily accepted. But governing a mass of independent frontiersmen, who had originally been brought together largely by their angry opposition to British rule, proved no easier than reaching a consensus upon where the Promised Land might lie. As the threat of the Matabele had faded, the bonds of fear that had held the trekkers together had loosened and the several treks nominally joined in the "United Laagers" had become quarreling factions.

Winter came and the winds from the Drakensberg justified the region's name, the "kaalveld." Drifting north, the trekkers argued interminably. Even after Nine Articles of Association were finally voted in June of 1837, which required absolute orthodoxy to doctrines of the Reformed Calvinist creed of any would-be citizen of their future Promised Land, the combined treks could still not decide where that land might be.

Potgieter and his large following still insisted that it lay to the
north, beyond the Vaal. Perhaps unwilling to face another confrontation with the Matabele, Retief and Maritz were inclined toward
Natal and had almost won the majority over when the scout Piet Uys,
who regarded Natal almost as a family preserve, arrived at the Sand
River with a sizable following to complicate the situation further by
quarreling with Maritz. As the "United Laagers" again disintegrated
into a collection of quarreling clans, Potgieter prepared to withdraw
his trek and move north across the Vaal. Discouraged, Retief, still firm
in his own conviction that the Promised Land lay east, set off in that
direction with only twenty wagons. He was headed for a confrontation with destiny that would cost him his life, give the trekkers a
martyr to revere and plunge them all into a time of terror that
would be remembered for generations.

18
IN SEARCH OF
A PROMISED LAND

October on the high veld is a glorious time. Spring in full spate paints
the grasslands with flowers of every hue. There is water aplenty,
sparkling in rivulets that by summer are streams of stone. Moving
east, Retief and his followers had left winter behind them on the
backened "kaalveld" and journeyed into spring. Around their wagons, herds of game grazing over the green veld opened and closed
like shoaling fish. Black "widow birds," trailing three-foot tails,
stitched through the air, and the whispering of the weaver birds busy-
ing themselves in the tall grasses sweetened the wind's song.

Retief was heading for a series of passes over the Drakensberg already scouted by his outriders and followed a route eastward that
led down a long shallow valley between buttes that glowed rose in
the slanting sun of early morning. Then, quite suddenly, as the
wagons rounded the thigh of a hill, there was nothing in front of
them but the sky, bellying down over the sheer face of the colossal
fault that is the Drakensberg into the fecund valleys of Natal.

Curving away to the northeast, the mountains were hurled upward to form a solid rampart of rock ten thousand feet high. To the east, swimming in light, far, far below, a seemingly enchanted miniature world of rounded hills, tiny streams, and clusters of green woods was spread out in a soft blue-green haze. And here, with the Promised Land in sight, Retief stopped his wagons—perhaps overwhelmed by the sheer power of the landscape and a sudden premonition of the difficulties that lay ahead. Only days before Retief's scouts had seen a mounted war party of black men, dressed in white men's clothing and carrying guns, driving a large herd of fine cattle and sheep up into the high veld. Identified as Batlokua, under their chief Sekonyela, with whom Potgieter had made a treaty the year before, they had evidently been returning from a raid on the Zulu with whose chief, Dingaan, Retief planned to negotiate for land. Uneasy about the vulnerability of his little party, Retief had made the decision to push on into Natal with a scouting party only when he learned that Maritz was finally coming up behind him with his sky-blue wagons.

Leaving the main body of his company in the lee of a hill on which a natural fortress of huge stones, thrown up by nature, would offer them refuge in time of trouble, Retief warned that no one was to venture down the passes into Natal until he had returned from parleying with Dingaan and then departed with fifteen men and four wagons.

Uncertain of what kind of a welcome he might receive from the Zulu, he made first for Port Natal, an unofficial English trading station on the Indian Ocean coast some 200 miles due east. The journey took the little commando over a series of steppes that led down to the sea. On the first plateau, there was fine grazing land on the hills and rich alluvial land in the valleys where crystalline streams, the head waters of the Tugela, snaked down through wattle groves. Here the land changed subtly into a semitropical thornveld of conically shaped hills and low ridges, furzed in a soft green that was punctuated by the strange, upright cruciform shapes of tall aloes brilliantly in bloom. It was hot in this second region by day, but it grew hotter the farther east the commandos went until Retief and his men found themselves in the tropics, skirting along the edge of a great tumbled gorge that was cloaked in opalescent mists by morning and evening but be-

came a sea of light and shadow by day. Runneled out of the earth by some colossal prehistoric flood, this was the Zulu "Valley of a Thousand Hills" and beyond it lay the palm-fringed coasts, the blue sea, and the little white settlement of Port Natal.

There were about 40 whites living at Port Natal, among them a former captain of the British Royal Navy turned missionary named Gardiner, who had repeatedly petitioned to have the little enclave declared a British territory and repeatedly been refused, although the Colonial Office had finally granted the missionary some loose powers to sign a treaty with the Zulu. Consequently, when Piet Retief arrived at the Natal trading station, the British were in vague possession of a tract of land, ceded by Chaka to them some years before, but had no official status with the British authorities at Cape Town.

From Gardiner and Alexander Biggar, a trader who welcomed his party, Retief learned much about the Zulu chief, Dingaan. Both warned that Dingaan, who had murdered Chaka, was cunning and had to be approached warily, but both also agreed with Retief that it was necessary to strike some kind of bargain with the Zulu before bringing his trekkers into Natal. Retief had therefore set off to meet with the Zulu chief, who styled himself variously the "King of Kings," "The Great Elephant," and the "Lion's Paw" and who, like Chaka, only received visitors on their knees.

The meeting took place inside Dingaan's royal kraal of Umgungundhlovu. Dingaan, tall and fat, greeted Retief and his companions ceremoniously by calling for a feast. During the festivities, Retief, perhaps hoping to impress Dingaan with the idea that the trekkers meant to be his "friends," boasted of their recent victory over his old enemy, Mizilikazi, before presenting his proposal for a treaty to the Zulu King. Dingaan, in turn, indicated his willingness to give the trekkers the same swath of land his predecessor, Chaka, had already ceded to the English traders, on condition that Retief retrieve the cattle Sekonyela had recently stolen from him. Satisfied, Retief had agreed to these terms, obtained a letter to this effect marked by Dingaan and left the royal kraal. In high spirits, he had dispatched a messenger to take the "good news" back to his main party waiting on the high veld, and then had ridden back to Port Natal to discuss the establishment of a new Boer nation in Natal with the Englishmen there.

In Retief's absence, the "headquarters" party waiting above the Drakensberg passes had lived through a fretful time. Lions had ravaged their stock, repeated rumors of hostile native tribes on the march had prompted them to draw up in a defensive laager around the natural stone fort. It was there on November 11, 1838, that they celebrated the "good news" Retief had sent. There was hymn singing, hubbub, and prayer. The next day, heedless of their leader's warning to remain where they were until he had returned, the trekkers prepared to leave for the "Promised Land."

Within a few days, hundreds of wagons, their back wheels locked to permit them to skid their way down the treacherous switchback trails into the valley thousands of feet below, had made their descent into Natal. Within a few weeks, hundreds more had followed. By month's end, almost a thousand wagons and more than 2,000 trekkers had streamed into southern Natal and were spread out along the upper Tugela where Retief, returning to his headquarters in late November, found them.

The trekkers' precipitous arrival in the land of the Zulus had not escaped Dingaan's notice, nor was the Zulu chief unaware of what had been happening on the high veld. There, in mid November, his traditional enemy, Mizilikazi, had suffered a second disastrous defeat at the hands of the war party under Uys, Potgieter, and a new arrival from Graaff-Reinet, Andries Pretorius, and had been driven into exile far to the north in what is now Zimbabwe. And if so formidable a warrior as Mizilikazi could be routed by the white man's guns, Dingaan wondered what might become of the Zulu nation with thousands of these invaders already in their land.

Well before Piet Retief's first visit to his royal kraal, Dingaan had been worried by the white man's arrival in the north. Chaka himself had prophesied that the whites had powerful knowledge that might destroy the Zulu, and Retief's brazen approach to Dingaan's own royal kraal and boasts about Mizilikazi's defeat had only deepened Dingaan's fears. Following Retief's first visit to Umgungundhlovu, he had sent a troop of his warriors to murder Retief and his followers but the plan had failed. Left to brood in impotence, the Zulu chief had learned of the trekkers' descent into Natal and of Mizilikazi's final debacle only a few weeks before he was also told that Retief not only had succeeded in retrieving his cattle from

Sekonyela, but also had stripped the mighty Batlokua chief of his horses and guns and was even then on his way to Umgungundhlovu with the stolen herd and 100 men.

Retief arrived back at Umgungundhlovu on February 3, 1838 and was welcomed ceremoniously by Dingaan. With Robert Owen, the English missionary looking on, there was dancing and feasting. Then the chief and Retief sat down to parley. During their talks, Dingaan repeatedly sought to persuade Retief to give him Sekonyela's guns and horses as well as the retrieved cattle, but to no avail. On the second day of talks, a Monday, a Zulu regiment not seen before in the camp marched in and signaled its arrival by dancing and beating upon its shields in a manner the survivors of Vegkop would have recognized but Retief did not. Robert Owen, alarmed, warned of trouble ahead, but Retief, so close to his goal, would not listen to the Englishman. On Tuesday, February 6, Dingaan finally signed a treaty giving "the Dutch Emigrant South Afrikans" a great tract of land stretching from the Tugela south to the Umzimvubu and invited the whites to share in a toast in his royal kraal. As the cup went round, he abruptly lurched to his feet and shouted "Bublani Abatageti!"—"Kill the Wizards." As he spoke, hundreds of warriors streamed from the surrounding beehive huts and fell on the unarmed Boers. Dragged to a hill just outside Umgungundhlovu, the corpses of Retief's party were left there for the vultures as Dingaan's impis formed and began a relentless three-hundred-mile run that would carry them north to the banks of the Upper Tugela in ten days.

19
DEATH ON THE TUGELA

The sky was moonless, the wind soft, the night a dark velvet cloak that wrapped the trekker encampments along the streams that feed the Tugela in summer's warmth. The Zulu struck from silence just after midnight on February 17 along a twenty-mile front. Every man, woman, and child at a place called Blaauwkrans was killed and the Zulu had overrun several other encampments before the sound of

distant gunfire roused their neighbors upriver, allowing them time to arm before the impis were upon them, surging out of the darkness, black on black, in wave after wave. At dawn, the Zulu were gone. They had taken with them more than 10,000 cattle and as many sheep and left 480 corpses and scores of wounded behind in the laagers and as many of their own number dead in the field. So began a siege that was to last for several months as the trekkers of the "United Laagers" fought for their lives and their tenuous claim to the Promised Land of Natal.

In the weeks after the first onslaught, Maritz rallied them near a place later to be called "Weenen"—"Weeping." There they mourned their dead and dying and wondered what to do. As it was assumed that Retief and his 100 men must also be dead, some argued that the entire trek should return to the high veld and follow Potgieter north. But the majority thought otherwise, and the women particularly were vehement about remaining where the "blood of innocents" had been sacrificed for their sakes. For did not the Book of Exodus reveal how God had tested His Chosen People? The Israelites, journeying out of Egypt, had "moved on from the wilderness of sin" to fight for their survival in the deserts and had prevailed. The Lord had said to Moses, "Write this as a memorial in a book and recite it in the ears of Joshua, that I will utterly blot out the remembrance of Amalek from under heaven."

And so they stayed, weathering a season of discontent that would have broken the spirit of a less stubborn and impassioned people. The rains came, miring the encampments and pinning the trekkers, who were short of draught oxen, down where they were. In April Piet Uys and Potgieter, who had come down from the high veld to help the stranded laagers, had led a disastrous expedition against the Zulu at Italeni where Uys and his 12-year-old son were both killed. Barely escaping with his life, Potgieter had read the disaster as an evil omen and left for the high veld with his own party. Closed in in their laagers the trekkers sickened with fevers that became epidemic, killing hundreds. Maritz succumbed and, as winter deepened, the impis returned and were barely beaten off, leaving more dead behind in the laagers, which were now almost without gunpowder and all but leaderless. But with spring, a new caravan of wagons not

only brought supplies but Andries Pretorius to them. Striding into the beleaguered encampment in a top hat, armed with pistols, a saber, and long rifle, the tall, handsome forty-year-old Pretorius took command of the weakened "United Laagers" on November 22, 1838, and six days later led a commando of five hundred men north to attack the Zulu.

Like the Huguenots of old, the commando rode out singing hymns. Each night, after a defensive laager was drawn, prayer meetings were held and Sarel Cilliers, who had been at Vegkop, read from the Bible. On December 7, Pretorius's scouts reported sighting the enemy, and two days later, a Sunday, the assembled company swore an oath that should God grant them victory, they would celebrate the day thereafter in His name and build a church to testify to their Covenant with Him.

One week later, in a vast saucer-shaped plain beyond the Buffalo River, cut by a small stream called the Ncome, their scouts told them the Zulu impis were near. As the sky darkened, the Boers drew into a laager and set a watch, singing hymns and keeping their lanterns burning. Nothing disturbed the silence of the night save the sound of the wind soughing in the tall grasses, but at dawn the Zulu were there, squatting in massed ranks that numbered between ten and fifteen thousand, their assegais sketching a wall of spikes against a silken silver sky and their many-colored plumes rippling in the wind. At five, the hissing began, and the impis danced forward, some of the Zulu firing guns, most armed only with their gleaming assegais. One who remembered the scene within the laager afterward, as all Zulu land came shrieking toward it, described it as one of "shouting and tumult, lamentation and a sea of black faces in a dense smoke that rose straight as a plumb line upward from the ground." Over and over the Zulu charged and were repulsed in a battle that continued unabated until the Boers' guns were burning hot and the laager was encircled with corpses. At eight, the Zulu finally fell back, leaving some 3,000 dead on the field and the Ncome flowed red with blood. The Boers, who had only three wounded, among them Pretorius, had been given a victory they believed confirmed their Covenant with the Almighty. Generations afterward, the Battle of Blood River was to obtain a significance for the Afrikaners that perhaps not even

the pious Sarel Cilliers, author of the vow of the Covenant, could have foreseen.

2 0

BLOOD RIVER

To reach Blood River today, one turns off a paved highway near the town of Vryheid in Natal and plunges for some distance down a narrow dirt road into a vast natural amphitheater where so many Zulu died. At the battle site, to which thousands of Afrikaners flock annually to commemorate the "Day of the Covenant," there are two monuments, the more impressive of which is a ring of 64 full-scale, cast-iron covered wagons. Turned the color of dried blood, it is positioned as Pretorius's laager was on that fateful December 16, 1838.

To stand alone within that ring in the dark is to invite delusions— to hear the crackle of ancient guns at daybreak, to smell the feral odors of sweat, blood, and fear and to feel the ground tremble with the dancing of warriors long dead as the ghosts that live on in this death-haunted place whirl in the wind. But it is also to find oneself speculating upon the perennial themes of the drama that was played out here and to begin to grasp why this place where 500 whites withstood the onslaught of thirty times their number has come to exercise such a potent hold upon the Afrikaner imagination.

By the time the trekkers had come to this place, they were already of Africa. Exiled from Europe long centuries since, born to Africa's earth, bedazzled by its suns and led on by its chimeras, they had become a tribal people bound by loyalties of kinship and clan to their leaders, by a language that testified to their adaptation to Africa in its "africanisms," and by a shared history of hardship that was already assuming the proportions of tribal legend. Little separated them from the Zulu but their guns, clothes, skin color, and stern Old Testament faith, and even the latter had been subtly Africanized by the year 1838.

Calvinism, at its core, was a creed based upon fear, fear of an omnipotent and inscrutable God, of the devil and his temptations, of death and damnation and of the corruptions of the "natural man" in

whose lusts for power, violence, and free sexual pleasurings John Calvin may have half recognized cravings in himself that Sigmund Freud was later to define as "libidinous." Evidently appalled by his own capacity for "sin," Calvin had sought to repress all that was "natural" in himself by complete submission to God and His laws and had called upon his disciples to do the same for the sake of their eternal souls. But dread of a lapse from perfect piety, of failure to conform to church law, dread of their own lustful appetites and of the chaos of the world had continued to haunt Calvin's disciples for generations, and dread was still a mainspring of the Afrikaner's rough-hewn faith centuries after the specter of eternal damnation had begun to fade from the minds of most European Calvinists. On the frontier, where nature was unsubdued, chaos *was* ever incipient, and the temptation for civilized men to regress to uncivilized ways and for law to give way to violence was explicit. The medieval Calvinist belief that this world was an arena of perpetual struggle between the forces of God and the devil, good and evil, order and disorder, civilization and anarchy had therefore not only been persuasive but necessary to the psychological survival of the trekkers; and the notion that God must have singled them out to bring His order into the wilderness helped these isolated wanderers to repress their own fears, maintain order and cohesion in their ranks, and rationalize the emotional and physical risks of the Great Trek itself.

For these reasons, it seemed to one who stood in that iron laager at Blood River not long ago, Dingaan's challenge to the trekkers would have had a near mythic significance for them. Savage and magnificent, the Zulu armies must have seemed to the outnumbered whites to be the forces of chaos incarnate, and it is possible that what the trekkers glimpsed in the gleaming faces that had come swarming toward their laagers out of the gloom was not only a specter of annihilation but a mocking spirit in whose lusts for blood and conquest they half recognized their own darkest cravings. And it was perhaps from this apparition of the "evils" lurking within themselves that the Calvinist warriors who pursued Dingaan's armies to Blood River recoiled with the greatest dread; for even before the killing had begun they had elevated it to the level of ritual by making a Covenant with God. By aligning their cause with God's, what the commandos with Pretorius apparently sought was not only to ensure

their victory over the Zulu but to exculpate themselves from the slaughter to come by turning their attack upon the Zulu armies into a "holy crusade" sanctioned by divine will.

And so, at Blood River a real battle was transformed into a mythic contest between "heroes" and "villains," "good" and "evil," "order" and "chaos" that was to reverberate with meanings for the trekkers' descendants down through the next century. In the triumph of the 500 defenders of Pretorius laager over some 15,000 Zulu, subsequent embattled generations were not only to see a paradigm for their own struggles to survive as a nation in the face of overwhelming odds, but evidence that God Himself willed that survival. Their destiny as a nation, many would come to believe, had been made sacred by their Covenant with the Almighty who had testified to His desire that they serve as the instrument of His order in Africa by protecting them from the forces of chaos and corruption which lurked there. Loyalty to the cause of their nation and to those whom God had called to lead it was consequently to become equivalent with loyalty to God in the minds of many Afrikaners and those who opposed them or attempted to subvert their faith in themselves risked being regarded as the devil's allies. Thus, at Blood River, the medieval spirit of Calvinism and the old Huguenot notion of divine destiny had been revitalized and recast in African terms. Cut off from the rest of the world on a continent that was to remain only half tamed until well into the present century, the Afrikaners were to linger in one of time's stranger back eddies, a people convinced that the Almighty had singled them out for a transcendent purpose: to stand against the devil in all of his guises so that they might bring His Kingdom into being in Africa. Persuaded that God Himself had guided them through their years of travail before, during, and after the Great Trek, many came to regard their own history with reverence once reserved for Scripture, to canonize their martyrs as saints, assign a prophetic role to their national leaders and, in this century, to elevate their own political causes to the level of a cultist religion that they would pursue with daemonic zeal.

BOOK THREE

———•◆•———

Dreams and Nightmares

MEN WITH A MISSION

Named for Andries Pretorius, who stood with his men against the Zulu at Blood River, Pretoria is the administrative capital of South Africa and the epicenter of the political and religious strength of Afrikanerdom. Erstwhile capital of the first ill-fated South African Republic, which forfeited its independence to Britain in 1902 after a bitter war, it is a country town that became a city at such a rapid rate that it still seems surprised by its own transformation. An agglomeration of architectural styles from "Boer" to "Bauhaus," Pretoria reflects the speed at which the Afrikaners have sought in recent decades to bring a new order out of the old in South Africa. On streets where one may also find shops purveying the necessary animal skins, roots, bones, and potions required by tribal shamans to an all-black trade, modern steel and glass buildings rise skyward above old-fashioned stoeped houses, and the tower housing South Africa's infamous Bureau of State Security (BOSS) and its dreaded interrogation center for political prisoners is only a few blocks removed from the modern Transvaal headquarters of the Dutch Reformed Church and the offices of its Ecumenical Secretary, the Rev. Eddie Bruwer.

Eddie Bruwer's life has spanned the tumultuous years in which Afrikanerdom "came of age" in South Africa. He was born in a little dorp in the northern Transvaal and his earliest recollections are of the 1930's, a decade in which the crippled Boer economy, still suffering from the devastations of the Anglo-Boer War, which capped the 19th century, was further crippled by drought and a worldwide depression.

"It was a terrible period for us," Bruwer remembers, "and one that was very much a part of my own life. My father was the pastor in the little village where I grew up and deeply engaged in his people's plight. The Afrikaners were abysmally poor then. They had nothing. No schools, no teachers, no future, no hope. Born to the

veld, they knew only their farms and the little towns like the one in which I lived. The world beyond, the world of the cities, was a mystery to them. And yet, one by one, as they lost their farms, they were being swept into the cities—into a world they barely understood. I remember when my father took some of us to the fair in Johannesburg in the 1930's. Many came barefoot or carrying their only shoes. Almost none had ever been away from the dorp where they had been born. They were as the blacks are now, reaching out for the first time, innocents in a world they'd never made. My father could see what was happening. He knew what evils awaited them in the cities where the English were in control, and like many of his fellow 'predikants,' he tried to be everything he could to his flock—their teacher, counselor, business advisor, protector, friend. They were so much in need of help then, so much in need of leadership. . . ."

The years that Eddie Bruwer remembers as the years of his own childhood were indeed tragic for the Afrikaners. Defeated in the Anglo-Boer War, they had literally lost their "birthright" in Africa and become as the Afrikaner poet van Wyk Louw described them— "Simple people who perform, true and singly bitter things and singly fall like grains of seed . . ." in a "wide and woeful land."

The trek behind them, they had held onto their independence as a nation for only fifty years, losing it to Britain in a war of surpassing bitterness. Lives, hopes, years of labor had all been forfeited to a mighty power that cared little for the Afrikaners' old-fashioned ideas, and when the Union of South Africa was brought into being in 1910 most Afrikaners faced a new age of British economic dominance in their country, ill-prepared for the changes it would bring.

During the Anglo-Boer War much of the veld had been devastated and hundreds of farms burned. In its aftermath, dispossessed Afrikaners had begun drifting toward the cities in search of work. Unsophisticated and unskilled, they soon found themselves competing for menial jobs in British-owned mines with black laborers who were paid a fifth of the wages commonly earned by whites. Mastered by the British and threatened by the blacks in the labor marketplace, the Afrikaners sought an antidote to their growing sense of inferiority to the former and fear of being economically overwhelmed

by the latter in political activism that in 1924 helped to bring an Afrikaner-Labor coalition to power. But even as this "Nationalist" government took legislative steps to protect white workers from being undercut by the British mine owners' exploitation of blacks by reserving certain jobs for "whites only," the number of "poor whites" among the Afrikaners increased steadily as droughts devastated the veld and rinderpest decimated what remained of the Boer herds. By the 1930's, with the entire world in the grip of a depression, one in every three Afrikaners was classified as indigent, and in country dorps like that in which Eddie Bruwer grew up, a proud people had been reduced to pauperism.

"It was in those years," Bruwer remembers, "that the Broederbond was formed. A secret society, made up of Afrikaner intellectuals and religious leaders, its object was to help Afrikaners regain their place in the world, for we knew by then that we could expect no help from the British . . ."

Strengthened by the commitment of men like Eddie Bruwer's father to his people's cause, the Broederbond and the Dutch Reformed Church took a leading role in organizing a "reddingsdaad," an attempt to redeem those who had fallen into physical and spiritual poverty by organizing self-help groups that drew "Die Volk" together. Soon, under the tutelage of the "predicants," almost half of whom were Broederbonders, this self-help effort began to express itself in political activism, and by 1938, when the Great Trek was reenacted at its Centenary, a new wave of Afrikaner nationalism had crested.

"My father *lived* that experience," Eddie Bruwer recalls. "The fires on the mountain tops were the fires burning in the hearts of the Afrikaner people, and I, as the great-grandson of one of the fighters who stood at Blood River, had the privilege to walk a few yards at the head of the ox wagons. It was an experience I shall remember all of my life. It brought us all together, made us one with one another, made us certain again of who we were. And out of that feeling of cohesion, we became again what we had always been—a tribal people—as clannish as the blacks with the mystic's sense of being a part of this land and the mystic's sense of having been given a mission here by God. It was out of that sense of calling, one that I believe began long ago out there on the veld, where the far horizons

speak of eternity, that the Afrikaner ideology of Christian National-ism grew. Out of that and our desire to become something in this world once again."

At the Centenary of Blood River, the descendants of the trekkers had reacted to their economic dispossession by the British and still unmastered fears of engulfment by South Africa's black majority by a reassertion of their old-fashioned faith in their vocation in Africa. But as the forties had progressed, the rhetoric of Christian National-ism, which had initially been aimed at inspiring a self-redeeming spirit among the impoverished and demoralized Afrikaner Volk, became ominously messianic as the church itself became increasingly politicized.

"The history of the Afrikaner," avowed Daniel Malan, an or-dained minister of the Dutch Reformed Church and a political activist who was to lead the Nationalist party to victory in the 1948 elections, "reveals a determination and definiteness of purpose which makes one feel that Afrikanerdom is not the work of man but a creation of God. We have a divine right to be Afrikaners. Our history is the highest work of the centuries. . . ."

"Die Volk," insisted Piet Meyer, Malan's associate and one of the Nationalist party's primary political theorists, had been "called" by "an All-Knowing Disposer" to a "divine task" and was to become "an organic wearer of authority with the patriarchal leader as the chief bearer of the authority of the nation. . . ." "The Boer people," Meyer proclaimed in the early 1940's, "had entered a Covenant with God so as to maintain themselves as God's people, to honor their separate calling as God's ordination. . . ." That "calling," he further avowed, could only be fulfilled if "The People" maintained its "unique life form," while it also imbued the entire culture with its Afrikaans Calvinist spirit.

"Separate development—'apartheid,' if you will—grew directly out of the heart of Christian Nationalism," admits Rev. Eddie Bruwer, in a tone edged with uneasiness. "The people believed in it because the Church itself had found it in accordance with Scripture, so long as it was done in accordance with 'righteous law.' "But it was not until the end of the war, after the British had so exhausted themselves in Europe that they had begun to lose their grip on Africa, that Afrikanderdom came into its own politically. I remember

"Calitzdorp, a town of a few thousand souls,
stands athwart one of the original routes
the trek-boers used as they drove . . . eastward."
The houses of Colored farmhands on
the outskirts of Calitzdorp resemble those
originally built by the trek-boers.

"Sam Brink's distaste for apartheid
is shared by his son Dirk, who would also
like to eliminate such vestiges of
the Afrikaners' patriarchal past as the . . .
wine ration to Colored farmhands . . ."
Dirk Brink distributes the "dop" (left).
Sam Brink (right foreground)
and his brother-in-law.

"Sam Brink can truthfully boast of producing . . . some of the best breeding stock for the ostrich trade." Dirk Brink leads the family ostrich herd to pasture.

". . . the trek-boers had driven their oxwagons . . .
upward over the heights of the first
dizzying escarpment . . . into a new world."

"Jac Faure's life at Vergenoeg retains
the shape of times past from which
present day South Africa evolved."
Jac Faure (left), master of Vergenoeg,
a Cape wine farm, and a black worker (right)
in Faure's wine cellar.

"We drove
country roads
down to Qwa Zulu."
Zulu woman
in the fields
near Tugela Estate,
Qwa Zulu.

"The city had become worldly and opulent."
Johannesburg.

". . . because the memory of these well-ordered
little worlds . . . went with those who
were forced to leave them . . .
generations of Afrikaners were to idealize
the benign life they seemed to represent."
The Faures at Vergenoeg,
their family home since 1820.

*Passes beyond Worcester, Cape Province,
that give access to the Great Karoo.*

"A land for poets, visionaries, and madmen, it was here
that Africa began to take possession of the Afrikaners
in spirit as it had claimed heart and hand in the Cape."

*The undulating reaches of the arid Karoo
along a route northward used during the Great Trek.*

"They were as the blacks are now,
reaching out for the first time,
innocents in a world they'd never made."
An outdoor classroom in Qwa Zulu.

when word of the Nationalist victory came in 1948. We were bewildered with joy. I remember how we students in Pretoria flocked
to Church Square to celebrate. Such tumult. Such excitement! Yet
standing in that sacred place for Afrikanerdom, I felt strangely awk-
ward—somehow outside of what was happening. Perhaps I sensed
even then that something was wrong. But it was too soon. Too
soon to know. Too difficult to turn against the tribe. We Afrikaners
were like a nation of adolescents then—just coming into our maturity.
You couldn't say yet that the child was bad. There was such burning hope in it, such conviction, such a passion to do things. Because
you see, we really hadn't expected power. It had come as a shock, so
that even as Malan was on his way up from the Cape after his election, he was still trying to formulate a clear policy for his government."

The governments of Daniel Malan and the Nationalist prime
ministers who succeeded him in the fifties were the governments of
zealots. Words like "independence," "cultural self-determination,"
"purity," "freedom," and "destiny" rolled from their tongues as they
formulated a new civil religion for the Afrikaner Volk, a religion
of political exclusivity and transcendence.

In 1938 Malan had told an audience at Blood River, "Here . . .
you stand on holy ground. Here was made the great decision about
the future of South Africa, about Christian civilization in our land,
and about the continued existence and responsible power of the
white race. . . . You stand here upon the boundary of two centuries. Behind you, you rest your eyes upon the year 1838, as upon
a high, outstanding mountain top, dominating everything in the
blue distance. Before you, upon the yet untrodden path of South
Africa, lies the year 2038, equally far off and hazy. Behind you lie
the tracks of the Voortrekker wagons, deeply and ineradically etched
upon the wide outstretched plains and across the grinning dragon-
tooth mountain ranges of our country's history. . . . The trekkers
heard the voice of South Africa. They received their task from God's
hand. They gave their answer. They made their sacrifices. There is
still a white race. There is a new People. There is a unique language.
There is an imperishable drive to freedom. There is an *irrefutable*
ethnic destiny. . . ."

"They did not see what had happened at Blood River as a manifestation of God's compassion," admits Eddie Bruwer. "They saw it rather as a confirmation that there must always be an Afrikaner nation in Africa and that their national survival was His concern. It followed from this that Christian National development was devoted to that survival, physically, economically, and socially. . . ."

Conviction carried the zealots of Afrikaner Nationalism forward at a mad pace in the early fifties as the ground rules of "apartheid" were laid down in a plethora of legislation. So that each nation might develop "rooted in its own national soil," the Nationalist government created a series of separate "homelands" for South Africa's tribal blacks and separate Group Areas for its Coloreds and Indians. To assure the "cultural survival" of these ethnic groups, social mingling was limited by law, education conducted in the "mother tongue," and restrictions placed on the movements of blacks, in particular, by "influx controls" and the rationalization of extant "pass laws" into a system of "reference books" to be carried by all African men. "Never," wrote one wag, "have so few legislated so much for so many." Dogmatic to the bone, like the true Calvinists they were, implacably logical and swept along by their inner convictions that "Right makes might," a new generation of Broederbond thinkers and politicians led by Hendrik Verwoerd rose to power in the 1950's, and the work of reordering South African society completely in accordance with Afrikanerdom's radical reactionary vision went on relentlessly as law upon law limiting, defining, and restructuring the life of its peoples was passed.

"We are trying to go down through the clay to the gravel and bedrock so that the nation of South Africa may exist to remote times in the future,"declared Verwoerd solemnly in the 1950's. "Perhaps it was intended that we should have been planted here at the southern point within the crisis area so that from this resistance might emanate the victory whereby all that has been built up since the days of Christ may be maintained for the good of all mankind. May you have the strength, people of South Africa, to serve the purpose for which you have been placed here." The message was messianic and spoken in the voice of a "true believer" willing to sacrifice the present to a millennial future.

"Verwoerd gave expression to the Afrikaners' vision," Eddie Bruwer commented somberly. "He had truly terrible powers of persuasion.

His logic seemed irresistible, and the power of that logic led us onward so that even today it is Canon if Verwoerd said it. His dream became our dream. His iron will, our will. Through him, we felt ourselves called once again, and we gave ourselves to our vision. We were all missionaries in those days. God had given us power to wield so that we might guide South Africa out of chaos and preserve His order by assuring that each tribe might develop according to its own heritage. But while we were all focused on the future, we neglected the present. And the present, for the black man, lay not in the homelands but in the cities. Yet even into the 1970's, we tried not to face this. We hid from the truth—the terrible simple truth—that we had failed to consider reality. And reality was the black man's desperation, the real pain of his condition and his rage. We dreamed of Order, but never, you see, escaped from the confusion we feared so; it was with us all the time. And when in 1976 Soweto exploded, it was like waking from a dream to find we were living in a nightmare."

22

APARTHEID: THE DREAM BECOMES A NIGHTMARE

Because of the riots that began there in 1976 and spread to the rest of South Africa, setting off a political chain reaction that continues to this day, Soweto looms large in the world's imagination as a symbol of all that is wrong in racially divided South Africa. What must be done to relieve the political oppression of its inhabitants, and of South Africa's non-whites in general, is discussed in college classrooms, "think tanks," in corporate board rooms, and in the counsels of heads of state as various as those of the United States, the Soviet Union, and Nigeria. But Soweto is also a *place* where people who must deal with its appalling social problems daily live and work, and as is often the case in South Africa, its reality is paradoxical.

To reach Soweto one takes a southbound highway out of Johannesburg, turns right at a fast-food stand selling "Boerewors" and beer to a mixed clientele and continues along the spine of a gaunt ridge, picked clean of all burnable vegetation by scavenging black hands.

When Baragwanath, the largest hospital in all of Africa, which serves non-whites only, appears on the left, Soweto comes into view on the right. Built in a great natural basin, the Southwestern Townships, better known by their acronym—Soweto—are subject to weather inversions and in winter seem to swim in their own smoke. Worst in the mornings and evenings, when Soweto's million and a half residents stoke their coal cookstoves, the thick yellow-brown smog has usually cleared sufficiently by midday so that from Baragwanath one can see Soweto for what it was: a planner's dream.

Begun in the fifties when the late Hendrik Verwoerd was South Africa's Minister of Bantu Affairs, Soweto was completed during his tenure as Prime Minister in the 1960's. It looks from a distance like an intricate sworled cache of insect eggs, planted with perfect precision upon the brown skin of the veld. Originally designed to provide low-cost housing for hundreds of thousands of blacks who had swarmed to Johannesburg in search of work prior to 1948, Soweto replaced a vast warren of tin and packing-crate hovels that had grown up around Johannesburg like one of those cinctures of misery that still encircle such cities as Lima, Calcutta, Rio, and Kingston. Built row on row, sworl on sworl, to cover some twenty-five square miles of low lying veld, the thousands of three- and four-room dwellings that make up the twenty-seven "townships" amalgamated as Soweto brought a certain monotonous order out of the noisome and colorful chaos of the shanty towns they replaced.

The men who conceived Soweto did not, however, want it to prosper. At the outset, this and the other townships, which were built on the outskirts of every major South African city in the fifties, were planned for obsolescence in a few generations. By then it was expected that a program of intensive development in the "homelands" would have brought the blacks close to economic self-sufficiency, creating a counterflow of black migration away from the "white core" cities. According to Henrik Verwoerd's own timetable for "separate development," the majority of the houses in Soweto and similar townships were expected to begin to lose their raison d'être in about 1976 when the flood tide of black migration was expected to begin to ebb. A grandiose make-do scheme from the first, Soweto was, therefore, planned with Teutonic thoroughness to provide decent interim houses for masses of blacks until such time as the greater attractions of their "homelands" would begin to lure them away, and was deliberately designed as a soulless entity with the word "Temporary" written large in the master plan of its construction.

Though each of its houses was provided with running water, very few had electricity or indoor plumbing, and none had telephones. There were to be no corner groceries in Soweto, no cobblers' shops, no small businesses, no industries, no opportunities for black investment. Home ownership and freehold of land were also disallowed and with them the right of property inheritance. In short, nothing about Soweto was to encourage its residents to think of it either as permanent or as "home." Instead, its very nature seemed meant to imply to blacks that they did not really belong in those areas that had been designated under the 1950 Group Areas Act as "white," and this notion was also carefully reinforced by a body of Draconian legislation that made life for urban blacks demeaning and difficult.

By law, no black was permitted to remain in a "white area" for more than 72 hours unless he could prove he had been born there, been employed there for at least ten years, and had no criminal record. Only those who met such criteria were to be considered legal residents of the townships and be entitled to have their families with them. Any black who did not was regarded as a legal resident of his or her tribal "homeland" and was allowed in the "white area" only as a migrant worker, subject to strictly enforced pass laws and influx controls that made it illegal for their families to accompany them to the cities and limited their labor contracts to 12 months.

What lay behind the Nationalists' ruthless attempts to discourage further black migration to the cities in the 1950's was, of course, fear. Newly arrived in power politically, still haunted by bitter memories of the recent past, the Afrikaners were a profoundly insecure people. Their historic dread of engulfment in black Africa, with them since the Trek, had been exacerbated in the first third of the twentieth century when thousands of Afrikaner poor whites had found their economic survival in the British-dominated cities threatened by the latter's willingness to exploit them as part of a vast labor pool that was predominately black. Even during the years of the "Union of South Africa," Afrikaners in the north, whose heritage was one of incessant struggle against domination by black man and Briton alike, had not learned either to trust or to like their British brethren, not only because the latter had managed to acquire most of the country's wealth at Afrikaners' expense but because, historically, British capitalism had consistently advanced its own interests in South Africa by exploiting the "native question," even as it had methodically misused both the blacks and the Afrikaners for its own benefit. The Afrikaners, therefore, not only believed they had reason to worry about the potential of a new alliance between "liberal" British capitalists and black power groups in the 1950's, but they were realistically concerned about the long-term socioeconomic and political implications of the creation of an enormous black lumpen proletariat in South Africa.

Population projections in the 1950's had indicated that by the year 2000 there would be six million whites and thirty-five million blacks in South Africa. Demographic and economic projections also indicated at the time that unless the extant trends were reversed, 70 percent of the country's black population would in fifty years be clustered in urban centers where there would not be enough work available to them. Shorter term economic forecasts furthermore indicated that a glut of unskilled black labor was already developing on the industrial labor market, and that black unemployment overall could only be expected to worsen in coming decades unless new jobs could be found on a large scale. The possibility that millions of half-starved, half-civilized semitribal blacks might soon be pounding at the gates of Johannesburg and other South African cities looking for work that did not exist, therefore, seemed real to Afrikaners of the 1950's. Coupled with this was the threat that, in such circumstances, South Africa's social and political order might founder in a sea of black unrest; for in the midst of the Cold War, militant Marxism was already on the march in Africa.

There was, therefore, an element of reasonableness in the Afrikaners' dread of the so-called "Swart Gevaar" in the 1950's. What was unreasonable was their response to it. Because it seemed to spell the end of the old social order that most Afrikaners had come to regard as in accordance with divine will, many of them could no more accept the inevitability of the black man's march to the cities and into the 20th century than they could conceive of a future in which blacks might come to dominate whites politically in South

Africa. Captives of their own frontier heritage, still as terrified of being overwhelmed in a sea of black primitivism as they had been at Blood River, and suspicious to the point of being paranoic about the motives of both the country's powerful English-speaking whites and its leftist-leaning black opposition groups, the Afrikaners' dread of a future in flux drove them to try to keep it at bay by clinging to the past. And so, like their Huguenot ancestors, they had begun to seek a model for what *should* be in what had been. Satisfied that God Himself had separated the nations at Babel, they also believed devoutly that it was His desire that Afrikanerdom should survive to bring a new order in Africa. It was, therefore, as zealots in what amounted to the "holy cause" of "separate development" that they had embraced Hendrik Verwoerd's policies in the 1950's and had embarked upon a radical program of social engineering that was in time to prove as ruthless as most such attempts to make reality conform to theory seem destined always to be.

In 1950, the cornerstone of "apartheid" was laid when the Group Areas Act was passed. It mandated specific areas of South Africa be reserved for its several racial groups, gave the largest share of its territory to its white minority and set aside ten separate semistates called "Bantustans" or "homelands" for the country's nine linguistically distinct tribes. Based on reserves that had been demarcated by the British for tribal blacks in the 19th century, these "homelands," when enlarged by land purchases, were to account for some 13 percent of South Africa's total territory and 40 percent of its arable lands. That same year, the government also appointed a study group, called the Tomlinson Commission, to explore the potential for "homeland" development and to recommend ways in which South Africa's tribal lands might be coaxed into providing livelihoods for the majority of its blacks.

In 1954, the Tomlinson Commission delivered its recommendations to the then Minister of Bantu Affairs, Hendrik Verwoerd. Almost 4,000 pages long, it advised that an investment of R208,000,000 be made in the "homelands," emphasized the need for the rapid development of their agriculture and light industry and detailed plans for creating fully diversified economies capable of supporting their populations. Fearful, perhaps, of the political implications of attaching such a price tag to "separate development," Verwoerd quietly shelved the Commission's full report, issued a brief precis of its proposals and suggested that only R72,000,000 would be necessary to implement them.

In 1955, he shepherded a second major piece of "apartheid" legislation, the Resettlement Act, through Parliament. Aimed at making South Africa's racial demography conform to the cartography outlined by the Group Areas Act, it resulted in the forced relocation of some three million people, most of them non-whites, in a program not unlike that which had been employed in the resettlement of America's Indians in the 19th century. South Africa's vigorous tribal blacks, however, not only survived the cruel uprooting, which continued for a decade, but began to multiply. Between 1955 and 1965 tribal birthrates climbed and though the black infant mortality rates remained ten times the white, the economic development of the "homelands" began to lag behind the economic needs of their burgeoning populations, driving a steady stream of blacks off the land and into the cities in search of work.

By 1970 there were approximately nine million blacks, half of the total black population of South Africa, living in areas officially designated as "white." By 1975, Soweto, a "temporary" housing scheme originally designed to accommodate 350,000, had become a permanent ghetto for a million and a half Coloreds, Indians, and blacks, only half of whom were legal residents. Crowded six to twenty-five to a house, they were to turn Soweto, a planner's dream that had grown in spite of itself, into a nightmare. This vast complex of 101,000 little boxlike houses was owned and run like some cumbersome Socialist welfare camp by the West Rand Administration Board. One of the largest cities in all of Africa, Soweto, by 1976, had more than a million black inhabitants. Of these, less than half had jobs, about half were living below the poverty line, and more than half were under twenty. The majority of its children were undernourished; the majority of its youth, unemployed; the majority of its schools, vastly overcrowded; the majority of its houses becoming dilapidated; and the majority of its neighborhoods, crime ridden. Murders averaged three a night. Gangs of thugs, called tsotsies, roamed its streets. The police were overworked and ill-trusted. Its teachers were ill-trained. Its administrators were largely corrupt; its services were vastly overburdened; and its instability was enhanced by a volatile mixture of tribal newcomers from the "homelands" and second- and third-generation urbanites whose own tenuous hold on security seemed to be threatened by an influx of too many unskilled, uneducated laborers for too few jobs. In short, Soweto had become a disaster waiting to happen, and in 1976 it exploded.

It was an ill-advised decision, made by Andries Treurnicht, another Afrikaner preacher turned politician and until recently the leader of the Transvaal division of the Nationalist Party, that ignited the Soweto riots. Newly appointed to the post of Deputy Minister of Bantu Education by John Vorster, South Africa's Prime Minister in 1976, Treurnicht was an arch conservative who still clung religiously to the principles of Verwoerdian "apartheid." Apparently determined to promote his own political career as a Nationalist hardliner, Treurnicht had insisted on implementing an outmoded rule which required that half of the subjects offered in Soweto's secondary schools be taught in Afrikaans, in spite of the fact that almost none of its black teachers spoke the language. Reaction to his decision had come swiftly. Black parents had complained, teachers had resisted, and on May 16, 1976, students at Orlando West Secondary School had walked out of their classrooms, indicating that they would not return until the language rule was rescinded. A month later, after a second student walkout at Naledi High School had ended in violence, all of Soweto had exploded in deadly rioting.

"We got a call on our radio that another patrol was in trouble and we drove over," said Martin Hatting, one of the one hundred white policemen who continue to serve with Soweto's eleven hundred black officers on regular street patrol. "We got caught as we went down a side street. All had seemed quiet, but suddenly a gang just roiled up out of the dusk. Two or three hundred of them attacked our van. They were throwing fire bombs and stones. The stones came right through the windshield of the van and both the driver and I were hit and bleeding. Then they were on us, rocking the van back and forth, screaming for our lives. That's when I shot three dead. My dog, a police dog trained for riot work, got loose then and ran at the mob. Some of them scattered and he followed. I went looking for him the next day. I saw a black fellow I knew—a friend of mine—who also had an Alsatian. He told me they'd caught my dog, mutilated it and then burned it alive. He took me to where its body was. I couldn't understand anybody doing that to a dog. After that first night the rioting seemed to go on and on. They'd come in mobs, mostly kids of fifteen and sixteen, mixed up with the tsotsies. The tsotsies seemed to want to stir things up. We call 'em the 'tackie brigades' because they always wear white tackies [sneakers]. They'd been terrorizing Soweto for years and still are. The riots just gave them a greater chance to do what they wanted, so while the kids marched and shouted and burned their schools and the West Rand Administration Buildings, the criminals stole liquor and took advantage of the turmoil—until the Zulu took to the streets and delivered their own kind of justice. And we're still contending with that—the Magkotlas [tribal courts] that deliver their own rough justice, the tsotsies, the factional fighing and political murders. Ach man, its madness what goes on here and what's strangest is that when the trouble's at its worst, it's always the white policeman they want because, these days, the parents think only the white cops can control their kids. . . ."

On the first day of the Soweto riots, police counted 250 injured and 25 dead. Among the latter was a lone white man, a social worker named Melville Edelstein whose recently published book, *What Do Young Africans Think?* had carefully documented the profound frustration of Soweto's youth. Edelstein had been beaten to death.

The violence continued for eight days. Unable to control the mobs, Soweto's predominantly black police force had been augmented by the government's dreaded "Swanepoel" riot units. While helicopters patrolled the township's perimeters, dropping tear gas, Swanepoel operations commenced inside Soweto and the death toll climbed to 176. Soon rioting had spread to other townships along the Rand, and state police operatives had begun arresting and detaining blacks by the thousands. Concurrently, the government held out an olive branch, promising to rescind the language rule, and the first spasm of violence began to subside. For a month there was quiet, but in July another outbreak of arson, this one directed chiefly at the schools, swept Soweto. In spite of an order to desist issued by the Soweto Student Representative Council (SSRC), which had organized the June protest, the fire bombings continued and soon new violence had enveloped townships from Johannesburg to Cape Town. This time, the government made no attempt to placate rioting blacks. Newly returned from conferring with Henry Kissinger in Switzerland on the touchy subject of "apartheid" and African-American politics, John Vorster, then Prime Minister, issued a despotic warning to blacks: "There is no way of governing South Africa other than by the policy and principles of the Nationalist party." Vorster warned, "If it [the violence] does not stop and stop immediately other steps will have to be taken . . ." The Minister of Police, meanwhile, had been making his own demagogic statements: "He [the black] knows his place," Jimmy Kruger had told a cheering audience of right-wing Nationalists, "and if not I'll tell him his place. . . ."

Apparently in response to the government's "hard line," the SSRC called a general strike in Soweto that all but paralyzed Johannesburg. In Cape Town, Colored students held solidarity demonstrations with the Soweto strikers, prompting marches into the center of Cape Town. These ended with rioting, which was brutally repressed by police in the full sight of stunned white Capetonians. As the newspapers filled with photographs of rioting mobs and dead black children, fear and guilt began to overtake white South Africans in general, and Afrikaner moderates in the Cape, particularly, began to plead for compromise and compassion. Daily, the situation grew more explosive as the rioting continued in townships throughout the country. When Cape police raided Colored and black schools, attacking children and teachers alike, Colored militants, polarized by their brutality, opened a terrorist campaign that continues to the present time. Reacting to the spread of violence, the impetuous Minister of Police sanctioned the formation of white vigilante groups. His action brought a spate of new attacks on white homes and businesses, which police answered by sweeping raids in the townships that, in Soweto, netted the entire civil leadership of the community. Young radicals countered in September of '76 by methodically fire bombing the government-owned liquor stores, bars, and beer halls patronized by many Soweto adults, serving notice in fire that they would not be co-opted as their parents had been. The racial division had now been complicated by a generational division among the blacks. This was a children's revolution. A new generation had taken charge. It was unafraid of the consequences of its action. It would, in fact, stand trial in 1980 to let the world know it was unafraid, while the revolution it had begun continued to simmer beneath the surfaces of South

African life. Shuddering on the brink of all-out racial warfare, white South Africans were at last forced to look squarely at the face of black rage. But what they saw in that face was regrettably not what the rest of the world saw—the rightful anger of a wronged people— but the specter of incipient anarchy that could destroy the black man and white alike. Products of a peculiar past, many Afrikaners responded to this dark vision by girding for a new confrontation with the same ancient enemy they believed they had glimpsed at Blood River: the devil, whose metier was chaos and whose legions they believed were assembling in this century under the banners of "godless communism."

23
SOWETO:
A SEARCH FOR SOLUTIONS

Among the concessions the government offered rioting blacks in 1976 was a promise to overhaul "Bantu Education." The man chosen to fulfill this promise in Soweto was Dr. Jaap Strydom. A Falstaffian figure, tough, jovial, and shrewd, Strydom was an old Soweto hand. A twenty-year veteran of "Bantu Education," fluent in Sotho and Zulu and a former inspector of Soweto's schools, Strydom was as well acquainted with its problems as he was with the political difficulties of trying to resolve them.

Strydom had joined what was then the "Department of Bantu Education" two years after it had begun implementing a new government program of black education in 1955. "I thought then," he remembers, "that I could make a contribution and believed that South Africa's problems could only be solved by educating *all* of its people to the same level." From the start, he found there was much to do. Until 1954, a year in which only 534 young blacks had received the equivalent of a high school diploma in South Africa, there had been no unified program of black education in the country and only the most rudimentary schooling was available to the majority. In the first half of the 20th century, the few secondary institutions that did exist for blacks were boarding schools, largely run by British missionaries and attended only by the very few blacks who could afford them. As part of its ambitious scheme of "separate development," the Nationalist government had been determined to systematize black education, and in 1953 had begun building and opening primary and secondary schools and training black teachers at a rate that was astonishing, given the limited funding allocated to the task.

In a scant twenty years, black enrollment in primary schools—where the rudiments of reading, writing, and ciphering were taught in the tribal tongues—had risen from 731,170 in 1955 to better than three million in 1976 and black literacy rates in South Africa had risen to become the highest in all of Africa. No mean accomplishment, "Bantu Education" had scored what seemed a stunning success, and as the majority of new black pupils registered for schools were in the "homelands," Afrikaners pointed with pride to these statistics as a measure of the success and sincerity of their government's effort at "separate development."

But Jaap Strydom, who had become a Soweto school inspector in the late 1960's, saw the opposite side of the picture in its swarming schoolrooms and realized that whatever had been obtained statistically by the general improvement in black education might well be lost unless the heightened aspirations education had created among young urban blacks were taken into consideration. Able to read and write, alienated altogether from their tribal past, a new generation was growing up in the townships that needed, wanted, and deserved new opportunities, and Strydom was among those who recognized early the dangers inherent in their growing frustration.

"The truth was," he said bluntly, "that the blacks of Soweto weren't 'Bantu' anymore and they couldn't be treated as such. It was like telling a child who has learned how to walk that he hasn't, that your schedule for his development says he's a toddler still and so he'll just have to get back down on all fours and creep and only stand up with your help. . . . Well, the kids especially wouldn't accept that kind of thinking anymore. This generation can read and write because we've taught them how, and they are not about to go back to the old way or to accept condescension from the whites. They are a generation halfway between what was and what will be and not only their future but ours depends on the way we treat them. . . ."

Aware of the pressures building up among young blacks well before Soweto exploded, Strydom had advocated a new program of technical and vocational education aimed at mainstreaming them into skilled jobs in industry.

"My kind of thinking wasn't exactly popular with the politicians then," he remembers. "To admit that we had to make room for blacks in skilled jobs, to admit that we *needed* them as much as they needed us, was also to admit that 'separate development' had its limitations, that the urban blacks had come to stay and that we were ignoring them at our own peril. But after Soweto blew up, I became a logical candidate for the job of trying to run what was left of its schools because the blacks knew I was with them and the white politicians regarded me as expendable."

The situation that Jaap Strydom inherited in December of 1976 was chaotic. Even before the riots Soweto's school system had been a patchwork affair. With the cost partially met by black parents, there were 280 primary "community" schools to serve an estimated 170,000 elementary school children but only 42 fully supported state secondary schools and two vocational centers to meet the needs of an ever-increasing army of teenagers. Student-teacher ratios in Soweto's classrooms stood at 60 to 1. The annual state expenditure on each black student was a mere R42 as compared to the R664 allocated to educate each white child, and these monies could not be stretched to meet the growing needs of township schools. Fees for materials were still being charged to parents in spite of the government's claim that education for blacks was entirely free. Black teachers were being paid far less than their white counterparts, and Soweto, burdened with a vast illegal population, had not for years received adequate financing to meet exploding enrollments in its schools. The riots had not improved things. Two of Soweto's extant secondary schools had been rendered useless by their students. The majority of the rest had been extensively damaged, and the student boycott, which had closed Soweto's secondary schools completely in June of 1976, was to keep them closed for another year despite Strydom's earnest efforts to reopen them.

"It was my job to get the kids off the streets and back into the schools as soon as I could," Strydom says, "and I was willing to bluff 'em, lie to 'em, and save them any way I had to. If we *could* have sold blacks on the idea that their languages, their heritage, their tribal history were fine and wonderful things and given them a sense of pride in their own past, that would have been fine. But we couldn't. A long time ago, way back when Philip first opened his missions, the British gave them the idea that they were worthless. They didn't know how to raise cattle, they didn't know how to write, to read, or even to pray. And then we Afrikaners came along and showed them that they didn't know how to fight either—that the assegai was no match for the blunderbuss. We had all the secrets of power, including a direct line to God, and we made *that* very clear. Well, if you tell a man he's worthless enough times, he's eventually going to believe it and hate you for it. And I suspect that what we are seeing in this century is not so much a unified desire for black power based on black pride as a negative fury with white superiority that is also all mixed up with an equal desire to emulate white society. Soweto's blacks, for instance, don't want to be reminded of their tribal past. They want a share in the future. That's why they left the 'homelands' and came to the cities like flies to sugar; they want to eat, they want to grow, they want to learn and it's my job to see that they do."

Strydom had plunged into the maelstrom of Soweto with considerable bravado. Convinced he had been put into his difficult job to "sink or swim" on his own, he attempted to set a course between the hardliners of his own Department of Bantu Education and the young black radicals of the SSRC. Repeatedly caught in the crossfire, he was helpless to prevent a new round of student strikes and a mass resignation of black teachers when his Ministry refused a black plea to revamp "Bantu Education" to make it identical with white education in the same week that Steve Biko, a brilliant young black leader of the militant South African Student Organization, was beaten to death in a government prison. Personally dismayed by Biko's death but still unwilling to abandon hope of a rapprochement between moderate whites and blacks, Strydom put the best face on a bad situation by agreeing publicly with Soweto's teachers about the reprehensible state of its schools. But what he proposed to do about the poor quality of black education stunned conservative whites and militant blacks alike.

"Let's face it," he insisted, "in the name of 'separate development,' we went ahead and Africanized black education too quickly.

We had 72,000 black teachers in black schools in 1976 and less than 1,000 whites. Of the blacks, not half were qualified. In Soweto alone less than 10 percent of the classroom teachers had passed matric [high school]. We'd been giving teachers with junior certificates jobs because they were black, with the result that we'd been running a social-welfare system for half-prepared teachers which had sacrificed the children. Well, that had to stop, because it's survival of the fittest in this world, and if you are frail and can't compete, you die. The kids were right. Soweto education wasn't good enough, but not simply because it was "Bantu.' We had a revolution of ignorance on our hands because the teachers couldn't teach what they didn't know, even in English, and what was needed right then was a drive, a big drive, to teach blacks all the things they needed to know to survive in the free enterprise system. What I wanted then, you see, was not fewer but more whites in black education—but try to tell that to anybody when the kids were still firebombing the schools."

Strydom's decision to create several "pilot" schools inside Soweto, using integrated faculties, came under immediate fire from all sides. Conservative Afrikaner ideologues saw the move as an insidious admission by a government appointee that "separate development" did not apply to the black township and hence as a dangerous departure from tradition. The bureaucracy associated with Bantu Education found the idea of such schools threatening to its raison d'être. Black teachers were infuriated by the implication that they were inferior educators, and the teenage black militants saw the move as a devious attempt to co-opt Soweto's middle class by offering them the bribe of better opportunities for their young in the hope of driving a wedge between moderates and militants that might cripple the black power movement in Soweto. And all were, of course, correct. Persuaded that the way to peace lay on a crooked road around the extremists, Strydom had become convinced that unless young urban blacks were given a reasonable stake in South Africa's capitalist system, they would necessarily ally themselves with Marxism against it. In Soweto's youth he knew he was dealing with the microcosm of a new black society whose furious yearnings must be met if a bloody revolution was to be avoided in South Africa. But he also knew that men of his "Verligte" (Enlightened) persuasion, who advocated too radical a departure from Nationalist tradition risked being ostracized by their Afrikaner brethren for challenging the sacred wisdom of "Die Volk" and their party.

Before the Soweto riots, the wisdom had held that the Nationalists' racial policies were both just and effective. Persuaded that "separate development" aimed at providing each of South Africa's black tribes with a secure territorial niche in which it would be free to evolve politically in accordance with its own heritage, most Afrikaners sincerely believed, as did their Prime Minister John Vorster, that "nowhere in the world have 4 million done so much for 18 million as in this despised South Africa." As ethnic independence was no less than what Afrikanerdom had sought for itself for several centuries, "separate development" for the tribal blacks still seemed to a majority of Afrikaners an inspired answer to their country's racial mixture. They were convinced that what was now and always had been at stake in South Africa was the survival of a white minority with an advanced "Christian" civilization on a continent dominated by underdeveloped black nations. So they had been willing to make what they construed to be major sacrifices within South Africa itself to ensure the separate freedoms of blacks, browns, and whites, and had subjected their country to what amounted to radical surgery to carve black states out of its body. Consequently, to imply that "separate development" could not be applied to nine million urban blacks, as "Verligtes" like Jaap Strydom had seemed to be doing in the aftermath of the 1976 riots, was to suggest that the policy many Afrikaners had been encouraged to equate with their nation's divine mission in Africa not only was inadequate but also implied that Afrikanerdom's fundamental faith in itself as an instrument of God's will might be misplaced.

Confronted with a rising tide of black hostility inside and outside of the country, and made suddenly aware of their own vulnerability, few Afrikaners, including even Jaap Strydom himself, were either able or willing to abandon altogether an ideology that had for centuries provided them with both a sense of their own national identity and psychological security. Consequently, when Strydom recalled his own decision to depart from "tradition" by recruiting whites to teach in Soweto's schools in 1977, he spoke of it in terms his ancestors at Blood River would perhaps have found perfectly understandable. "It was the rage of those who opposed me that convinced me I was doing the right thing," he remembers, "'and I suppose it was about then, if you were the religious sort, that you might have begun to believe in divine guidance. Because the people who joined me were all Afrikaners who felt they had been called to the work, and those who stayed with it have come to recognize, as I have, that what we are up against here in Soweto are dark forces. Not the old devil, mind you, but the new one—the godless ones—the Communists. . . .''

24
A COVENANT WITH THE FUTURE

Violence directed at the schools and police stations continued to rock South Africa for several years after 1976. In Soweto itself, an estimated 27,000 teenagers eligible for secondary schooling simply stayed away from classes and a partial boycott persisted into 1980. Pupils who were enrolled by their parents in Soweto's vocational training centers and the few junior and secondary schools Jaap Strydom had reopened were often made the targets of gang attacks on their way to classes. As time passed it became difficult to determine whether the majority of Soweto's youngsters were staying away from school for purely political reasons or because they also feared retaliation if they attended.

At Dobson, one of the two "model" junior high schools Strydom had managed to open late in 1977, the beginning of classes each morning was heralded by the approach of an armored van, nosing its way cautiously through the potholed streets of Orlando toward the former high school. Equipped with two inches of double steel plate, a three-quarter-inch unbreakable perspex windshield, and solid rubber tires, the van had been assigned by the Department of Education to Dobson's five white faculty members in 1977 to assure them a safe crossing of Soweto on their way to and from work each day. Driven by a mild-mannered young man named Thys Lourens, one of Dobson's two science teachers, the van's arrival signaled that the gates of the chain-mail fence surrounding the school were about to be unlocked and that a new day, in which teachers and students at Dobson would observe the rituals of learning like mummers playing at normalcy,

was about to commence with "morning prayers" in the school court-
yard.

Much as were the children whom he had come to teach at Dobson,
Thys Lourens was an innocent caught in the toils of a society in
conflict. An idealist with an admitted penchant for the "underdog,"
Lourens had become imbued with a sense of "mission" while study-
ing for a degree in social care at Potchefstroom University in the late
1960's. Long a bulwark of church education in South Africa, Potchefstroom was then in the throes of a religious revival, heavily influenced
by the liberalized Calvinism of Holland's Reformed Churches. The
campus was populated by groups that were beginning to agitate for
changes in South Africa's racial and political policies to give all its
people, regardless of race, an "effective share" in their own gover-
nance. Religiously inclined in any case, it was at Potchefstroom that
Thys Lourens decided to become a minister. Here he also met and
married his wife, Emilie, another young Afrikaner committed to social
change, and the great-granddaughter of the founder of the Reformed
Church of the Transvaal, the Reverend Postma. Immediately after
graduation, Lourens was drafted into South Africa's universal military
training program and had been taught the skills of armored warfare
before he could take up his training for the ministry. During his year
of service he had glimpsed, for the first time, his country's prepared-
ness for racial warfare. Convinced by this experience that reform was
urgently needed, he had come away from his year in the military
even more deeply committed to a "mission" of peaceful change for
South Africa. Ordained a minister of the Reformed Church, after
completing his studies at Potchefstroom in the early seventies, Thys
Lourens had come to Soweto precisely at that point in time when
blacks, asserting their own demands for a share in the affluent white
society, had chosen to exchange pacific protest for violence.

"You know," he mused quietly one evening as he sat with Emilie
and their three children in the kitchen of the suburban home that
Emilie, contrary to South African custom, runs without black servants, "most people believe that a minister's only 'calling' is to the
pulpit. But at Potchefstroom I had a professor who had a profound
influence upon me. He made me see that each one's true 'vocation'
in this life is to make ourselves worthy by helping those who need
us most. Before the riots in Soweto, we lived in a house in a section

overlooking the townships that has since been declared 'Colored.' In the evening, we could see the smoke of cook fires rising over Soweto and hear singing. It made us feel a special kinship with the people living there, and so when the rioting started and you could see the fires shooting up and hear the guns bang, banging, we felt their suffering keenly. Afterwards, when the call came for teachers, I answered, and a year later, as things began to calm down a bit, Emilie also signed up. . . ."

When Thys Lourens began teaching at Dobson, the former Orlando North High School, it was a windowless hulk, its doors torn off, its brick façade scored by gunshots. Groups of angry youngsters still roamed through Orlando. Armed police still made raids on the school, and no teacher, white or black, felt safe at Dobson. Each day, as Thys Lourens drove the school's armored van to work from his home in the pleasant Afrikaner suburb of Florida, he felt Soweto's dumb rage breathing about him. He saw its poverty in the faces of people buying a penny's worth of coal from carts drawn through its murky streets by spavined donkeys. He understood the message of a hand-lettered sign offering infant coffins to a needy public, which was almost lost in a forest of slick billboards advertising laundry detergents and toothpaste to a city largely without indoor plumbing. Gaunt reminders of Soweto's new politics of violence were everywhere: in the blackened brick heaps of what had been the WRAB buildings, in the names "Mandela," "Biko," and "Machel" scrawled upon its walls, and in the faces of the young that glowered malevolently as he passed them by. But the fury of Soweto worried Thys Lourens no more than the signs of a growing militancy among whites, many of whom seemed convinced, even as Jaap Strydom appeared to be, that Communist agitators and not spontaneous rage had led to the uprisings in the black and Colored township of South Africa.

"I suppose it's natural for people to be afraid," remarked Lourens. "And it's pretty common when you're afraid, to be angry, to want to strike back. So we do hear a lot of comment about not building back up what the blacks have torn down. And there's a lot of antipathy to what we are trying to do in black education, just as there's resistance to mission work in Soweto. But thinking South Africans know that we need the blacks as much as they need us, and I'm also convinced that the majority of Afrikaners recognize that the cry that went up from Soweto was a cry from the heart that must be heeded. And that's why I'm there. Because I believe that the way to the heart of Africa lies through Soweto; that we must be *with* the black man and *for* his well-being *now* to redeem our country. I'm not pessimistic. The Afrikaner conscience has been awakened, and there is a new sense of purpose among us to redress the wrongs of our society, and not wholly because we are afraid of the consequences if we do not. Our biggest problem, in fact, is not to give in to fear, to keep our courage. I realized that last year when a boy in my class told me, 'I like you, but I don't know if I can trust you.' That summed it up for me. That is what has crippled us in the past—fear."

But the fear is there, nevertheless. Though the majority of Afrikaners were and are dismayed by the brutality, which has been used to suppress black and Colored protest in South Africa, most are also resigned to the idea that, in the final analysis, the "security" of their country is paramount. Therefore, while the latest Nationalist Prime Minister, Piet Botha, has been quietly dismantling the apparatus of "petty apartheid" and encouraging the reform movement of which Thys Lourens is a part, by repeatedly warning Afrikaners that they must "adapt or die," his government has remained as militantly prepared to suppress any sign of black unrest within the country as it has been to meet the challenge of subversion from without. And the essential ambivalence of Afrikaner society—of a will to reform coexisting with a will to continue the repression of the black majority—was plain on the day that Thys Lourens accompanied Dobson's children and their parents on an outing to the Rand Trade Fair.

Acres of halls set in a park made up the fair and the school groups browsed through them wide-eyed. There were expositions of consumer goods, of machinery, foods, and fancies of every imaginable sort. On restricted access to blacks, until the recent relaxation of the "apartheid laws" designated many such public facilities as "multiracial," the Rand Trade Fair made the disparities of South African life visible to Dobson's children, many of whom had never been outside of Soweto before. There, laid out before their eyes, were all the perquisites of white privilege, which they, as blacks, would continue to be denied unless vast changes could be worked within their society. And at the very center of the fair, a display of military hardware underscored the grim capacity of the government to resist any attempt to force those changes by revolutionary means. Excited by the sheer power of these machines of war, many boys with Thys Lourens had scampered to talk with a Colored officer about enlistment in South Africa's multi-racial army while their teacher had paused to examine a lesser display of automatic weapons, stacked above a Bible, which was opened to Psalm 111: "Great are the works of the Lord" the young minister read. "He is ever mindful of His Covenant . . . He has shown His people the power of His works in giving them the heritage of nations. He has commanded His Covenant forever. . . ."

BOOK FOUR

The Past
That Shaped the Present

25

RENEWED QUARRELS
WITH BRITAIN

FAITH HAD provided the Calvinist Afrikaners with a refuge from the
anxiety of their isolation in Africa as the trek-boers and Voortrekkers had wandered northward into its wilderness in the 18th and
19th centuries. They had come to believe that like the children of
Israel, they were directed and protected by God and the further they
had withdrawn from civilization, the more deeply ingrained this
belief had become. But it was not until their fears had become flesh
at Vegkop and Blaauwkranz that the Voortrekkers had pledged themselves to God in the manner of their Huguenot ancestors, and even
then, the idea that they were a Covenant People had not become
the central tenet of an all-encompassing national religion until it was
articulated as such by their first great political leader, Paul Kruger,
after a war with an enemy far more formidable than the Zulu—
imperial Britain.

There had been renewed friction with the British almost from the
moment the trekkers had arrived in Natal. Pretorius's victory at
Blood River notwithstanding, there had been little peace in the
"Promised Land" and skirmishing with Dingaan's impis had continued for several years until the Boers had finally managed to divide
the Zulu's forces by offering Dingaan's half brother, Mpanda, his
throne. In the first flush of their triumph at Blood River, Pretorius's
commando had ridden on to Umgungundhlovu and there, among the
skeletal remains on Execution Hill, had discovered Retief's leather
pouch, containing the treaty Dingaan had marked, ceding to the
"Emigrant Dutch" much of the same territories Chaka had once
given to the British at Port Natal. As Great Britain had never officially
accepted this cession, Pretorius had claimed it freely and in 1841 had
announced the annexation of the "Promised Land" to those lands
already claimed by Potgieter on the high veld, and the creation of a
new independent Voortrekker Republic.

The British, meanwhile, had watched the northward progress of the trekkers with increasing misgiving. Britain's primary concern in Africa was to protect its trade route to India and it had made its displeasure with the trekkers' arrival on the Indian Ocean coast in 1838 evident by briefly investing Port Natal with troops. But it was not until coal had been discovered in Natal and two foreign steamers had called in on the newly "independent" Afrikaner republic that the British decided to abort its independence.

Using as an excuse the Boers' continuing conflicts with the Zulu, who outnumbered them seven to one, the new British Governor of the Cape, Sir George Napier, invaded Natal in 1842 on the pretense of keeping the peace and "protecting the natives." The Boers had greeted the arrival of his regiments with forbearance and asked that they be removed. When they were not, however, a pitched battle ensued at a place called Congella. The Boers won, but their victory proved pyrrhic. Napier had soon flooded Natal with troops, and in 1843 Great Britain had announced the annexation of Natal to its African Empire.

The Natal Afrikaners reacted to the forfeiture of their independence by once again "withdrawing" from British rule. Trekking back over the Drakensberg, they had hauled their wagons up inch by inch into the high veld, singing psalms and praying as they went. Left behind them among the dead in the "Promised Land," were three of the men who had originated the Great Trek—Piet Retief, Piet Uys, and Gerrit Maritz. Of its principal leaders, only Potgieter and Pretorius now remained alive.

Potgieter, who had always held that the "Promised Land" lay beyond the Vaal, had established his conservative Dopper clans there at a place called Potchefstroom and it was to Potchefstroom that Pretorius now repaired to discuss the future of the Voortrekker republic. As a result of their talks, the two leaders agreed to the formation of a new republic. Stretching from the Orange River in the south to the Limpopo in the north, girded on the west by the Kalahari desert and on the east by the Drakensberg, it encompassed the great horseshoe of territory left partially vacant by the Difaqane. It abutted the kingdoms of the Mashona, Bechuana, and Matabele in the northwest, the Makapan, Pedi, and Swazi in the northeast, the Zulu beyond the Drakensberg in the east, the Barolong and Sotho in

the southeast, and two communal, multiracial kingdoms in the south-
west, which were established by Afrikaans-speaking Colored folk
called Griqua, who had made their own trek from the Cape.

Sprawling, largely semiarid, the new landlocked republic seemed
worthless to the British, and they were briefly content to leave it alone.
But in 1845 renewed disputes between the Sotho and the Boers and
the British and the Xhosa along the Cape Colony's northern frontiers
had prompted a change in Colonial Office policy with regard to South
Africa's "natives" that, in December 1847, brought a flamboyant
new Governor to the Cape, Sir Harry Smith. Smith had earned his
reputation in the Peninsula Wars and improved upon it by his dashing exploits among the Sikhs in India. Making straight for the Xhosa
border lands, Smith had demanded an immediate audience with a
group of their rebellious chiefs. To mark the opening of the conference, he had blown up a wagonload of munitions. As the smoke
cleared, Smith had shouted to his terrified audience, "*That* is what
I shall do to you if you do not behave." Then, forcing one of the
chiefs to his knees and brandishing his saber, Smith had delivered
a brief address in English to the astonished Xhosa in which he
instructed them to wear clothes, speak English, give up polygamy, and
abandon their witch doctors. In conclusion, he had also announced he
was annexing all of their lands to the British Cape as Victoria East
and British Kaffraria. The new "natives policy" implemented with
regard to the Xhosa, Smith had mounted up and led his little army
north into the Boer republic beyond the Orange River.

Arrived in "Transorangia," the swashbuckling Sir Harry had first
extracted a pair of treaties from the Sotho and Griqua. These signed
he had again brandished his saber and announced magnanimously
that he was annexing all of the lands between the Orange River and
the Vaal as the Orange River Sovereignty. Then, without so much
as a nod in the direction of the Voortrekker republicans—whose
territories he had just unilaterally reduced by half—Smith had returned to Cape Town to notify the Colonial Office of his accomplish-
ments.

The Governor's actions left the Boers as dumbfounded as the
Xhosa, but at odds with one another about how to respond. Potgieter
wanted no quarrel with Britain because he believed that to challenge
them was to invite their intervention beyond the Vaal. Pretorius,

more choleric, had ridden south immediately to attack a garrison of troops Smith had left at the new "capital" of the Orange River Sovereignity, Bloemfontein. His attack brought the British back across the Orange in force, but it also established Pretorius, whom Smith declared to be an "outlaw," as Britain's chief adversary and the Boers' undisputed leader.

In 1851 an opportunity to regain what had been lost to the British by means other than war presented itself to Pretorius when Moshesh of the Sotho, tiring of vassalage to Britain, offered to ally himself with the Boers. Shrewdly, Pretorius had indicated to the British that he would decline the offer if they would in turn give up Transorangia and acknowledge the Transvaal's independent status. Weary of dealing with the fractious folk of the north, the Colonial Office had instructed a dismayed Governor Smith to comply, and in 1852 a series of Conventions were drawn up in a farmhouse on the banks of the Sand River opening the way to the restitution of the Orange Free State's independence and acknowledging that of the South African Republic beyond the Vaal. The Voortekkers had, it appeared, finally achieved the goals of their Trek: a truly independent republic. Among the witnesses, as Pretorius signed the Sand River Convention, was his young aide, Paul Kruger.

26

PAUL KRUGER:
THE MAKING OF A PATRIOT

It had taken almost twenty years for the Afrikaners to achieve independence, and only a year after the Sand River Convention was signed, the last of the Great Trek's leaders were dead. The deaths of Potgieter and Pretorius did not, however, end differences between their followers. In 1856, when Pretorius's son, Marthinus, became president of the Transvaal Republic, men who had followed Potgieter defied Marthinus and something very close to anarchy reigned in the Transvaal. Then the bull-headed Marthinus Pretorius decided to extend his authority as president to the Orange Free State, which had won its independence from Britain under the Convention of Bloem-

fontein in 1854. The infuriated Free Staters promptly sent a commando to Transvaal, but thanks, in part, to the mediation of Paul
Kruger, a clash was avoided. Eventually, a treaty of friendship was
signed acknowledging the independent existence of the two Boer
republics.

Already of note in his northern district of the Transvaal, Kruger,
then 35, was soon to emerge as the most important leader the Afrikaners had yet produced. And the man he was to become during the
difficult years when he led his people in the tragic Anglo-Boer War
of 1899–1902 was already apparent in the man he had become by
1860. Born in 1825 on a backveld farm in the Colesberg district of the
Cape Colony, just south of the Orange River, Stephanus Johannes
Paulus Kruger was the third son of Elsie Steyn and her husband,
Kasper Kruger. When he was eleven, the entire Kruger clan, con-
sisting of his grandfather, uncles and their families, his mother, father,
brother and sisters, had uprooted itself and joined Sarel Cillier and
Andreis Potgieter on their trek northward to escape from British rule.

With Potgieter when the Matabele had attacked at Vegkop and
afraid of continuing north thereafter, the Krugers had gone east in
the wake of Piet Retief's trek to the lovely butte country lying above
the Drakensberg passes. But after only two years, they had once more
inspanned their oxen and followed Potgeiter north to the wide, green
lands beyond the Vaal. Along the way, at fourteen, Paul Kruger had
killed his first lion. The next year, during a Matabele attack, he had
killed his first man.

From the time his family left Colesberg until they settled in the
green hills of the Magaliesberg region, just north of the Witwatersrand, Paul Kruger's education was almost wholly practical. His
formal education had lasted only three months and was received in
1838 during the winter the Combined Trek lingered at Thaba Nchu.
In that period, Robert Lindley, the American Wesleyan missionary,
had been influential in young Kruger's religious education—broaden-
ing his narrow "Dopper" faith somewhat. A religious man-of-action,
Lindley became a model for Kruger, and it was perhaps from him
that the future president of the South African Republic learned to
combine the natural earthiness of his character with a religious
mysticism.

Manhood had come early for Kruger. As was Afrikaner custom,

he had become a "burgher" with the full rights of adulthood at fifteen. At sixteen he had staked out two farms in the Magaliesberg region. At seventeen he was married to Maria du Plessis, a girl he had met during the trek. When he was twenty-one, Maria and their newborn son had died. Inconsolable, Kruger had wandered off alone into the mountains where he was found some time later in a delirium by a search party. Carried from the mountain, Kruger told his rescuers that he had had visions and been "reborn to God. He has shown me everything. . . ."

Other stories were told of young Kruger, some true, others perhaps apocryphal, which had made him a folk hero in the Magaliesburg well before he was known to the world beyond. It was said that he could outrun a horse and that he was gifted with a second sight, which permitted him to visualize game in their hiding places and thus to find prey when no other man could. That he was in fact a skilled and avid hunter is indisputable. Once while hunting rhino alone, his gun had exploded, mangling his thumb at the critical moment of the rhino's charge. Forced to ride for his life, he had later amputated the thumb and cauterized the stump himself with turpentine. On another occasion, when his horse had fallen on him, crushing his leg, Kruger, again alone, had set the leg himself and ridden a full day before reaching home. Though the leg had mended, he had ever afterwards walked with a slightly lurching gait.

Just under six feet, powerfully built, able to outride, outshoot, and outlast most of his fellow frontiersmen, the God-fearing, shrewd Kruger always seemed to live on a scale just a bit larger than life. A trekker at ten, he had become a deputy field cornet and leader of men a good bit older than himself at seventeen. Married a second time in his mid-twenties, he had fathered 16 children by his second wife, "Tant Sien," and was grandfather to 120. A full field cornet at twenty-six, when he had helped Andries Pretorius negotiate with the British at Sand River, Kruger was to spend the rest of his life defending Afrikaner independence against black man and Briton alike.

Only months after he returned from Sand River, Kruger led his first full commando against the Bechuana, whose chief, Secheli, was charged with harboring another black accused of murdering Transvaal citizens. After a skirmish with Secheli's men, Kruger had approached the LMS representative then living with the Bechuana,

Dr. David Livingstone, to ask his assistance in arresting the wanted man. At the mission, he later avowed, he had not only found Livingstone but a cache of arms he was apparently keeping for Secheli. As the sale of guns to tribal blacks had been strictly prohibited by the Sand River Conventions, Kruger regarded their presence in the mission as evidence of a breach of its terms and one more example of British perfidy. Convinced that Britain had repeatedly used the "native question" to further its own aims in Africa at the expense of the Boer, Kruger regarded the activities of the LMS among tribes bordering the Transvaal as particularly suspicious in the light of developments in Natal.

There, Theophilus Shepstone, a young man who had first come to notice as a Colonial Service specialist in "native affairs" when he had defended Harry Smith's annexation of "Transorangia," had recently become Minister of Native Affairs. Determined to impose the "Pax Britannica" among Africa's warring tribes, Shepstone had resolved Natal's problems with the Zulu by herding some 80,000 of them into specially created "reserves" under his direct supervision. As the primary Zulu kingdoms and several reserves abutted the South African Republic, Kruger did not trust Shepstone's power among the Zulu any more than he did his avowed determination to spread the "Pax Britannica." Shepstone had put himself on record from the outset as being opposed to both the Sand River and Bloemfontein Conventions that had given independence to the Boers. As it happened, events would prove Kruger's suspicion of Shepstone correct.

In 1853, however, Kruger had more immediate threats to deal with. That year, the Venda, under their chiefs Mapela and Makapaan, had resorted to terrorist attacks on whites along the Transvaal's northeastern borders. Sweeping down on the outpost of Schoemansdal, they had killed twenty-eight whites in their first assault, none more hideously than Herman Potgieter, the eldest son of the old Voortrekker leader, Andreis Potgieter. Captured by Mapela, Potgieter had been forced to watch fifteen of his companions hacked to death before he was himself flayed alive and disemboweled. Roused to fury by the reports of his death—given by a witness who had managed to hide in Potgieter's wagons—the Transvaalers had sent a detachment of commandos to the Waterberg under Marthinus Pretorius and Paul Kruger. Makapaan's and Mapela's kraals were overrun, and both had contained evidence of further savagery—the dismembered bodies of a number of white men, women, and children captured in another raid.

Incensed, the Boers had driven Mapela's forces onto a precipitous mountainside. There, Kruger had himself led a charge on a position that sent many hundreds of Venda plunging to their deaths over the cliff face. Makapaan's clans, almost a thousand strong, had meanwhile retreated into caves in the Waterberg, which Pretorius had ordered sealed off with the intention of starving his enemy to death. Not wholly without mercy, Paul Kruger is said to have entered the caves through a fissure and led some hundred Venda women and children out as prisoners. The action infuriated Pretorius but it was consistent with Kruger's convictions. A strict Dopper, Kruger took the Decalogue literally.

Kruger's church, the Christelijk Gereformeerde church, founded by the Reverend Postma at Rustenburg, was a throwback to the original church of the militant saints of the Dutch Reformation, based closely upon the canons promulgated at Dort in 1618. To "dop" a candle meant to extinguish it, and the Dopper church eschewed all Enlightenment influences, regarding them as corrupt. Seeking instead a return to the forms of early Christianity, it required a strenuous piety of its members. Kruger was a lay preacher in the church, and his faith was as fundamental to his character as his love of the land he called "ons land"—a bountiful land, mild of climate, rich in grasses and fruits, swarming with magnificent game, where self-reliant men could live freely, on close terms with God and Nature, untouched by the corruptions and sophistications of the world beyond.

27

AN AGE OF EMPIRE:
EUROPE IN THE 19TH CENTURY

While Paul Kruger was coming of age in a land that seemed untouched by time, the world beyond Africa was changing at an ever accelerating rate. In Britain, the transmutation of ideas that had brought capitalism out of puritanism had been completed during the

*"Illusion and revelation would have their place in the Anglo-Boer War,
but its outcome was a foregone conclusion. The Boers would be crushed."
Wagon Hill at Ladysmith, Natal,
site of a pivotal battle early in the war.*

"Few Afrikaners can forget the past.
Their national pride and prejudices are rooted in it."
A survivor (above left) recalls life in British concentration camps
where 25,000 Afrikaner women and children,
memorialized at Bloemfontein (below left), perished.
The Harrismith monument (above)
celebrates the heroism of the local Boer commando.

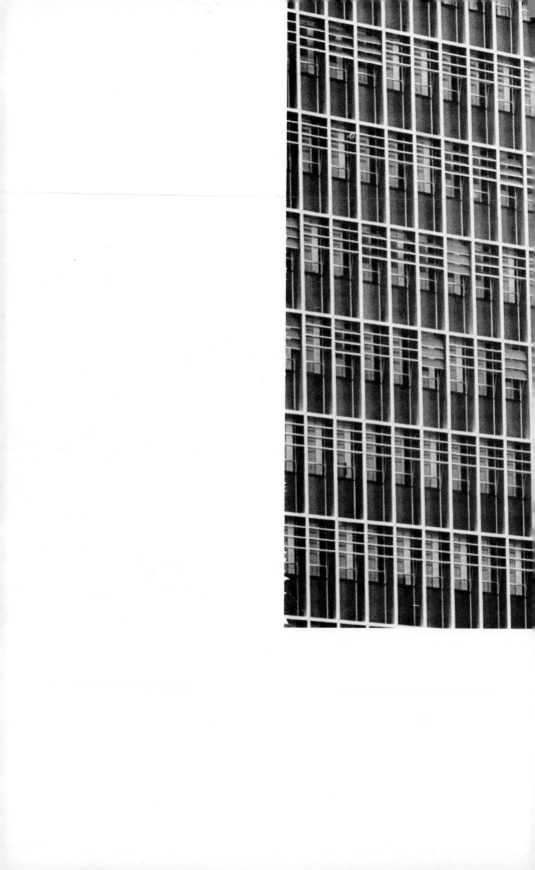

"Paul Kruger . . . appears in the theater of the imagination
as a great, bulking figure, dressed in top hat and rumpled tailcoat,
lurching across history's stage toward inevitable tragedy."
Kruger's statue at Church Square, Pretoria.

"*The British who controlled the Union's economy were its 'power elite';
the Afrikaners remained second-class citizens* . . ."
*Uncut diamonds at DeBeers Consolidated (above),
the Kimberly company Cecil Rhodes organized and used
to further his imperial ambitions in Africa.
(Right) South Africans of British descent play bowls
on greens overlooking Cape Town's beaches.*

"While their predicants preached a return to purified Christian Nationalism . . .
the Broederbond had guided investment . . . to develop
a few Afrikaner enterprises in banking and business."
The Sanlam insurance building in Johannesburg,
symbol of Afrikaner economic achievement.

Enlightenment, and as the 18th century gave way to the 19th, a burst of new inventions had ushered in a new age of technology, which had changed Britain from a nation of farmyards into one of factories. As coal began to replace wood as the primary fuel of Britain's textile industry, manufacturing capacity increased and with it the need for an unending supply of cotton, flax, wool, and other raw materials. By 1820, the first steam engines were operating on newly laid railroads in England, the first steamship had crossed the Atlantic and, by 1825, Britain's burgeoning new coal, iron, and steel industries at home were linked by a network of railroads, canals, and Macadam roads.

As her industry grew, so did its demand for labor, and a vast shift in population took place as masses of people were drawn into the cities and, inevitably, slums began to overspread London, Manchester, and other cities. Appalled by the grinding poverty of the working classes and the misuse of their children in the factories, many British writers, among them Wordsworth and Shelley, cried out for reforms, and the Tory reaction that had given conservatives complete control of the government in the aftermath of the Jacobin revolution in France abated. From 1830 onwards, one reform act after another passed through Parliament, widening the franchise, improving the lot of the poor, protecting the working classes, and accomplishing a social revolution that had been obtained on the continent only by a series of violent political upheavals.

The Whig-Liberal governments that had made social reform their business at home, however, had made the entrenchment of British power their business abroad. As Victoria's fleets and regiments expanded her Empire, one "little war" followed another. In the fifty years after Waterloo, British troops had fought in Aden, on the Gold Coast, in Burma, Malaya, Afghanistan, and Baluchistan. They had subjugated the Sikhs, Sinds, and Ameers in India, fought a costly war against Russia in the Crimea, taken control of Persia, opened the way to the lucrative opium trade that carried the poppy dreams of Turkey to China, and, by further enriching the Empire, had accelerated the pace of intellectual and social change in England.

By 1859, Charles Darwin was already elaborating his concepts of evolution to fascinated audiences in England, and Karl Marx was engaged at the British Museum in the researches that would lead to the publication of his masterwork, *Das Kapital*. Both Darwin and Marx reflected in their works the logical progression of ideas that had had their origins in the Reformation, which had opened the way to the Enlightenment, and the Enlightenment in turn had produced the new "faith" in science and progress. Darwin's speculations on the *Origin of Species* replaced the old Calvinist notion of "Election" with a new concept of "natural selection," whereas in Marx's thought, the tradition of protest and the passion for social "righteousness," which had begun with Luther and Calvin, was brought to another more explosive conclusion.

But even as Marx sat penning the social dynamite that was destined to set off a series of bloody revolutions in the 20th century, the desperate conditions of the British working classes, which had stirred his quasi-religious passion for change, were being ameliorated and the potential for political revolution in Great Britain was being defused. Consequently, it was to be Darwin's rather than Marx's thought that was destined to have the greatest intellectual impact in Britain. His ideas inadvertently inspired a new secular creed, based on his concept of the "survival of the fittest," and this new creed would capture the imagination of a new generation of British imperialists who, in the closing decades of the 19th century, would come to regard the expansion of the British Empire as an expression of Nature's, if not God's, Grand Design.

28

BRITISH IMPERIALISM AND THE DISCOVERY OF DIAMONDS

There was little intimation in faraway Africa at mid-century of a whirlwind in the making that would soon bring time and change rushing after the upcountry Boers. The middle decades of the century were ones of drift for the Afrikaners, and Britain's colonial government at the Cape had been content to leave them in fine isolation in the "worthless" north after the signing of the Sand River and Bloemfontein Conventions in 1854 and 1856. Great Britain, in any case, was preoccupied by a rash of new problems accruing from the growth of her Empire. As a result of the failure of the potato crop, Ireland was

facing starvation and famine had been translated into a revolutionary rage against the British landlords who ruled the country. In
the aftermath of the Crimean War, popular resentment of Britain's
imperial adventurism had already been running high when the Sepoy
Rebellion in India had further stunned the British public by its
ferocity. There was, therefore, little enthusiasm at the Colonial Office
for any expansion of British rule in Africa in 1858 when the latest
of the Cape's governors, Sir George Grey, dispatched a plan to the
Colonial Secretary in Whitehall, suggesting the creation of a new
"federation" there.

Sir George had been presented by Britain's old adversary, the Xhosa,
with an opportunity to bring all of the Indian Ocean coasts from Cape
Town to Natal under the Union Jack. Perennially at war with
white settlers along the Kei—Sir Harry Smith's annexation of their
lands notwithstanding—the Xhosa had put an end to Britain's incessant problems with them in 1857 by what amounted to an act of mass
suicide. Led on by one of their seers, Mhlakaza, the Xhosa had been
persuaded that with the right spells they could at last defeat the
whites by raising their warrior ancestors from the dead. To bring these
legions to life, they were told, they must sacrifice all of their cattle
and destroy all of their crops. Then, so Mhlakaza prophesied, the sun
would turn in the sky, a hurricane would roar across the land, and
the dead would rise with spear in hand to harry the white invaders
into the sea. Once the whites were gone, the Xhosa were assured,
their cattle would also be reincarnated and their lost crops replenished.

In February of 1857, therefore, the slaughter of the Xhosa's cattle
and destruction of their corn lands was begun. In the next year, at
least 25,000 Tembu and Xhosa had died of starvation, and another
30,000 had been driven south into the Cape in search of food. As
a result, the power of the Xhosa chiefs had been broken. Suddenly
freed of the onerous business of keeping the Xhosa in check, Sir
George Grey saw the opportunity to implement the federation scheme
he and Theophilus Shepstone had devised. Using as his excuse renewed disturbances along the Free State's borders by Moshesh,
Grey advised the Colonial Office in London that the time had come to
bring some discipline to the north by bringing it under British sway.

"South Africa," Grey had cabled the Colonial Secretary, Sir Edward Bulwer Lytton—a man more noted for his authorship of *The*

Last Days of Pompeii than as a statesman—"seems to be drifting by not very slow degrees into disorder and barbarism. . . . Nothing but a strong federal government, which unites within itself all the European races in South Africa, can permanently maintain peace in this country and free Great Britain from constant anxiety for the peace of her possessions here."

Unimpressed, Bulwer Lytton had opposed Grey's plan. "In a federation with those Dutch Republics," he countered coolly, "we have much to risk and nothing to gain. . . . It would thrust their Dutch nose into all sorts of black squabbles from which the British giant would always have to pull him out with the certainty of more kicks than a half pence. . . ." Satisfied that the landlocked Boer republics offered no possible threat to British hegemony in the Indian Ocean the Colonial Office's policy toward the Boer republics remained one of calculated indifference until diamonds were discovered in the northwestern corner of the Free State in 1867. Then it underwent an abrupt shift that was soon to bring history rushing upon the isolated Boers.

It was a Griqua child, living on a farm owned by a Boer named van Niekerk near the settlement of Hopetown on the Orange River, who found the stone that started the diamond rush in Africa. The boy had discovered his "blinklippie" in a river wash and carried it home where, ultimately, it was shown to a prospector named O'Reilly. Suspecting what it might be, O'Reilly had asked to keep the stone and later sent it for assay. First examined by a man named "Gregory," whose name ever afterwards would mean "blunder" to diamond men, it was not recognized as a diamond because Gregory did not believe any diamond ground existed in Africa. Unpersuaded, the persistent O'Reilly had sent the stone to two more assayers, the last of whom confirmed that it was indeed a diamond with a value of roughly £500. Two years after its discovery, the farmer on whose lands it had been found, Schalk van Niekerk, learned that a neighboring Griqua shaman was using an even larger "blinklippie" in his healing rituals. Approaching him, van Niekerk had offered to barter 500 ewes, 10 oxen, and his horse—the entire stock of his farm—for the stone, which he later sold for £11,000. Assayed at a massive 83.25 carats,

it proved to be one of the most perfect white diamonds ever discovered—the magnificent Star of Africa.

The discoveries at Hopetown brought a rush of thousands to the
region. Almost overnight, tent cities, inhabited by as rowdy a spectrum
of humanity as one might expect to find in hell, had grown up along
the Vaal and Harts rivers. Soon, the once pristine veld had been
turned into a moonscape by diamond diggers, and the search had
spread from the first sites at Klipdrift and Pniel eastward after two
Boers named De Beers had found a few diamonds on their lands.
Persuaded to part with their farm for £6,000 by a shrewd Englishman named Richard Jackson, the De Beers brothers' diggings were
to produce £199 million in diamonds within fifty years, but even
from the first the richness of Jackson's finds at "De Beers" had focused the main rush in the region around present day Kimberley where
the world's richest pipes of blue diamondiferous ground were soon
to be discovered.

Located in a wedge of land where the Vaal and Harts rivers approach their confluence, the main body of the diamond grounds lay
in an unprepossessing stretch of the veld claimed jointly by Griquas,
under their King Nicholaas Waterboer, the Free Staters, and the
Transvalers. By 1870, however, there were more newcomers living in the region than there were Boers in the entire Transvaal,
and the quarrels of the three original claimants had been further
complicated when the "outlanders" had announced they were forming
their own independent state and elected as their president a former
British seaman named Stafford Parker. Parker's presidency however
proved short-lived, for in January of 1871 the British announced the
formation of an "impartial commission," under Natal's Lt. Gov.
Robert Keate, to judge the merits of the rival claimants. Notified at
the outset of his deliberations by the new Colonial Secretary, Lord
Kimberley, that "HM's government" would look "with great dissatis-
faction" on any extension of Boer interests in the Griqua's territories,
Keate, not surprisingly, had found in favor of Nicholaas Waterboer
in October of 1871. A month later, at his "request," the newly named
territory of Griqualand West had been annexed to the Cape Colony—giving the diamond lands to Britain. The Griqua, who
had claimed their portion of the land communally, were soon to

find they had no land left to claim, and the multiracial experiment of these simple folk ended with their dispossession and impoverishment. But the Keate Award had also added another grievance to the already long list of complaints against the British which the Afrikaners harbored, and it drew the Orange Free State and the Transvaal together in a sense of shared injury.

29
CECIL RHODES:
AVATAR OF A NEW AGE

The man who was to become Paul Kruger's primary adversary in the final decades of the century arrived in the diamond fields in the year of the dubious Keate Award. Cecil John Rhodes had come to Africa at 17 to save his own life. Consumptive, he had sought the sunshine of Africa, where his brother Herbert had gone "farming," as a tonic for his poor heart and weak lungs and had settled on Herbert's Natal cotton farm in 1869. But after diamonds were discovered in the Vaal-Harts region, Herbert and then Cecil had decided there was too little future in farming and had gone west to seek their fortunes in diamonds. Cecil had made the journey alone in a donkey cart from Natal to the "dry-diggings" and arrived in 1871 at the tent town of "New Rush," which was destined to become Kimberley.

Rhodes was an unprepossessing youth. Slim, pale, and shy, he affected white flannels, stood with a slouch and was publicly reticent. When he did speak, his voice sometimes broke into a high falsetto and there was little about him as an adolescent to augur the man he was to become or to excite the interest of his fellow diggers at New Rush.

New Rush, on the other hand, excited Cecil Rhodes as England never had. A sprawling collection of mud huts and tents, it was the boom center of a diamond field that, within a year of his arrival there would outproduce every other known diamond field in the world six times over and become by 1872 the largest "city" outside of Cape Town in all of Africa. An ugly place, it was the home of pickpockets, prostitutes, savvy diamond merchants, world bankers, blacks, whites, browns, Germans, French, Italians, Americans, Canadians, Irish, Australians, and Englishmen of every stripe and social station. Cecil Rhodes, the son of a minister, found it nonpareil as a place to learn about life.

The labor on the extensive diggings was provided largely by the Griqua and by tribal blacks. Newly arrived from their kraals, the latter worked like beasts for their white masters, sweating in the 110-degree heat to earn the money to buy two things: guns and whiskey. Half-naked, less than half-civilized, they were at once magnificent and strangely intimidating and, like most Englishmen, Rhodes regarded them as "barbarous and a subject race." "We are to be lords over them," he was later to declare simply. But there were other equally exotic denizens of diggings to whom Rhodes did not condescend and from whom he learned much—the slick European entrepreneurs, shrewd diamond merchants, and daring fortune seekers, not a few of whom, like Charles Rudd, Alfred Beit, and Barney Barnato, a former London music-hall comedian, Rhodes made his partners. From such men, as from hundreds of other nameless adventurers whom he bested in these years, Cecil Rhodes learned the art of financial wheeling and dealing, that, in later years, he called simply "The Game," and which was to fascinate him for much of his life.

In 1872, however, the Rhodes brothers had little more claim to fortune than three plots of earth, each 31 square feet, atop a hill some 30 feet high and 220 long at Colesberg koppie, where some 600 similar claims were also located. Each was worked by white overseers and their black and brown diggers in an assemblage some 10,000 strong. In a letter written to his mother at this time, Rhodes gave a sparse description of the diamond fields. "Fancy an immense plain with right in the centre a great mass of white tents and iron stores and to one side of it all, mixed up with the camp, mounds of limelike anthills; the country round all flat with just thorn trees here and there." Going along the narrow trails on the koppie, Rhodes continued, were mule wagons which drew the sieved debris away from the diggings. These often tumbled into the ever deepening holes that pockmarked the surface, to everyone's amusement. But Rhodes did not write of the other amusements of New Rush— of the saloons and gambling halls and drinking, of the regular auctions of prostitutes, or of the spider fights that had here come to provide "sporting men" with an opportunity for wagering. Instead, he says simply, "I average about £100 a week" and signed his letter simply, "yrs, C. Rhodes."

Early in 1873, Herbert persuaded Cecil to embark on a new adventure. Herbert, the quixotic Rhodes, who was always ready to look for a new adventure and was eventually to die when he ignited his own store of gin while on trek alone in the Transvaal, had heard that gold had been found at "Pilgrim's Rest," in the far-off eastern reaches of that wild republic. Leaving still another new arrival in Africa, a third brother—Frank Rhodes—behind in charge of their diamond diggings at New Rush, Cecil and Herbert had traveled north by ox-wagon—inadvertently following a portion of the route used by some of the Voortrekkers.

It was apparently on this trip, made at the slow pace of the ox through the wild high veld, that the magnificence of Africa had taken hold of Cecil Rhodes just as it had taken hold of Kruger some thirty years earlier. For when Rhodes returned to newly named Kimberley, he had decided to go to Oxford to study and equip himself in the service of a dream—a dream of somehow controlling Africa's future.

Had he not gone to Kimberley to "average £100 a week," it is unlikely that Cecil Rhodes could have afforded to attend Oxford. One of the younger sons of a family of two sisters and nine brothers, two of whom died young, Cecil came from a well-connected but not particularly well-to-do "county" family of the village of Bishop Stortford. His father was a parson and by the time Cecil, who was born at the vicarage on July 5, 1853, came along, the Reverend Rhodes was unable to afford for Cecil the kind of education he had provided for his elder brothers. They had attended two of England's most prestigious public schools, Winchester and Eton. Cecil, instead, was sent to Bishop Stortford Grammar School where he did not distinguish himself. Withdrawn from school at 16 due to poor health, he had been sent out to Africa as so many of England's "younger sons" were sent to "the colonies" in this era to make their own fortunes. There was consequently little about Cecil Rhodes to recommend him at Oxford, a place where Eton mattered and Bishop Stortford Grammar did not. Rejected by prestigious University College, he was sent by its Provost to Oriel with the suggestion that "They are less particular there." He was only grudgingly admitted to Oriel by its master, who complained of being sent only "the failures."

For the next seven years, Rhodes commuted between Oxford and Kimberley—mixing a study of classics with business—slowly amassing a small fortune in Africa, selling diamonds in London, and buying hydraulic equipment for his diggings in the diamond fields. At Oxford, he attended lectures in a desultory manner, making no mark by which he is particularly remembered. He was, however, captivated, as all of England was then, by a sense of great expectations. Social Darwinism had fired the Victorian imagination with a sense of Britain's manifest destiny in the world. Disraeli, on becoming Prime Minister, had launched on aggressive new imperial policy and encouraged the British to take pride in their dominant position in the world. At Oxford, John Ruskin lectured the undergraduates with unabashed patriotism, urging upon them "a destiny now possible to us, the highest ever set before a nation . . . She [England] must found colonies," Ruskin advised, "as fast and as far as she is able; seizing any piece of fruitful waste ground she can set her food on and teaching her colonists that their chief virtue . . . is to advance the power of England by land and sea. . . ."

Here were words to inspire a youth like Rhodes with a sense of destiny. Back in Kimberley—after recovering from a near-fatal heart attack in 1874—he penned a document in 1877 that he was later to send to his friend, the newspaperman W. T. Stead. "It often strikes a man," Rhodes had mused on paper in his twenty-fourth year, "to inquire what is the chief good in life. To one the thought comes that it is a happy marriage, to another great wealth, to a third travel, and so on, and as each seizes the idea, he more or less works for its attainment for the rest of his existence. To myself—thinking over the same question—the wish came to make myself useful to my country . . . I contend that we are the first race in the world, and that the more of the world we inhabit, the better it is for the human race. I contend that every acre added to our territory provides for the birth of more of the English race. . . . The absorption of the greater portion of the world under our rule simply means the end of all wars." And so Rhodes vowed that henceforward he would work "for the furtherance of the British Empire, for the bringing of the whole civilized world under British rule, for the recovery of the United States, for the making of the Anglo-Saxon race into one Empire!"

Later in the same year he made a will in which he left all of his earthly fortune to promote just these aims. In it, he proposed the formation of a "secret society" that would oversee the extension of British dominance through the creation of business cartels, which would quietly take control of the wealth of the continent, of Africa, South America, the Middle East, southeast Asia, China, Japan and, eventually, the United States as well as India. To himself, Rhodes modestly assigned the task of bringing all of Africa, from the Cape to Cairo, under British sway. Despite the adolescent megalomania of this vision, it was to possess Rhodes all of his days, and in each of subsequent wills but one, which were penned as he slowly amassed the means to bring its accomplishment within his grasp, Rhodes was to reiterate his "Grand Design" and leave his fortunes to promote it.

Rhodes, the product of a very particular British tradition, was not alone in his fevered imperialism. Victorian England produced "Jingoists" in this period as regularly as she did steam engines. Her entire educational system was geared to turn out young men who believed in "duty, God, and Country" and who regarded the goals of ordinary mortals—to marry, to raise families, to survive, to live in peace and die at home—as beneath them. Shut off in "public" schools for boys where discipline was rigorous and normal sexual development stunted, they absorbed the vocation of Empire, the way novices in convents absorb the vocation of the Church, and later became married to its ideals and to its service, rather than to wives. And it was, perhaps, precisely because Cecil Rhodes could *not* claim he had been educated at Eton or Winchester that he longed to surpass those who had been. He became, in Kimberley, at least superficially, the replica of a public school boy-man, devoted to his male friends and absorbed by grandiose notions of empire. For women never interested Cecil Rhodes any more than they did most of his brothers, only one of whom ever married. Whatever sexual desires he may have felt, it seems, were, instead, sublimated into a passion for the conquest and domination of Africa for the sake of the British Empire. From the time in the mid 1870's when he began the shrewd dealings which eventually gave him control of the world's diamond markets through De

Beers Consolidated, until his death at 49, he devoted himself to this goal heart and soul. He found his principal pleasures in life to be the manipulation of power and the companionship of the men who conspired with him in his grandiose scheme to make all of Africa, from the Cape to Cairo, British.

30
AN AFRIKANER REACTION

Rhodes was not original. The dream of a British Africa had captured the imaginations of Englishmen since Somerset had first set foot at the Cape. But not until after the explorations of Richard Burton, John Speke, David Livingstone, the Bakers, and Henry Stanley—begun at mid-century and nearing completion in the 1870's—had revealed the contours of the once dark continent and shown the chain of lakes that lay, like a watery highway through its heartland, had it begun to seem plausible that one nation might, in fact, possess it all.

Imperialism had taken on the dimensions of a secular religion in Britain by then. Carried to power on a wave of "Jingoist" passion, Disraeli had advocated what Ruskin preached. At the Colonial Office, a scheme to federate South Africa, which Bulwer Lytton had rejected in 1858, had been revived by the new Colonial Secretary, Lord Carnarvon, as part of a much larger design to color much of the map of Africa British "pink." But while Disraeli and Carnarvon schemed to create a new union in Africa, Afrikaner resentment of the Keate Award and British high-handedness generally had brought a revival of Afrikaner folk-feeling from the Cape to the Limpopo.

In the Cape Colony itself interest in the Afrikaans language had been revived and the first Afrikaner nationalist association, the Afrikaner Bond, had been founded. Politically assertive, the Bond had been influential in the decision of the new Cape Parliament to reject the decreed annexation of Griqualand West under the Keate Award, and it had also openly opposed Carnarvon's suggestion of a new "federation."

In the Transvaal, too, the Keate Award had had its repercussions. Because he had failed to defend the South African Republic's claims to the Vaal-Harts region, Marthinus Pretorius had been forced to resign as president in 1872. Still in an aggressive mood, the Transvalers had then improbably selected as his replacement a young Dutch Reformed minister from the Cape named Thomas Burgers. An avatar of modernism, Burgers, a Calvinist who did not believe in the devil incarnate and who quoted Comte, was elected over the misgivings of traditionalists like Paul Kruger because he promised to build a railroad to the sea and thus to release the Transvaal from its long economic bondage to the British Cape Colony as a landlocked nation. Sent to Europe by the Volksraad to raise funds for such a project in 1875, Burgers had talked of "federation" with Carnarvon but had gone on to Europe to raise the money to build his railroad—utterly infuriating the Colonial Secretary.

Rebuffed by the Cape and spurned by the Transvaal, Lord Carnarvon had next tried to solicit support for his plan to federate South Africa by being conciliatory to the Free State. In 1876, a suit brought by the Free State's president, Thomas Brand, for damages resultant from Britain's annexation of the diamond fields, was accepted by a London court, which later awarded the Free State some £90,000 in lieu of its lost territory. But far from being conciliated by the court's award, Brand, like most Afrikaners, regarded it as an admission of British guilt.

Thomas Burgers' adventures in Europe had worried Carnarvon, not only because the Transvaal's president seemed to be inviting European states to take a direct interest in a region he regarded as a solely British province but because Burgers' plan to drive a rail line to the sea at the Portuguese port of Delagoa Bay raised another troublesome specter in the Colonial Secretary's mind. In 1875, Britain had lost Delagoa Bay in a dispute with Portugal, which also had holdings in west Africa. The probability that the Portuguese and the Transvaal Afrikaners would now form an alliance also presented the possibility that Britain's expansion northward into the heart of Africa might be blocked—an eventuality that the Colonial Secretary was simply unprepared to accept. He had begun to seek another way to bring the recalcitrant Boers of the north to heel when Thomas Burgers inadvertently presented it to him in 1877 by going to war with Sekhukuni, king of the Pedi tribes, whose legions had begun to drift into territories claimed by the Transvaal.

Burgers' campaign against the Pedi was disastrous from the first. Sekhukuni led a nation almost as populous as the Zulu, and his well-armed, well-disciplined legions were more than a match for the paltry force Burgers sent against him. Routed in battle, the Boers had fled, convinced by their defeat that God had deserted their cause because their modernist president did not cleave to the old faith. Unable to rally them or to check the marauding Pedi, Burgers had lost face with both the blacks and the Boers and left precisely the opening Carnarvon was looking for. He sent Theophilus Shepstone up from Natal to mediate the dispute.

With Sekhukuni still unchecked in the north, Shepstone had met with the Volksraad in Pretoria early in 1877. "In your country," he told them, "there is no government. Your president is not supported. As a friend, I offer you England's aid." Then he announced, almost casually, a few weeks later, that he was annexing the South African Republic to Natal, and on May 24 he ordered that the Vierkleur (four-color flag) be lowered and the Union Jack raised over Pretoria. To placate the stunned Boers, Shepstone acceded to one recent Volksraad resolution, which had installed Kruger as vice president of the Transvaal. It had seemed a politic if meaningless gesture, since the republic was soon to lose its independence. But it was one nevertheless that was to have unexpected results. It had given Paul Kruger preeminence in the Transvaal at a singularly bitter moment in Boer history, and he was soon to use his position, as the former vice president of the defunct republic, to confound both Carnarvon and Shepstone and to frustrate Britain's imperial ambitions and all of Cecil Rhodes's dreams for Africa.

31
KRUGER IN CONTROL

Paul Kruger was 52 when he assumed leadership of the South African Republic. He would govern it for 25 years. A man molded to the needs of pioneer life, he seemed ill cast for the leading role he was about to play in world events and appears in the theater of the imagination as a great hulking figure, dressed in top hat and rumpled tailcoat, lurching across history's stage toward inevitable tragedy as if buffeted by invisible winds. Other figures were to join him as the play of events unfolded: Carnarvon, Shepstone, and the leonine British statesman, William Gladstone, were to be his foils in Act I. Rhodes, a man called Jameson, and later Joseph Chamberlain would dominate Act II. But in Act III, raging legions were to take center stage, setting it afire amid the cries of the dying. Kruger would be old in Act III—old and cynical and wise and yet somehow as full of simple faith as before the play had begun—an ugly, sad old man, destined to die in a far country at the end of a bitter war.

Kruger's first reaction when the Transvaal was annexed was to go to London to protest the decision directly to Lord Carnarvon. His first meeting with the Colonial Secretary, at Carnarvon's home, a mansion modeled on the Houses of Parliament, was a meeting of opposites: Carnarvon urbane, condescending, deft in his use of language; Kruger rough, unworldly, direct in speech and secure in his conviction of the rightness of his cause. Bluntly, Kruger asked Carnarvon to restore the Transvaal's independence. "This was," Carnarvon informed him, "impossible" as "an act performed in the Queen's name could not be questioned." A republican to the marrow of his bones, Kruger found such a notion incomprehensible and suggested that a plebiscite be held to determine the Transvaalers' will in the matter. To this Carnarvon also demurred, offering instead smooth assurances that under British rule the Boers would "enjoy the fullest legislative privileges compatible with the circumstances of the country and the intelligence of its people" and indicating then that the meeting was at an end.

After the interview, Kruger remained in England for only a few weeks, trying to rally support for his cause. He met with little sympathy, but his presence in London was noted. Disraeli described him as "an ugly customer." Sir Bartle Frere, whom Carnarvon was soon to send to Africa as the instrument of his plan to press for federation, recognized "considerable ability and shrewdness under his somewhat clownish appearance." Gladstone, who was soon to seek reelection as Prime Minister, perhaps sensed something dangerous in Kruger's mission and kept him at a distance.

The mission was a failure: Kruger sailed for home in 1877 a disappointed man, leaving behind him at the Colonial Office the impression that he was resigned to the Transvaal's new status as a British vassal. Back in the Transvaal, however, it immediately became clear that he was not, for at a mass meeting in Pretoria only a few days after his return, he announced that he was calling a plebiscite on the issue of annexation. Over Shepstone's express objections, it was held in April 1878. Of some 8,000 enfranchised white males in the Transvaal, 6,591 voted against annexation, 587 for it.

Armed with this proof of his people's real sentiment, Kruger sailed again for England in 1878, taking with him another trusted Boer leader, Piet Joubert, and a Hollander named Bok. In London, the deputation had been refused an audience with the Colonial Secretary, but those officials with whom they did confer indicated firmly that the annexation must stand.

Returned home, Kruger was forced to play a waiting game until what seemed an opportunity to regain the Transvaal's independence presented itself in 1879. In December of the previous year, Cetewayo, the new King of the Zulu, feeling betrayed by Shepstone, who had engineered the slow diminishment of his territories, had raised an army of 60,000 and begun threatening to invade Natal. Ordered to disband, he had refused and, in January of 1879, the British Commander in Natal, Lord Chelmsford, had marched into Zululand with three columns of redcoats to put down the Zulu revolt. On January 20, Chelmsford had encountered Cetewayo's impis at a place called Isandhlawana where they had paraded as a warning to the outnumbered British to withdraw. Foolishly, Chelmsford had instead given chase to the Zulu impis and then encamped his men. Thirty-six hours later, the Zulus had attacked and in the ensuing battle Chelmsford had lost some 1,600 officers and men. Ultimately relieved of his command, he had begun a war that was to drag on for six more months and require Britain to commit a vast army equipped with 36 batteries of heavy artillery to defeat the Zulu.

Watching the progress of the war in Natal impassively, Kruger had done nothing to help the embattled British, evidently in the hope that their difficulties would aid Gladstone, who was running for re-election in Britain against Disraeli. Campaigning against the latter's rampant imperialism, Gladstone—who had promised to restore the Transvaal's independence—had made much of Chelmsford's disasters as an example of the dismal results of Disraeli's policies, and his cause had prospered as the Zulu wars dragged on. Inclined to trust in Glad-stone because he quoted the Bible, Kruger had chosen to disregard the opinion of the Cape's latest Governor, Sir Bartle Frere, that he "might as well ask to go back to the Garden of Eden" as to hope to regain the Transvaal's independence, and had hoped for the best.

Gladstone won, but Kruger gained nothing from it. Immediately embroiled in the Irish question, Gladstone and his cabinet voted to let the annexation of the Transvaal stand, and even as a petition from Kruger and Joubert, asking that he "rescind the Annexation of our poor country" was in transit to London, a letter drafted by Lord Kimberley but signed by Gladstone was on its way to Pretoria. "Our judgment," it read, "is that the Queen cannot be advised to relinquish her sovereignty over the Transvaal. . . ." Gladstone, his campaign promises notwithstanding, had subscribed to Disraeli's imperialist schemes for Africa. Britain was tightening her grip on the continent and unless forced to do so would not release the Transvaal.

32
A COVENANT RENEWED

Kruger had recognized that a war with Britain was possible. He had traveled widely in South Africa in 1879, trying to determine how much support there might be for the Transvaal should push-come-to-shove with Britain. Chelmsford's disasters in Zululand had revealed the tactical weaknesses of the British military machine to the Af-rikaners, who now suspected they could challenge Britain with some hope of success. Wherever Kruger had gone he had found that a new spirit of nationalism had been awakened among the Afrikaners by Shepstone's annexation of the Transvaal. In Cape Town he had heard Jan Hofmeyer of the Afrikaner Bond ask Parliament if the British meant to "dragoon the Transvaal" into a confederation, and in the Free State the mood had been martial. Therefore, when the letter, indicating Gladstone's intention to proceed with Carnarvon's plan for confederation, was received in Pretoria, Kruger began to prepare for war.

On December 8, 1880, a "volksvergadering" was called at "Paardekraal," a farm halfway between Pretoria and Potchefstroom. Though the British authorities had warned that anyone who attended would be charged with high treason, some 6,000 Boers had ridden in, among them delegations from the Free State and the Cape. The meeting lasted a week, elected a new Volksraad, appointed Kruger, Joubert, and Pretorius as its ruling triumvirate, and declared the Transvaal independent. Before the old four-color flag of the South African Republic was raised on December 16, however, Kruger had called upon the assembled Boers to pledge themselves anew to the same oath their fathers had sworn before the Battle of Blood River. Amid psalm-singing and prayers, the men came forward, one by one, and placed a stone signifying a renewal of the Covenant on a cairn raised to mark the occasion. Then, on December 16, they had ridden out to war with Britain.

Within three days the 3,000 British troops in the Transvaal were besieged in their garrisons. Stunned, General Colley, now in command in Natal, had hastily gathered 1,500 men and rushed north to put down the rebellion. Colley's unwise advance led him directly onto Boer lines along the Transvaal's eastern frontier, and he was repulsed at Laing's Nek. Apprised of Colley's defeat, Gladstone's government—absorbed by Britain's ongoing troubles in Egypt and Ireland—decided to offer Kruger generous peace terms. But when ordered to indicate the Colonial Office's willingness to negotiate, General Colley reacted by launching a second unsuccessful assault on Boer positions near Ingogo and also sent off a furious dispatch to Lord Kimberley. "Am I to leave Laing's Nek in Natal territory in Boer occupation and our garrisons isolated?" he demanded.

"We do not mean that you should march to the relief of garrisons or occupy Laing's Nek," Kimberley had responded firmly. "Fix reasonable time within which answer must be sent by Boers. . . ."

A frustrated General Colley had done as instructed. He had conveyed the Colonial Office's peace offer to the Boers, who forwarded it to Kruger in the hinterlands. But he waited only two days for a reply from Kruger that he knew could not possibly reach him in less than a week. Then, on the night of February 26 Colley secretly positioned himself and some 584 riflemen atop a hill overlooking Boer positions at a place called Majuba. At dawn, he opened fire on the laagers, expecting a rout. Instead, the Boers counterattacked and swept the

British from the hill, leaving Colley and 91 of his men dead, wounding another 134, and taking scores of prisoners while sustaining only one casualty themselves.

In the tangled play of events, the impetuous Colley was odd-man-out, dead on Majuba Hill. But by dying he had transformed himself into a martyr in the cause of Empire and so inflamed British opinion against the Boers that it became impolitic for Gladstone's government to be "generous" with Kruger. As a result, when the Transvaal did regain its independence in August of 1881—as the South African Republic—the terms of the Pretoria Treaty left it subject to the "suzerainty" of Britain. Yet considering the David and Goliath proportions of the Boers' challenge to Britain, Colley had also given the Boers a victory that seemed little short of miraculous to Paul Kruger, who was to find in it the final proof of God's concern for the Transvalers as a Chosen People.

On December 16, 1881, a festival of thanksgiving was held at Paardekraal to celebrate the Boer victory. Called upon to address the throng, Paul Kruger had delivered a sermon rather than a political speech. Convinced that the Lord had led "Die Volk" into the wilderness to chastise and purify them—just as He had done with the ancient Israelites—Kruger had insisted that He had vouchsafed His protection to them at Blood River and again at Majuba so that they might remain a nation apart, independent and uncorrupted by any alien influences, fit to serve His holy purpose in Africa as a Covenant People. The power of his belief in the sacred destiny of the Afrikaner nation was to catalyze the patriotism of the Boers and transform it into a religious nationalism every bit as militant and exclusive as that of the Calvinist saints of old. For after Majuba Paul Kruger had become convinced that the Afrikaners' continuing struggle with the British was but one more manifestation of God's eternal struggle with the devil's legions.

Kruger's distrust of the British had been intensified when he had traveled to London in 1877 and 1878. Brought face to face for the first time, at the age of 52, with a world in transition as a result of the industrial revolution, Kruger—a frontiersman of the high veld—must have found it a frightful place. London was crowded with poor who labored in noisome factories for the rich. Its leaders were devious men who did not speak the truth, and it professed a proud faith in "Progress," based on Darwin's concept of "survival of the fittest," which made a mockery of the holy truth Kruger had affirmed under Africa's pulsating stars—the Truth according to the Book of Genesis that God was sole author of the Creation. Convinced of the evil of "progress," Kruger had evidently become persuaded that if it were ever permitted to overtake the Transvaal, it would bring corruption with it to destroy not only the lives but the very soul of the Afrikaner "Volk," and he had reacted against it with a radical religious conservatism worthy of the original Calvin.

After Gladstone had reneged on his promise to restore the Transvaal's independence, the pattern of the future seemed self-evident to Kruger in the pattern of the past: Britain wanted mastery in Africa, and she meant, if she could, to master the Boer as she had the black man. Though the Transvaal had broken free of her imperial grip, it remained in jeopardy. It seemed plain to Kruger that if she were permitted to do so, Britain meant to surround and suffocate the Boer state by taking Bechuanaland and Matabeleland. To prevent this, Kruger had sought to galvanize a spirit of continuing resistance among the Transvaalers at Paardekraal by reminding them of their "sacred tradition" and encouraging them to take up their African birthright by trekking again into lands farther north.

Within a few months of the "volksvergadering" at Paardekraal, the wagons were rolling again as trekkers from the Transvaal set off to stake new claims beyond its northwestern borders—in territory along the so-called Missionary Road, which connected the Cape Colony with Bechuanaland. By 1882 two satellite Boer republics, named Stellaland and Goshen, had been established in the region and trek-commandos were trading their fighting skills as mercenaries for farms in intratribal wars farther north in Bechuanaland. Without contravening the terms of the Pretoria Convention, Kruger had indirectly bid for, and evidently won, a foothold in the hinterlands that effectively blocked British ambitions there. The timing of his move had been exquisite. Engaged in simultaneous wars in Egypt, Ireland, and Afghanistan in 1882, the British had little desire to start another war with the Boers, who had proved their mettle at Majuba. Inclined to temporize, the Colonial Office sent two "commissions" to Bechuanaland to investigate, the first headed by an LMS missionary named

Mackenzie, the second by the newly elected member of the Cape Parliament from Griqualand, Cecil John Rhodes, who was on record as opposed to giving the Boers "so much as one inch" of that strategic territory. Meanwhile, the Colonial Office also bowed to Kruger's request to renegotiate the Pretoria Convention and in 1883 invited him to London for talks.

Kruger won several key concessions in the new Conventions, signed in London in January of 1884. A British Resident, left behind in Pretoria in 1881 to oversee "native affairs," was recalled, and the entire punitive preamble of the Pretoria Convention, defining continuing British "suzerainty" in the South African Republic, was deleted from the new agreement. But Kruger did not gain any rights vis-à-vis the two Boer mini-republics, and when he sought to extend his protection to them later that year, his action brought 5,000 British troops under General Warren rushing northward to hoist the Union Jack over Stellaland, Goshen, and Bechuanaland. Their work of annexation completed, Warren and his little army, along with MacKenzie and Cecil Rhodes, had then ridden south to warn Kruger personally against any further ambitions in the north. When it became clear that Mackenzie meant to see that the new Bechuanaland protectorates were entirely cleared of Boer settlers and reserved only for Englishmen, Rhodes had resigned his appointment as commissioner and apologized to Kruger. But his conciliatory mien had left Kruger unimpressed. "That young man," he had said of Rhodes presciently, immediately afterward, "is going to cause me trouble one day."

33
RHODES AND KRUGER

Rhodes and Kruger were to dominate the historic drama played out in South Africa over the next fifteen years. Acting out the compulsions in his own nature, each would reflect the historic compulsions that led inevitably to a second and far more devastating war between Boer and Briton at the century's end. Ironically, both were John Calvin's spiritual descendants. Kruger, a "Dopper" absolutist, believed that in attempting to preserve the traditional pastoralist society of the Boers, he was also defending God's own order in Africa. Rhodes, the capitalist and Darwinian, was a New Man. A descendant of all those radical Enlightenment thinkers who were in turn Oliver Cromwell's spiritual grandchildren, Rhodes arrogated to himself a task that Kruger would have preferred left to God: the creation of a New World Order dominated by those whom Rhodes regarded as evolutionary Super Men, the "Anglo-Saxon races."

Viewed separately, the two men seem simple opposites: Kruger the immovable object, Rhodes the irresistible force. The old and the new. The true believer and the doubter who truly believed in his messianic role as an agent of change. For Kruger never questioned God and doubted the possibility of "progress," while Rhodes, doubting His existence, also sought to become His instrument by extending the benefits of Britain's "civilizing influence" to the world in general and to Africa in particular. Antagonists in the classical sense, it was inevitable that the two men would clash, and it was only incidental that the discovery of gold in the Transvaal in the year of their first encounter helped to precipitate the conflict that was to destroy both.

Rhodes was 32 when he met Kruger for the first time. Though already established as an important figure in the Cape Parliament, and one of the wealthiest men in the diamond fields, he was no more prepossessing on sight than he had been at 24. Still lanky, he had begun to thicken at the waist and walked with a forward thrust like a man in a perpetual hurry. His face was built around an aquiline nose that overpowered a lesser chin, and his expression combined an element of rapacity with an aloofness that he fancied gave him an Augustan look; for by 1885 Rhodes had laid the foundations of a power a Caesar might have envied, and which had made his dream of bringing all of Africa under British sway seem possible.

Rhodes had emerged as one of the richest men in the diamond fields in 1880 when he helped to found the De Beers Company and had used his wealth, after the former Griqualand was finally annexed to the Cape that year, to stand for and win election to the Cape Parliament. In Parliament he had put himself squarely behind Britain's plan for federation, for Rhodes believed that the unification of South Africa was the necessary first step in his own grand scheme to push British control northward through Bechuanaland,

Matabeleland and the east African highlands to meet the southward thrust of the British Empire along the Nile tributaries leading toward the Sudan. "I went down to the Cape Parliament thinking in my practical way," he would later write, " 'I will go and take the north.' " But Kruger's successful 1881 rebellion, the restoration of the Transvaal's independence, and an upsurge of anti-British sentiment among Afrikaners generally, persuaded Rhodes that the best way to overcome Afrikaner resistance to the spread of British power in Africa was to draw Boer and Briton into partnership, and he had openly begun to court the help of Jan Hofmeyr of the influential Cape Afrikaner Bond in order to advance his own "colonial scheme" for Bechuanaland.

"I was a rabid Jingo once," he told his fellow Cape M.P.'s in a confessorial tone. "I am that no longer. But you are dealing with a question upon the proper treatment of which depends the whole future of this Colony. I look upon this Bechuana territory as the Suez Canal of the trade of this country, the key of its road to the interior. Some honourable members may say this is immorality. 'The lands,' they may say, 'belong to the chief, Mankoroane. How improper! How immoral! We must not do it!' Now I have not these scruples. I believe that the natives are bound gradually to come under the control of the Europeans. . . ."

"If we do not settle this ourselves," Rhodes had continued, "we shall see it taken up in the Houses of Commons, on one side or the other . . . We want to get rid of the Imperial Factor [Britain] in this question and to deal with it ourselves, jointly with the Transvaal. . . . I solemnly warn this House that if it departs from control of the interior we shall fall from the position of the paramount state in South Africa, which is our right in every scheme of federal union in the future, to that of a minor state. . . ."

It was a persuasive speech. It pleased the Cape's British population with the notion that greater Africa must someday be brought under the influence of a government in the British mode. It admitted to Afrikaners that Rhodes was not an ally of LMS and believed that Africa's blacks were "bound to come under the control of Europeans" as had the thousands who worked for De Beers at Kimberley. And most important, it seemed to concede to Hofmeyr and the Afrikaner Bond Rhodes's promise to "Get rid of the Imperial Factor" in Africa and to "deal jointly with the Transvaal" in the creation of a self-governing colonial union in which the Cape Afrikaners would have a particularly powerful political influence. Won over by the idea of a reunified Afrikaner nation, the Bond had taken the leadership in promoting a new customs union between the Cape and Natal and the two Boer republics as a first step toward federation, and Rhodes had been freed to turn to other business he considered urgent: the amalgamation of power that would make it possible for him to "go and take the north."

34
RHODES,
DIAMONDS, AND DREAMS

Diamonds appealed to Rhodes. He could "feel the power in them," he said and Rhodes had returned to Kimberley from Cape Town in 1886, meaning to use the power he perceived implicit in diamonds to bring his dreams of unifying Africa to fulfillment. "My plan is to gradually assimilate all of the territory south of the Zambezi," he had told Jan Hofmeyr. Later, reflecting on his plan, he would write: "When the thought came to me to get through the continent, it was a mad thought. The idea of a lunatic. It is now not the question of the lunacy of the project; it is merely a question of the years it will take to complete. . . ."

The thought of getting "through the continent," of possessing Africa, seems to have haunted Rhodes the way the thought of possessing a woman haunts some men. But because he knew by 1886 that he had rivals for her, Rhodes had evidently begun to feel a sense of urgency about his plans. By then, there were Germans in South-West Africa. The Belgians and French, led by the explorers Stanley and diBrazza, were in the Congo, the Italians in the north, and the Portuguese in the east. Furthermore, another gold strike had been reported in the Transvaal, and though Rhodes believed the Witwatersrand fields would finally prove as unprofitable as those near Pilgrim's Rest had been, he also realized that the Witwatersrand strikes could jeopardize his own schemes by tempting one of the other colonial powers in Africa into an alliance with Kruger's republic. There was, it appeared, no time left to wait for its "gradual assimilation." To secure the north, it seemed to him imperative to encircle the Transvaal and plant the British flag in Matabeleland. Rhodes now sought to accomplish this without alienating the Cape Afrikaners by replacing the power of the British government with that of a private company capable of claiming an Empire on its own. To create such a giant, however, he not only needed vast capital but a leverage among the world's financiers and power brokers that would ensure his freedom of operation in Matabeleland. The key to both, he recognized, lay in monopolizing the world's diamond markets, and in 1886 he moved to take total control of the single most important source of gemstones and industrial diamonds in the world: the Kimberley fields.

Rhodes had only two rivals for the diamond fields in 1886. One of them, Alfred Beit, who had taken the fortune he had originally accrued as a tin-shack landlord in Kimberley in the early 1870's, parlayed it into diamond holdings and left Kimberley to become a powerful financier in an international firm called Wernher-Beit. His other rival was Barney Barnato.

Barnato had come to Africa in 1873 with £30 and 40 boxes of cheap cigars and headed straight to the diamond fields. With the money he gained from selling his cigars, he had begun what he called "Kopjewalloping"—buying diamonds directly from the men who dug them for resale to the diamond merchants. He had often seen Rhodes at the digs in the early days. The young Oxonian had supplemented his income at Kimberley then by selling ice cream and renting a steam pump to diggers on those rare occasions when rain flooded their claims.

It took no particular genius to recognize that the key to Kimberley's real wealth lay in amalgamation. Every year, as the "digs" had grown deeper, the difficulties of mining narrowly cut individual shafts had been compounded. As the covering yellow sands had been stripped away, the true diamondiferous ground had been revealed to lie in great vertical pipes of volcanic blue magma, rising out of the very bowels of the earth. To mine these pipes, men had to sink deeper and deeper shafts, side by side, and by 1885 the consolidation of these shafts had not only become a physical but an economic necessity. Diamonds lying deep in the pipes could be recovered only by quarrying, and quarries like the great "Blue Hole" owned by Rhodes' De Beers, which began to yawn at the center of Kimberley, could be dug only by the concerted use of massed labor gangs. Such gangs, further-more, seemed to be most easily organized by providing tribal blacks and Griqua with housing and forcing them to keep to their contracts by cloistering them in "compounds," as Rhodes had done at De Beers. It had been Rhodes's success in perfecting the "compound system" that had helped to put De Beers into the highly competitive position at Kimberley and permitted Rhodes to challenge more powerful rivals.

By 1886 three companies controlled the diamond fields: Rhodes' De Beers, a partnership called the French Company, in which Beit had interests, and Kimberley Mines, dominated by Barney Barnato. Bent on amalgamating all three, Rhodes had approached Beit and the Rothschilds in London with a scheme to monopolize the entire dia-mond industry by absorbing the two rival firms into a single company called De Beers Consolidated. Beit had applauded the plan, a loan of two million pounds had been written to Rhodes by the Rothschilds, and the French Company had swiftly capitulated. Barney Barnato, however, had refused to be bought out, even after Rhodes had taken control of every outstanding share in his company except the ones Barnato himself owned.

It was at this point that Rhodes, sensitive himself to the meaning of British class distinctions, is said to have offered Barnato, in whom he perceived a yearning for acceptance by his "socal superiors," election to both the Cape Parliament and the exclusive Kimberley Club, heretofore off limits to Jews, if he would assent. "This is no mere business transaction," Rhodes is said to have told Barnato. "I mean to make a gentleman of you." Barnato had accepted Rhodes's offer but had added his own terms: five million pounds and a life governorship in De Beers Consolidated.

The two agreed to finalize the deal in the Kimberley cottage of one of Rhodes's closest friends, Dr. Leander Jameson. Barnato approached the meeting expecting to hear about contracts, mergers, and finances. Instead, Rhodes lectured him with passionate intensity on his "Grand Design" for Africa. Pacing back and forth, quoting statistics, Rhodes revealed to the astonished Barnato that De Beers Consolidated was but a stepping stone to the creation of a much greater enterprise, a com-pany capable of opening and controlling the heartlands of Africa. Unrolling maps, he indicated those territories already painted "British pink" that lay like a half-closed fist around the two small Boer republics and then swept his hand northward, over the great green bridge of territory leading into the interior and upward to the Sudan. The keystone of that bridge was Matabeleland and it was there, Rhodes insisted, that the fabled treasures of King Solomon's gold mines would be found. The meeting lasted eighteen hours and when it had ended, Barnato had not only agreed to the creation of De Beers Consolidated —a company that until very recently retained its complete monopoly on the world's diamond markets—but to Rhodes's grandiose schemes to go prospecting in Matabeleland. "He had a fancy then," Barnato was later to remark, "for making an Empire."

35
GOLD AND A GRAND DESIGN

In 1885, two Transvaalers—the brothers Willie and Frederick Struben—found gold on their Witwatersrand farms. That same year, two Englishmen—George Walker and George Harrison—made a second strike on the ridge at Langlaate. The Strubens had discovered the legendary Confidence Reef; the two Georges, the main Witwatersrand Reef. Together, they had struck the world's richest goldfields, but the true value of the Rand's treasure, which lay embedded in veins of hard quartz that rippled in frozen waves for sixty miles deep within the earth, would remain incalculable until new ways of extracting it were developed in the 1890's. Nevertheless, the Rand strikes worried Paul Kruger. He feared they might invite British reannexation of the Transvaal and had at first tried to suppress news of them. But as word of the finds spread anyway, gold hunters by the thousands had swarmed to the Witwatersrand, and Paul Kruger's anxieties for the future of the S.A.R. had multiplied with the predominantly British population of a newborn boom town called Johannesburg that grew up at the very heart of the Transvaal.

Kruger had good reason to be afraid. By 1886, the S.A.R. and its sister republic, the Orange Free State, were almost entirely surrounded by British-held territories. To the west, Griqualand had been absorbed by the Cape in 1880 and on the S.A.R.'s northwestern borders, the whole of Bechuanaland had been annexed by Warren in 1885. To the east, a wall of British protectorates stretched from the Cape Colony to Natal and beyond. Cetewayo's Zulus had gone down to defeat in 1879. Swaziland had become a British protectorate in 1880, and late in 1885, the Pondo and Tembu had agreed to British "protection" after Cecil Rhodes had personally demonstrated the power of the new Maxim machine gun to them by cutting down a field of their maize with it. By 1887, only two tribal kingdoms bordering the Boer republics remained independent, those of the Mashona and Matabele and time was running out for both when Kruger sent a representative to Bulawayo, the royal kraal of the Matabele King, Lobengula, to negotiate a mutual protection pact.

Though the British tended to discount Lobengula's grasp of recent events, the Matabele king could not have been unaware of the fate that had overtaken most of the once mighty black nations whose territories bordered on his own. Britain's "modus operandi" had become obvious by then. "First come the traders," Cetewayo had remarked. "Then come the missionaries, and then come the men in the red coats." There were LMS missionaries in Mashonaland and Matabeleland by 1887, and Lobengula had greeted the S.A.R.'s delegate, Pieter Grobbler, cordially and agreed readily to a treaty with Kruger's government. But before the pact was signed, Grobbler was mysteriously murdered, and very shortly after his death four Englishmen appeared at Bulawayo. John Moffat, the son of the LMS missionary who had ministered to Lobengula's uncle, Mizilikazi, had come as an agent of the Cape's government, but Charles Rudd and his two companions represented Cecil Rhodes. All four made it plain to Lobengula that the "white Queen" disapproved of his pact with Kruger, but the latter three also offered to reward the King if he would repudiate it and agreed instead to grant "concessions" to Rhodes's company to prospect for gold in his kingdom. Similar "concessions" had already been obtained by Rudd from the Mashona in exchange for a promise of protection against the Matabele, who had made vassals of them. But Lobengula did not assent to Rudd's proposition until he had been promised 1,000 Martini-Henry rifles, 100,000 rounds of ammunition for them, an armed steamboat for patroling the Zambezi, and a monthly stipend of £100 for life. As he put his mark on the agreement, however, Lobengula had no idea that he was simultaneously closing the South African Republic's northern border and signing his own nation's death warrant.

By 1888, the initial "boom" at Johannesburg had begun to falter as the difficulty of mining the Rand's ore and prizing the gold from its quartzite matrix became apparent. At the outset, Transvaal Boers had neither the skill, the means, nor the inclination to work the Rand, but by 1888 even the smaller British entrepreneurs were being eliminated by large combines, dominated by the men of Kimberley—Beit, Barnato and, belatedly, Cecil Rhodes.

Rhodes had organized his Gold Fields of South Africa Company with Charles Rudd shortly after the latter returned from Bulawayo. He had done so, not because he had abandoned his belief that the real "Mother Lode" would be found in Matabeleland, but evidently to provide himself with another trump card to play when he went to London to seek a royal charter permitting him to form a new company modeled on such great ventures of the past as the British East India Company, for the purpose of exploiting central Africa. Rhodes had three things to offer would-be shareholders in his proposed "British South Africa Company" when he arrived in London the next year: De Beers Consolidated and its recently acquired monopoly on the production and marketing of Kimberley's diamonds, a respectable share in the Rand's gold and a promise of even greater riches to come in the "concessions" he held to hunt for gold in Mashona and Matabeleland. They were enough to win him both the charter he sought and the financial support he needed, and in 1889, Rhodes formed the British South Africa Company by amalgamating his holdings with those of two British exploring companies and a third company, called the African Lakes Corporation, associated with the LMS. The newly formed "B.S.A." took title to a vast ill-defined region, over five hundred miles in breadth, which stretched southward from the shores of Lake Nyasa some 1,200 miles to the border of Bechuanaland and the South African Republic. Rhodes had got himself an Empire comparable in size to India. His actual hold on it, however, was as tenuous as the "concessions" Rudd had extracted from the Mashona and Matabele to hunt for gold in their territories. It was to remedy this that Rhodes, on returning to South Africa, had bought the B.S.A. a small army and a column of "pioneers" and dispatched both from Kimberley, under the leadership of his old friend Dr. Leander Jameson, to establish a white settlement called Fort Salisbury in Mashonaland.

Though Lobengula had been persuaded by Jameson to give his "pioneers" safe passage through Matabeleland, the Mashona did not welcome the whites who had come to claim their hereditary lands at rifle point. In reprisal, they had cut the telegraph wires being strung from Kimberley to Salisbury and had taken some 500 yards of it. With consummate cheekiness, Jameson had charged the Mashona with theft and demanded a fine in cattle. When it was paid, however, the cattle proved to belong to Lobengula—the Matabele's King Overlord from whom Charles Rudd had promised the Mashona protection. At this point, Jameson chose to send a message to Lobengula informing him of the affair, which the Matabele King construed as an invitation to collect his lost cattle. But when his impis went to Mashonaland to retrieve them, they were ambushed by white pioneers. Thirty-three of Lobengula's men were killed, the cattle were not retrieved, and even before Lobengula could protest, trumped-up reports of Matabele atrocities were being circulated in the outside world. Jameson then prepared to lead a column of 900 men, which soon was reinforced by 4,000 "volunteers" rushed north by Rhodes, into Matabeleland to "avenge" the white pioneers.

The war lasted from October to December. In the first encounter between Jameson's forces and Lobengula's impis, more than 1,500 Matabele were killed outright and thousands more were wounded. Armed only with assegais and the old Martini-Henry rifles, the impis were scythed down where they stood, falling like sheaves of maize before the fire of the Maxim guns. Turning to terrorism in reprisal, the Matabele justified earlier fictional reports of their atrocities by attacks on white farms, but were ultimately no match for the murderous Maxim machine guns. When the war was over, Rhodes went north to distribute the spoils of victory. At Bulawayo he magnanimously gave a farm to each of Jameson's 900 men—some five million acres of land that had formerly belonged to Lobengula's people. Out of the death of the Matabele nation, a new state was being born. It would be called Rhodesia.

It had been a period of accomplishment for Rhodes. In five years, by moving with a singlemindedness that was both ruthless and bold, he had extended his grip on Africa from the Cape to Lake Nyasa and taken the bridge of territories required to color the map of Africa "British pink." In the east and west, German and Portuguese expansion had been simultaneously checked by the creation of the B.S.A. Though Paul Kruger had one chance left to reach the sea via a narrow corridor of land leading down through Portuguese Mozambique, he and his Boers were otherwise sealed within their borders with no hope left of continuing the northward roll of their trek wagons. Rhodes, furthermore, now wielded unprecedented political power in the Cape where he had been elected Prime Minister in 1890, after he returned from Matabeleland as a conquering hero who had destroyed the "cruel military system of the Matabele." At the peak of his financial and political powers, he seemed to hold the future of Africa in the palm of his hand.

Often likened to a "god," Rhodes at this point seemed rather to think of himself as one of the world's natural emperors. Asked how long he thought he would be remembered, he had answered "four thousand years." Yet for all of his successes, the colossal Rhodes had feet of clay. His primary objective, the creation of a colonial Union in South Africa, had not yet been achieved. The Rand's gold belonged to the independent Transvaal. His old adversary, Kruger, was still defiant, and Rhodes now realized that his own time was limited. In 1891, he had suffered a second heart attack and was never to regain his health.

36
A CONTEST OF WILLS

Rhodes was 38 when his health began to fail. The illness was not unexpected. His weak heart and lungs had troubled him since youth and the thought of death seems seldom to have been far from his mind. By 1891, he had written four wills, expressing in each a similar wish that his worldly fortunes be used for the furtherance of an Anglo-Saxon world empire.

Born as Britain was approaching the pinnacle of her imperial and industrial powers, Rhodes had never questioned that the future belonged to her. Though he only half believed in God, his faith in the civilizing destiny of England was absolute. A zealot in this cause, he seemed all of his days to be rushing forward to meet the future, determined to impress his Grand Design upon it. And that was perhaps what defined the essential difference between himself and Kruger. For Rhodes, a death-haunted young man, wanted what he could not have, tomorrow, whereas Kruger, an old man, looked back upon a simpler age that was fast slipping away and dreamed of preserving it.

Rhodes, grasping at life, still hoped to possess all of Africa. One of a new breed of men who put their faith in maps, telegraph wires, and technology, he wanted to penetrate its dark heart with the iron rods of the railroad, to break its secrets, open it to commerce, subdue its gorgeous tribes and give them all to a squat Queen to rule. Kruger, on the other hand, had for a long while dreamed of a trek that would never end, of the slow northward drift of blue ox-wagons across the green plains of Africa through lands where great herds of wild animals grazed. But as an old man, Kruger knew change was inevitable, and one of his last gestures, just before it had become plain that the S.A.R. would have to fight to hold onto its independence, was to set aside the great tract of wilderness, known today as Kruger Park, as a monument to the world of primal splendor he had known as a boy.

In 1889, Kruger had entered into a mutual protection pact and customs union with the Orange Free State, having rejected a similar union with the Cape the year before. He had then turned to fight fire with fire—after Rhodes had blocked his hope of finding "liebensraum" for his Boers in Matabeleland—by proposing to bring the S.A.R. into contact with the outside world by driving a rail line to the sea at the Portuguese port on Delagoa Bay. It was to be financed with funds taxed from the Rand gold fields and engineered with help from the Netherlands. Construction of the Netherlands Railroad was about to begin when Kruger had signaled British authorities at the Cape that he would accept Rhodes's recent acquisitions in Matabeleland, if they would accept the S.A.R.'s claim to a swath of territory leading down to the sea through Swaziland.

The move infuriated Rhodes. If completed, the Netherlands Railroad not only threatened to break Britain's stranglehold on the South African Republic's trade with the outside world but to invite its alliance with other colonial powers and interfere with Rhodes's own plan to claim Delagoa Bay for the B.S.A. But because he did not wish at that moment to risk a quarrel either with Kruger, the Portuguese, or the latter's German allies, Rhodes had restrained an immediate impulse to annex the Portuguese port. Instead he had attempted to persuade Kruger to accept several alternate routes to the sea. His distrust of Rhodes confirmed by what had happened to Lobengula, Kruger had rejected every proposition until Rhodes, hoping to win him by personal persuasion, had journeyed to Pretoria for talks.

"We must work together," Kruger records Rhodes said to him. "I know the republic wants a seaport. You must have Delagoa Bay. . . ."

"How can we work together?" Kruger claims he responded. "The harbor belongs to the Portuguese, and they won't hand it over."

"Then we must simply take it," Rhodes said flatly.

"I can't take away other people's property," Kruger indicates he replied. "If the Portuguese won't sell the harbor, I wouldn't take it even if you gave it to me, for ill-gotten gains are accursed. . . ."

Rhodes, who had once boasted, "I have never met anyone in my life whom it is not easier to deal with than to fight," had found Kruger unwilling to listen either to blandishment or to bribe. Almost bewildered by the old man's continuing resistance to the benefits of "Progress" and the "Pax Britannica," Rhodes was to resort increasingly to coercion in his subsequent efforts to force the S.A.R. into accepting both. As his own health failed Rhodes's methods were to become progressively more ruthless until, in 1894, he was to enter into a plot to overthrow Kruger's government that was not only to destroy his own political career but to precipitate a bloody war between Briton and Boer that has left a legacy of bitterness in South Africa to the present day.

For the next two years, however, Rhodes made no direct effort to bring Kruger into line but devoted himself instead to strengthening his own political base and promoting the cause of a colonial federation. Soon after a rail line linking Cape Town to Johannesburg, which undercut Kruger's project economically, was completed in 1892, Rhodes had turned to the elaboration of a "Natives Policy for Africa" meant to enhance cooperation between Briton and Boer by rejecting the pro-forma liberalism of previous British imperial governments.

"I will lay down my own policy on this native question," he had told the Cape Parliament. "The native is to be treated as a child and denied the franchise. . . ." In 1892 and 1894 Rhodes had put these policies into law by pushing two important pieces of legislation through the Cape Parliament. The first, by limiting the franchise to owners of property valued at £75 or more and who could read and write their own names, effectively eliminated most blacks and many Coloreds from the Cape's voting rolls, undoing much that previous more liberal British governments had done for them. The second, called the Glen Grey Act, was to have even more far-reaching effects on South Africa's future as the forerunner of much of its present controversial "homelands" legislation. Modeled in part on Shepstone's "native policy" for Natal, the Glen Grey Act, which Rhodes and Hofmeyr sponsored jointly in Parliament, created a number of carefully defined "locations" in the Transkei in which Pondo and Xhosa were to be given freehold farms on condition that they learn to work them. The Act also imposed fines on landless blacks for idleness, which forced them into the white man's employ and so assured that white farms and the mines would have a reliable labor supply. Furthermore, it transferred control of the "locations" from the traditional tribal chiefs to Cape-appointed magistrates, whose power was enhanced by the fact that the law allowed no other whites but themselves, and traders and missionaries they selected, into the reserves. Thus, by invoking strict separation of the races, the Glen Grey Act strengthened the Cape government's grip on most of the territory lying behind the high veld Boers and the Indian Ocean coasts. Though perhaps an incidental result of this sweeping land reform, the law had also, as one of its consequences, lent even greater strategic importance to the S.A.R.'s last free outlet to the sea, Paul Kruger's Netherlands Railroad.

Shortly after the Glen Grey Act went into effect, Rhodes had gone north to visit Bulawayo, where an unproductive search for a New Rand was still being conducted. More and more, the evidence indicated that the legendary "Vigiti Magna" of Africa had already been found in the Transvaal, but Rhodes was as yet unwilling to abandon all hope for Matabeleland.

The difficult trip and his own frustrations had taken their toll on Rhodes's heart, which had weakened steadily after 1891, and during this journey the evidence that it was failing had become undeniable. At 41, Rhodes looked 60, relied increasingly upon brandy for the energy he needed to persevere, and his moods had become noticeably extreme. Stopping in the company of Dr. Jameson on his return trip from Bulawayo, Rhodes had found Kruger's port facilities nearing completion. On seeing them, he had apparently flown into a rage and offered on the spot to buy the whole of Delagoa Bay outright from the Portuguese. When the offer was politely refused, he and Jameson had hastened on to Pretoria where Rhodes bluntly warned Kruger not to use his new railroad at the expense of British colonial interests.

"If you do not take care," Rhodes reportedly stormed, "you will have the whole of South Africa against you. You are a very strong man, but there are things you may do which will bring the whole of the Cape Colony and, indeed, the whole of South Africa against you and so strongly that you will not be able to stand against it!"

It was after this final confrontation with Kruger in November of 1894 that Rhodes evidently committed himself to a scheme to foment an "outlander" revolution in the Transvaal and overthrow Kruger's government. Though the plot gained the explicit approval of the Colonial Office in London, it involved a cast of characters on whom Rhodes, in a more rational state of mind, might never have depended and a scenario that in its disregard for reality brings to mind equivalent political fiascos of a more recent vintage both in South Africa and the United States.

37
JAMESON'S RAID

The world's appetite for gold had become insatiable by 1895, and wherever the yellow metal was in short supply, economies faltered, wages lagged, and depressions ensued. It followed, therefore, that Britain sorely regretted having let the Transvaal slip from her grasp in 1881—four years before the Rand had been discovered—and that by 1895, her ardent wish to have the Rand back had placed Paul Kruger's S.A.R. in extreme jeopardy.

Kruger realized, soon after its discovery, that the Rand's treasure might hold a deadly threat to his republic. "Every ounce of gold taken from our soil," he had warned his advisors somberly in 1888, "will have to be weighed up with rivers of tears and the life blood of thousands of our best people in defense of that same soil."

Anathema to him two years after its founding, Johannesburg, the city that bore his name, had grown more so with each passing year as it had drawn to itself in ever increasing numbers precisely the kinds of people Kruger had learned to distrust on his several journeys abroad. Arriving by the thousands—principally from England—these adventurers not only brought with them the dubious ethics of the new social Darwinism but all of the corruptions and sophistications of the Victorian demimonde, and under their tutelage Johannesburg had grown into a godless, greedy, pleasure-loving city. Dominated by a ruling clique who called Cecil Rhodes their friend, it was to Kruger's way of thinking a city devoted entirely to Mammon, to be shunned.

What troubled Paul Kruger as much as Johannesburg's corruptions and connections, however, was its growth. By the 1890's the Rand's population of "outlanders" had outstripped that of the rest of the S.A.R. and the Boers had become a minority in their own republic. The political implications were obvious and Kruger had twice revamped the rules for enfranchisement to prevent the "outlanders" from seizing political power. He then responded to their resulting complaints by setting up a Second Volksraad to represent their interests to his government indirectly. But as this left the real control of the republic in the hands of its Afrikaner minority, the "outlanders" had organized a "National Union" in 1892 and had begun to clamor for a series of "rights and reforms" which included an end to the tariffs on goods coming into Johannesburg and to the government monopolies on dynamite and liquor, a reduction in the 10 percent tax on gold production, a switch from Dutch to English as the medium of instruction in Johannesburg's courts and schools, and the right to vote on matters of "importance" to them without becoming

Transvaal citizens. But neither Kruger nor his Volksraad were willing to accede to these demands and friction between the "outlanders" and the government had increased steadily. When Rhodes and Jameson visited Johannesburg in 1894 the unrest in Johannesburg evidently persuaded Rhodes that the time was opportune to topple Kruger's government.

The plot was simple: a reworking of what Jameson had used against the Matabele, it would use the same somewhat theatrical devices of "ruse and rescue." The ruse was to be an "outlander" uprising in Johannesburg. Staged on cue by Rhodes's allies there, they were to demand immediate reforms from Kruger and, when these were not forthcoming, to take up arms to seize Pretoria. The "rescue" was to be provided by a column of well-armed men, led by Jameson, who were to march into the Transvaal from the north on the pretext of protecting British citizens in Johannesburg. To "prevent further bloodshed" at this juncture, Rhodes was to plead for British intervention in the Transvaal, and the British High Commissioner would be sent north to mediate in the conflict. Under his "impartial" aegis, "free" elections would subsequently be held in the S.A.R., the intransigent Paul Kruger would be removed from office and replaced by a new president sympathetic to Britain's interests, and the Transvaal and all of its gold would be brought under British colonial control.

It was to be child's play, one of those "imperial picnics" of which the Victorian English had become so fond. It was to be financed surreptitiously by Rhodes, secretly approved by the Colonial Office, and publicly executed in the cause of "good government" by the "outlanders" and the dashing Dr. Jameson. That there was an element of adolescent fantasy in all of this disturbed no one and, for a while, things went according to plan.

Early in 1895, with Dr. Jameson as his traveling companion, Rhodes had gone to London. Warmly received at Victoria's court, he was honored by having the new colony he had added to her dominions named "Rhodesia" and was installed as a Privy Counselor in her government. When the Queen had complained of the loss of the Transvaal "which we ought never to have given up," Rhodes had confidently assured her that it would be restored to her Empire. And in consultation with her new Colonial Secretary, Joseph Chamberlain, Rhodes had evidently laid out his plan for retrieving it.

The ambitious Joseph Chamberlain, who had disavowed any further British expansion in Africa by force earlier in his career, had become an ardent Jingoist by 1895. Already worried that Germany might advance her interests on the Rand by forming a friendship with Kruger, he had evidently given his assent to the plot to raise a revolution on the Rand and had asked Rhodes to keep him informed of its progress.

Soon after Rhodes had returned to Cape Town, plans for "Jameson's Raid," had gone forward at an accelerated rate. To arm the "outlanders," guns were secretly shipped north from the Cape in oil drums to Rhodes's brother Frank, the Administrator of his Goldfields Company, and to Hays Hammond, its chief engineer. To provide Jameson with what he needed, a new "Rhodesian Horse" company was formed to reinforce the old Matabeleland police by an addition of several hundred men. Simultaneously, as the "outlanders" began to increase their agitation for "reforms" by filing a petition for their rights in London, the men who ran the railway line from Capetown to Johannesburg had increased tensions by deciding to circumvent Kruger's rail tariffs by transshipping goods from the Free State to the Rand by ox wagon. Reacting, Kruger had closed his borders along the Vaal and kept them closed until Chamberlain in London had begun making very threatening noises. The Colonial Office, meanwhile, had quietly granted Rhodes a strategic corridor, which connected Bulawayo with the Cape via Mafeking. By November, the date of the "uprising" had been tentatively set for December 28, and Jameson had begun his southward march toward Mafeking at the head of a column of well-armed troops.

In Johannesburg, tension mounted steadily. Talk of rebellion was everywhere, and Kruger heard it clearly in Pretoria. On November 16, Jameson slipped into Johannesburg to meet with his co-conspirators. He took an undated letter away with him, in which the "Reformers" pleaded for the protection of Johannesburg's "women and children." The letter was to be published after the rebellion had begun, but Jameson was sternly instructed to await a signal from the city before beginning his march from Mafeking.

As Christmas approached, Britain became embroiled in a quarrel with the United States over British Guiana. Chamberlain, worried lest his administration be faced with a dual crisis, cautioned Rhodes that he must either undertake his venture immediately or postpone it indefinitely. Rhodes went forward by confirming the date for the uprising as December 28.

Christmas approached and telegrams began to fly back and forth from Johannesburg to Cape Town, from Cape Town to London, from Mafeking to Johannesburg. Some referred quite openly to the coming rebellion and when Kruger's advisors—who now knew almost as much about Jameson's plans as he did—asked him why he did not stop the rebellion before it started, the old man answered: "You must give the tortoise time to put out its head before you can cut it off."

Chrismas passed. On December 26, Chamberlain informed Prime Minister Lord Salisbury that a revolution was imminent in Johannesburg, and Rhodes wired a *London Times* correspondent to "Inform Chamberlain I shall get through all right if he supports me. Today the crux is I shall win and South Africa will belong to England."

But at this point, the ludicrous began to happen. It was race week in Johannesburg and, in the holiday atmosphere, few of the "Reformers" were inclined to give up sport for the sake of a revolution. On December 27 Jameson's co-conspirators called off the plan and reset the date for January 4. Frustrated, Jameson had decided then and there to begin celebrations for the New Year and had given his troopers a party that lasted three days. On January 1st—full of enthusiasm—he had fired off two more telegrams to the "outlanders" intelligence chiefs in Johannesburg, signaling his imminent departure from Mafeking. However, as both had gone away on holiday, these signals were never received. Nor did Jameson get the last despairing message from Rhodes, telling him to abort his mission for reasons later succinctly described in an article in the *Cape Times:*

"An essential part of the plan," wrote the *Times* editor, F. E. Garrett, "was the cutting of the telegraph wires—'secure telegraph office silence' as one of the cipher telegrams put it. And one wire was cut, sure enough. The southward wire to the Colony was cut south of Pitsani and again south of Mafeking. But the really important wire running to Pretoria was not cut by reason of the trooper being sent to cut it being, in plain words, drunk. He started his errand carrying with him the most detailed and elaborate instructions. He was to cut the wire in two places so many yards apart, take it so far into the veld, and bury it so deep He did cut certain wire and he did make an effort at least to bury it in the veld. But the wire cut was the peaceful fence by which a farmer kept his cows in. Then with good conscience he reeled back. In the whole tragi-comedy there is no grotesquer touch than this which the writer had from a resident on the spot. . . ."

Having consumed three wagon loads of whiskey and 36 cases of champagne, Jameson's column—some 1,000 men short of the originally planned for 1,500 men—rode out of Mafeking on the first of January into the blazing summer heat of the Transvaal. Kruger, who had been privy to the telegraph traffic that had passed through Pretoria, had his men waiting. As Jameson's troopers rode southwest, expecting to be met by a relief column the vacationing "intelligence chiefs" were to have sent from Johannesburg, they were met instead by Boers on horseback. The Boers did not attack the column. Instead, they simply rode southward alongside it on either flank in perfect silence.

At this point, had things gone according to the original plan, there should have been an uprising in Johannesburg and an attack on Pretoria. Another *Cape Times* article of the period indicates why there were no attacks. "The Johannesburg leaders," wrote Garrett, "had just discovered that the Boers keep Nagmaal. At the end of December and the beginning of January, Church Square at Pretoria was white with the tents of outspanned wagons . . . and in each wagon, along with the Bible, came a rifle. . . . Pretoria was a ready-made garrison . . . Once again the Boers say, 'We were saved by our religion.' "

Meanwhile outside of Johannesburg, the Boers on Jameson's flanks had begun to close on his column, herding it along, as they might have herded their cattle, into a valley between two long ridges letting onto a swamp. At this point either Jameson or his co-commander, Sir John Willoughby, ordered that a barrage of shells be laid down on the hills. When it was over, a scout was sent forward to survey the damage and returned to report that all the Boers he had seen in the hills were prostrate and presumably dead. A charge on the

Boer positions was ordered and one hundred of the troopers rode forward, directly into the fire of Boer sharpshooters lying flat behind every rock. Sixty were killed. The column moved on, crossing the swamp under steady harassing fire from the Boers. At dawn, however, the Boers were mysteriously gone and Jameson's column, now badly off its original route, pushed forward until it came upon two small boys of whom Jameson asked directions. They were given, in English, and they did not direct the British toward Johannesburg, but into a cul-de-sac near the village of Krugersdorp where hundreds of Boers awaited them. After an hour's fighting, Jameson's men laid down their arms and, in surrendering, laid to rest all of Cecil Rhodes's grand dreams.

On January 3, Rhodes learned the worst. Jameson and all his men were in prison, and in Pretoria, Kruger was receiving congratulatory telegrams. Among them was one from the Kaiser, which praised Kruger for having restored order in the Transvaal "without appealing to the help of friendly powers."

In Cape Town, Rhodes was pacing, ashen, when Jan Hofmeyr arrived at his home, Groot Schuur, to demand his resignation as Prime Minister of the Cape. To Hofmeyr, Rhodes, by his involvement in Jameson's Raid, had betrayed Afrikanerdom's trust in him. He felt, he was afterwards to say, "as one who finds his wife has been deceiving him." When Rhodes began to rant, crying, "What am I going to do? Live it down? How can I? Am I to get rid of myself?," Hofmeyr had coldly recommended that Rhodes exile himself forthwith to Rhodesia.

For Rhodes, the rest was denouement. Dismissed as Prime Minister, he did betake himself to Rhodesia, where, after Jameson's defeat, the remnants of the Matabele nation had staged another uprising. But he did not repent of his actions in the Transvaal, except as they had created a new obstacle to his Grand Design. Returning to the Cape in 1898, he had formed a new "Jingo party." Still unable to comprehend the depth of Afrikaner nationalism, Rhodes had continued to denigrate it and, until the eve of the Anglo-Boer War, maintained that Kruger would "give" at the "final push." When he died at the Cape in 1902, unaware that at the end Hofmeyr had sent a telegram to him which said simply, "God be with you," the war was three years old, and the train that carried Rhodes's body north for burial in Rhodesia passed through a blackened country where ragged bands of Boers on horseback still fought the artillery of the British Army for a lost cause.

38
THE WAY TO WAR

Rhodes's fall shook the British government and very nearly toppled Joseph Chamberlain. Though the Colonial Secretary's direct involvement in Jameson's fiasco remained secret, British policy in South Africa suddenly seemed feckless. Victoria's honor had been besmirched, the Transvaal not only still had its independence but its gold, and the Colonial Office's only remaining ploy was to insist that the Pretoria Convention of 1881, which had given the Queen "suzerainty" in the Transvaal, took precedence over the London Conventions of 1884.

In South Africa, meanwhile, Paul Kruger's position had been vastly strengthened. A reawakening of "Volk" feeling among Afrikaners from the Cape to the Limpopo had transformed "Oom Paul" (Uncle Paul) into a folk hero and made him the undisputed spiritual leader of his people. The defense alliance between the Free State and the S.A.R. had been tightened, and in the Cape, the resurgence of Afrikaner nationalism had brought a government dominated by the Afrikaner Bond to power in 1898. But contrary to Jingoist propaganda, which insisted that Kruger and his cohorts were conspiring to take over all of South Africa, Kruger's attitude toward Britain in this period was publicly conciliatory. Though he had pressured Britain to indict Rhodes, dissolve the British South Africa Company, and admit there was no truth to Chamberlain's claims with regard to the Pretoria Convention, he had nevertheless released Jameson and his raiders for trial in London and signaled a willingness to compromise on the "outlander" issue by appointing a moderate Cape-born, Cambridge-educated attorney named Jan Smuts as his Minister of Justice in 1898 after his own relection to a fifth term as president of the S.A.R. Chamberlain, however, had evidently already decided that there would be no compromises with the Transvaal. Instead, he saved his own political skin by taking the offensive, insisting that Kruger was the real culprit, both because he had created an intolerable situation for British subjects on the Rand by failing to extend the franchise to them, and because he had invited interference from Germany in a region where Britain's interests were paramount.

It is debatable whether Chamberlain actually meant to precipitate a war in South Africa when he appointed Sir Alfred Milner, one of the most implacable "Jingoists" of the age, as Britain's spokesman there in 1897. Perhaps he simply believed that an unrelenting application of pressure, backed by a show of Great Britain's astonishing strength, would be sufficient to bring Kruger to heel. He had, at any rate, launched a "war of despatches" with Pretoria almost immediately after the Raid. Though the Colonial Secretary was fully aware that there was no legal justification for his insistence that the Transvaal was a "suzerain" British dependency, he may have believed it possible to regain control of the S.A.R. and its gold simply by bullying Kruger under the pretext that the Pretoria Convention still applied. If that was his object, the man he sent to represent him in South Africa was well chosen.

Constitutionally incapable of being anything but "firm" in his approach to the Afrikaners, Sir Alfred Milner was a man as stiff and pretentious as his own waxed mustache. Aloof to the point of arrogance, he had little of Rhodes's charm and all of his ambition, and his own predilections made him utterly unsympathetic to a man like Kruger, whom he regarded as a peasant politician, parading a lot of religious humbug to gull his people into resisting subjection to British rule.

Used to treating the "natives" with condescension, Milner's style did not endear him to the Boers from the outset, and he seemed to go out of his way to give insult to Afrikanerdom generally when he began to insist that Kruger give in immediately to the "outlanders'" continuing demands for the franchise.

Kruger had reacted sharply to Milner's demands by dismissing a judge favored by the "outlanders" from the S.A.R.'s supreme court and despatching an ambassador to Europe to see the Kaiser. In so doing, he may have fallen into a trap. From this point forward, Cham-

THE WAY TO WAR

berlain made much of the "German" question in Africa, and Milner was unrelenting in his pressure for "reform" in the Transvaal.

Moving deftly, Chamberlain made it clear to the Kaiser that Britain would brook no interference in Africa. He had, however, softened this by offering to divide Portugal's African territories with Germany on condition that Britain be given carte blanche in the Transvaal. Soon after the Kaiser signaled his agreement to these terms, Milner stepped up his pressure on Kruger. "There is no way out except reform in the Transvaal or war," he cabled Chamberlain late in 1898. "They are armed to the teeth and their heart is black." By November, the High Commissioner had gone to London to lobby in person for a showdown with Kruger. When he returned to the Cape in January of 1899, it was plain that he did so with every assurance that, if a confrontation came, Whitehall would be ready for it.

The storm clouds of war were gathering and all could see them. In March, Milner solicited a petition from "outlanders" on the Rand, calling for immediate British intervention. Kruger stood firm and, in May, Milner sent a cable to Chamberlain for publication in the London press: "The case for intervention," it read in part, "is overwhelming . . . The spectacle of thousands of British citizens kept permanently in the position of helots . . . does steadily undermine the influence of Great Britain. . . ." Chamberlain responded, "Our response will be a very strong one. . . ."

Was it then, all preplanned? Did Britain want a "little war" with the Transvaal, one that would take a few lives, end in a few weeks, give Britain control of the Transvaal's gold and an open road north all the way to Uganda and beyond? One more attempt at conciliation was made in May when Kruger met personally with Milner at Bloemfontein. Coldly polite, Milner remained absolutely unyielding. After five days of fruitless discussion, Kruger, exhausted, frustrated and frightened, cried out, tears streaming down his cheeks, "It is my country you want!" There was no reply. With a wave of his hand, Milner indicated the meeting was at its end. "Mr. Kruger procrastinates," he remarked caustically afterward. "He dribbles out reforms like water from a squeezed sponge."

It was now only a matter of time—time for Britain to move troops to South Africa, time for the grasses to grow green on the high veld so that the horses upon which the Boer commandos would depend for mobility would have the grazing they needed, for both president Steyn of the Free State and Kruger of the S.A.R. now believed Britain meant to have her war.

In mid-September, Kruger told his Volksraad that the British had "asked for his trousers, and he had given them; then for his coat, he had given that also; now they wanted his life and that he could not give. . . ." Soon he was urging his burghers to read the 83rd Psalm: "They have taken crafty counsel against thy people . . . they have said, Come and let us cut them off from being a nation . . . Let them be confounded and troubled forever; yea let them be put to shame and perish. . . ."

On October 10, 1899, Chamberlain was awakened at 6:15 and read a cable drafted by Jan Smuts, demanding that the British government immediately withdraw its troops from the S.A.R.'s borders and send away the reinforcements being posted to South Africa. "They have done it!" he shouted exultantly. That evening the British Government cabled the Queen's repudiation of the Boers' ultimatum, and on the morning of October 11, 1899, the South African Republic and Orange Free State were at war with Great Britain and all her vast empire.

39
A BLACK WEEK FOR BRITAIN

Illusion and revelation both would have their place in the Anglo-Boer War, but its outcome was a foregone conclusion. The Boers would be crushed. How could it be otherwise? Britain in 1899 was the world's mightiest power. Her empire encompassed 100 million square miles. Her supply of manpower seemed inexhaustible, and she had a variety of new weapons and ammunition at her disposal from Maxim guns to the explosive, lyddite. The two Boer republics were backward, small and friendless, the gold of the Rand notwithstanding. Locked within British territory, sealed within British-dominated seas, their isolation had been made complete on October 14, 1899, when Portugal had agreed to a pact with Britain prohibiting the passage of arms through Lourenco Marques. Their weaponry was limited. They were without any regular army. Their generals were amateurs. Yet to the astonishment of Britain and the world, they were to withstand the onslaught of British imperial might for three years. Before the war could be ended, Great Britain was required to field an army of 449,000 trained troops to defeat some 70,000 Afrikaner irregulars. Her victory, moreover, lost the peace, for to gain it she was to resort to tactics that were to leave a legacy of bitterness in South Africa from which only evil could grow.

The war was fought in three phases. In the first phase, it was a strangely anachronistic conflict of sieges, a chivalric war in which the troops on both sides conformed to certain ritualistic rules of conduct. In the second phase, Britain, embarrassed to be stalemated by an army of amateurs, poured men and matériel into South Africa at an awesome rate and launched a juggernaut that swept north from the Cape along the western railway lines, overrunning one town after another until Pretoria itself was taken. The third and bitterest phase of the war was fought thereafter by a ragged army of Boers who refused to admit defeat and by a British command that meant to bring them to their knees by whatever means were necessary.

The Boers had a small advantage in numbers at the commencement of hostilities. Though Great Britain at the time had a standing army in excess of 170,000, the majority of these were colonial troops—Indians, Egyptians, West Indians, and West Africans. To employ non-whites in a "white man's war" was deemed unwise in London, perhaps for fear that it might spark a mutinous spirit among Victoria's dark-skinned subjects elsewhere. Britain's "household" and "line" regiments, however, were under strength in 1899. Though 50,000 reserves in Britain were immediately activated, reinforcements were not expected to begin to reach South Africa—where some 25,000 British troops were on hand—for at least two months.

The Boers, meanwhile, could field 30,000 men almost overnight, and on the dawn of October 11, the vast inland veld was alive with men on horseback, riding out to war equipped as always with a rifle, hard biscuit, dried meat "biltong," and a bedroll. Within a few days the commandos had swept south, west, and east to the frontiers. Only in three places, however, did they overrun republican borders to lay siege to Kimberley and Mafeking, in what had once been Griqualand

West, and to close on Ladysmith, the gateway to Natal. Their unwillingness to press on to seize the rail junctions of the Cape Colony and the Natal port of Durban may have been a strategic blunder. By opting for siege warfare, the Boer generals, Piet Cronje and Piet Joubert, tossed away the one chance they had to prevent Britain from reinforcing its under-strength army in South Africa, and so may have lost the war at its beginning.

The sieges at Kimberley and at Mafeking were carried on in a singularly leisurely style that pinned down the Boers as well as the British for months. At both places bombardments were conducted with ritualistic punctuality, as if to avoid killing anyone. At one point General Cronje warned the young British commander at Mafeking, Lieutenant Baden-Powell, who would make himself famous as founder of the Boy Scouts, that he was about to put into use the Boers' biggest weapon, one of four Creusot "Long Tom's," which could fire a 94-pound shell six miles. Following this preannounced shelling, Baden-Powell had amused all of England by cabling: "Four hours of bombardment. Killed a hen. Wounded a dog. Smashed a hotel window."

There was, however, suffering in both places. At Kimberley, the British, unwilling to feed the black diggers from the diamond mines, sent thousands of them out to forage for their survival in the 14-square-mile enclave of semidesert enclosed within the Boer lines. At Mafeking, where Baden-Powell and his aristocratic staff had laid in a sizable store of tinned salmon, pressed duck, and champagne for the duration, black troopers slowly starved to death on a cornmeal gruel, which they were forced to buy from the British commissary, though it was they who supplied the white man's table with beef by raiding Boer farms.

Though more serious from the start, the war on the eastern front also had its bizarre moments. When the Boers captured a British armored train trying to break through to Ladysmith (named for Harry Smith's wife) at the rail junction of Elandslaagte on October 19, 1899 they entertained their British captives at the local hotel with a drink and songfest. "God Save the Queen" and the "Volksleid" were sung with equal fervor right up until dawn, when a British counterattack sent the Boers scurrying back to positions in the nearby hills for a grim battle that was to prove the precursor of many similar ones to follow.

The Boers controlled the rail line, which would open the way to the relief of Ladysmith, from a hogback hill just outside of Eland-slaagte where they had positioned a few hundred men and a single big gun. Hoping to break out, General Sir George White had brought a total of six regiments on horse and foot and 18 pieces of heavy artillery up to the rail junction. On the morning after the impromptu songfest, he began hurling wave on wave of men at the Boers' hilltop position. His losses were terrible. In one attack, a Boer reserve detachment had caught an entire British light horse battalion in a flanking operation and killed most of its complement; on the hilltop, charge after charge by the Gordon Highlanders had produced walls of bodies around the Boer positions. Finally overrun by the Devons at dusk, the Boer survivors of this incredible onslaught had tried to break away but had been caught in a slashing charge by two British cavalry units. The fighting had continued until nightfall, when a "cease fire" was sounded. As darkness came, each side had permitted the other to collect its dead and wounded and on the blood-soaked hill Boer and Briton had passed each other in silence as they searched by lantern light for friends among the mutilated corpses.

The next day, wrongly informed that the Boers were bringing up reinforcements, General White had abandoned Elandslaagte hill as untenable, leaving Ladysmith unrelieved and the way to Durban open to Joubert's commandos. Urged to take swift advantage of the opportunity by his second in command, Louis Botha, Joubert had hesitated to move on Durban. "If God offers you his finger," he told his junior officer, "do not take his whole hand." Joubert reflected the conviction of the Boer high command that God would again deliver His Chosen People so long as the Boers did not challenge Britain's honor directly by a full-scale invasion of her territories. It was a fatal, if foxy, notion. Even then, British troop reinforcements were on their way to South Africa by the thousands.

Belatedly, the Boers had launched an attack on the Cape Colony in December to take control of its strategic rail junctions and had successfully invested Stormberg and Magersfontein. By then, however, several British battalions had been landed at Cape Town, and on orders of the British Commander in Chief in Africa, Gen. Redvers Buller, had been sent north with their generals, Wauchope and Methuen, to relieve Kimberley.

It was midsummer in the Karoo. Forced to carry full packs, rifles, and bayonets, the red-coated Highlanders, Irish Rifles, and Northumberland Fusiliers were marching toward disaster through temperatures ranging in the low hundreds. At Stormberg, 90 were killed outright in a Boer ambush and another 600 captured. At Magersfontein the Highland Brigade had been marched by night straight onto unseen Boer positions. Designed by one of the younger Boer commanders, Jacobus De la Rey, and described as "one of the boldest and most original conceptions in the history of war" by the august *Times History,* they consisted of a series of trenches, twelve miles in length, which crisscrossed the veld at the foot of Magersfontein Mountain and secreted some 8,000 men. Protected with barbed wire and camouflaged with brush—as were the trenches designed on De la Rey's model in World War I—they were almost immune to artillery fire and virtually invisible to the oncoming Scots. At one moment they had been marching half asleep toward a mountain dimly defined in the predawn, and the next moment found themselves in a hell of enfilading fire.

The battle at Magersfontein, which began with slaughter at dawn, had continued all day as Wauchope and Methuen had thrown the full force of 13,000 men into repeated assaults on the Boer trenches. Cronje, the Boer commander of the western front, who witnessed it all from Magersfontein Mountain, called the courage of the Scots' regiments "sublime," but it was also appallingly wasteful. When the numbed British army finally turned in retreat, it had left more than a thousand men—most of them Highlanders—dead on the field. Said one young Scotsman, whose General Wauchope also lay among the dead, the Highland Brigade "had been taken into a butcher shop and left there."

Britain was to be staggered by worse news within the week when word reached London that General Buller, who had taken the relief of Ladysmith upon himself, had marched into a similar trap set for him by Louis Botha at a place called Colenso on the eastern front. As at Magersfontein, Botha's men had made themselves all but invisible in trenches along the Little Tugela River. Buller, who counted himself an "up-to-date soldier," had marched his men onto the trenches in tight-packed formations of the sort that had been employed by the British in battle since Marlborough's days, 200 years before. The result at Colenso, as at Magersfontein, had been carnage. Buller had lost 1,127 men, killed outright, ten cannons, 600 rounds of artillery ammunition, thousands of wagons and horses and uncountable wounded. Botha, who had 40 killed, granted the British an armistice the next day. As Buller collected his dead and wounded from the field, Botha's men spent the day in solemn Thanksgiving. "Black Week," as the British press called it, had ended on December 16, the Day of the Covenant, and the commandos kept it as a "sabbath" before riding north toward Ladysmith.

Pivotal to the control of the whole eastern front, Ladysmith was considered the gateway to Natal, and Botha believed that if it could be taken the Boers might move on Durban with impunity. But General White's garrison of 14,000 men was well deployed in its defense, and the hills that ringed the town bristled with British gun emplacements. Still unwilling to risk an all-out assault on them, Joubert had not given Botha permission to attack until he learned that Buller was once more marching north with reinforcements in the week after Christmas.

Botha called his commandos in from the surrounding veld on January 3, and the British knew immediately that an attack was forthcoming. The men manning the gun emplacements along the southeastern ridge, comprised of Wagon Point, Wagon Hill, and Caesar's Camp, that evening could hear the Boers singing psalms and see their campfires twinkling below, and on January 4 General White had ordered the Wagon Point batteries reinforced by some 33 Royal engineers and 170 Gordon Highlanders. Protected from the rear by a sheer precipe some 300 feet high, the guns of Wagon Hill were strategically placed to lay a raking fire along the entire face of the hill behind them. This, by White's reckoning, should have made the position impregnable to any assault.

Botha began his attack just before dawn on January 6 by sending his men creeping forward under the cover of darkness along the entire length of Wagon Ridge. At the foot of the cliff face, guarding Wagon Point from the rear, a tall, lean field cornet named "Japie" de Villiers, already well known to the British for his conspicuous bravery, turned to his 14-year-old son Paul and handed the boy his watch and Bible. "I will not come back," de Villiers told the boy. "I believe I will stay on this hill, so you must have these as head of the family." Moments later he had signaled to his friend, Zacharias de Jagar and twenty other volunteers, and led them up the cliff, hoping to take the British guns on Wagon Point from behind. Though only he, de Jagar, and one other man actually made it to the crest, the assault was very nearly successful. Looming out of the dawn gloom, de Villiers had appeared suddenly at the mouth of one of the British gun emplacements and informed its astonished defenders that they were his prisoners. " 'Japie' de Villiers came over the top," one British eyewitness remembered, "and told us to surrender! A bloke put up his rifle and missed him! Can you imagine him standing over a gun pit, sixteen feet across and full of armed men, telling everyone to surrender!"

Suddenly there was firing everywhere in the gloom, but it was not de Villiers or de Jagar who ran away. "Those men," wrote another British eyewitness, "were apparently incapable of going backwards." Spilling out of the trenches, the terrified British ran to and fro— shooting in all directions and often killing their own men. De Villiers now ran toward a second gun emplacement and tried to scale the wall. "Bayonets were thrust at him, which he parried with his rifle until a revolver was fired point-blank into him. He sank below the wall where he sat rocking to and fro . . . and then another bullet found him," reported another British witness.

Firing had now begun along the face of all three hills. As wave on wave of Botha's men attacked from the east, Wagon Point's guns, finally brought into action, rained a withering fire on them, but the assault continued and British lines began to waver. The Boer forces, however, were not inexhaustible and, unlike Buller, Botha was not willing to buy victory at the price of thousands of lives. As inconclusive hand-to-hand combat continued on the hilltops, a retreat was ordered. Ladysmith had held. The Boer initiative, begun in Black Week, had faltered for the first time. Three days later, when the new British Commander in Chief, Lord Roberts, seconded by Lord

Kitchener, arrived in South Africa with several thousand more men, the war quietly entered its second phase.

40

ROBERTS AND KITCHENER

Black Week had staggered Britain. Victorious in half a century of "little wars," she had expected an easy victory in South Africa. Instead, the notion of British invincibility—one of the bulwarks of the Empire—had been challenged by a ragtag army of amateurs. Buller's losses of 3,000 men in a single week had exposed the deficiency of Britain's military machine to all the world, and the British were determined to correct this situation by an unparalleled show of military force. On December 19, Lord Roberts superseded Buller as Commander in Chief in South Africa, and Lord Kitchener was named as his Chief of Staff.

Frederick Sleigh Roberts seemed a logical choice to lead Her Majesty's forces against the Boers. A former Commander in Chief of the Indian Army, "Bobs" as he was popularly known in the Victorian press, had earned his reputation during the Afghan Wars of 1878–80 by his celebrated rescue of besieged British garrisons at Kandahar. Called out of semiretirement in Ireland to accept his command, Roberts, 67, learned on the day of his appointment that his only son had been killed in action in South Africa. When he sailed for Cape Town four days later, he went as a hero in mourning to avenge the grief of a nation in shock.

His second in command, Lord Kitchener, was a hero of more recent vintage, lionized for his relief of Khartoum in 1898. Known to the men who served under him as an utterly ruthless soldier, Kitchener had confirmed British control of the Sudan that year by smashing the Mahdists—a Moslem nationalist movement—at Omdurman in September of 1898. Rewarded by elevation to Commander in Chief in Egypt, Kitchener had been called from that post to serve with Roberts in South Africa.

Both "Bobs" and "K," the sobriquet by which Kitchener was

known in the press, were of that breed of military men who put their faith in numbers and fire power. They planned to hurl men and material on an unprecedented scale into an effort to secure the towns and rail lines of the Free State and Transvaal while a much reinforced Buller cleared Natal.

On January 10, 1900, when Roberts and Kitchener landed at Table Bay, they were in the van of an army that would soon outnumber every Afrikaner man, woman, and child in Natal, the Free State, Transvaal, and Cape Colony combined. By February the British troop build-up in the Cape alone had surpassed 180,000 men, and on February 11 Roberts launched his juggernaut.

Fifty-one thousand men strong, his armies swept north, overrunning Stormberg and Magersfontein in two days. Cronje, who narrowly escaped capture, glimpsed an army five miles long marching toward the Magersfontein passes before he and his 4,000 men and their families slipped through British lines by night and got away. On February 15 a cavalry division relieved Kimberley, while Kitchener, who had replaced the ailing Roberts as commander in the field, force-marched his infantry toward the Free State capital of Bloemfontein in pursuit of Cronje's army. At Paardeberg, a hill overlooking the Modder River south of Bloemfontein, he caught up with the Boers and Cronje turned to fight.

For ten hellish days, Cronje's army withstood the onslaught of more than ten times their number, under ceaseless bombardment by 100 British guns. When the Boers finally surrendered, Roberts himself commended Cronje on a "gallant defense" before ordering that his remaining men be marched forthwith to Cape Town and shipped to St. Helena to spend the duration of the war as exiled prisoners. Conan Doyle, a war correspondent with Roberts's command, described them as "the most singular lot of people to be seen at that moment on earth, ragged, patched, grotesque, some with galoshes, some with coffee pots, umbrellas and Bibles their favorite baggage. So they passed out of their ten days of glorious history. A visit to the laager showed that the horrible smells that had been carried to British lines and the swollen carcasses that had swirled down the muddy river were true portents of its condition. Strong-nerved men came back white and sick from contemplation of the place in which for ten days women and children had been living. From end to end, it was a festering mass of corruption, overshadowed by incredible swarms of flies. . . ."

Stripped of its defenders, Bloemfontein was taken by Roberts on March 13. Six weeks later, when Mafeking was relieved, all of Britain exploded in celebration, expecting an imminent end to the war. Another English war correspondent named Winston Churchill was on hand when Roberts marched into Johannesburg on May 27, four days after an exultant Milner had announced the annexation of the Free State as a British Crown Colony. "For three hours," rhapsodized Churchill, "the broad river of steel and khaki flowed unceasingly, and the town folk gazed in awe and wonder at these majestic soldiers whose discipline neither perils nor hardship had disturbed and whose relentless march no obstacle could prevent. . . ." That week Paul Kruger abandoned Pretoria. When it fell to Roberts on June 5, another eyewitness gave a different description of the occupation of Church Square. "In perfect order but weary unto death, the British troops marched in," wrote Johanna Brandt. "Thousands and thousands of soldiers in khaki, travel-stained, footsore, and famished, sank to the ground at a given command in the open square facing the government buildings. Some of them tried to eat the rations they had with them; others, too exhausted to eat, fell into a deep sleep." One old warrior, looking up into the face of a girl who stood above him, said in a broken voice, "Thank God the war is over." She bent toward him and in a voice hoarse with rage whispered, "Tommy Atkins, the war has just begun."

Two days later a commando under Christiaan deWet, one of the younger Boer leaders, struck at Kroonstadt, the main rail junction linking Johannesburg with the south, took 700 prisoners and cut Roberts's supply lines. The war, which should have been over, was not. Soon commandos had arisen like dust devils in the wind across the breadth of the veld. Their appearance signaled that the war was entering a third phase, and that the Boers would no longer fight battles in conventional "European" style. Instead, they would rely on techniques of the hunt and mastery of the horse and gun, bred into them by their frontier heritage, to fight what the British labeled a "guerrilla war." For if the towns belonged to the British, the men who rode in the commandos with deWet, De la Rey, Hertzog, Botha, Smuts, Beyers, and Scheepers owned the veld from the arid stretches of the Little Karoo to the Soutpansberg, and none needed more than his horse, his gun, his Bible, biscuits, and "biltong" to sustain him in a land as familiar to each as his own father's face. And that was what Roberts did not comprehend: the spiritual and physical connection between the Afrikaner and Africa. They were the land's and the land was theirs. They could come and go as freely as the wind, not only because they knew every koppie and drift and could find provisions, horses, recruits, friends, and family wherever they rode but because they were bound to the veld by ties that went generations deep. They could no more conceive of surrendering it to the British than they could conceive of surrendering their memories. It was, they believed, the heritage God had given them, and the only way the British could subdue them was to kill the living land itself.

Tragically, this was precisely what Lord Roberts, operating with a numb logic, decided to do when he initiated a scorched-earth policy in the regions where the Boer commandos were most active. It was not, however, a decision Roberts wanted publicized. Slated for advancement to Commander in Chief of the British Army in June of 1900, when he had cheerfully reported that "the Boers have melted away like the snows of spring," he had no wish to revise his optimistic estimate or to shock the sensibilities of the British public by permitting unfavorable press reports of farm burnings to reach England. Censorship of press dispatches was, therefore, carefully maintained until Roberts finally sailed for England and Kitchener took command.

41

FORCE AND SPIRIT

Lord Roberts had seen no reason to revise his view that the war was virtually over, even after the Boer commandos had begun harrying his supply lines to Johannesburg. A man who liked to rely on "facts," the "facts" had argued in his favor. Afrikaner forces in the field had been reduced to roughly 15,000 fighting men after the fall of Pretoria, whereas there were almost a quarter of a million men in the British command. Both Boer capitals were safely in British hands.

President Steyn of the Free State was wandering like a nomad with de Wet. Paul Kruger—old, ill, and grieving—had gone into exile in Holland in October, leaving Vice President Schalk Burger to a peripatetic existence with Botha in the bush. The Rand belonged to the British. Natal had finally been cleared of "rebels." The Free State and Transvaal had both been annexed to the Crown. Milner had declared that the remaining Boers in the field were to be regarded as "outlaws," and when Roberts sailed for England in December expecting a hero's welcome, he was sure that only "mop up" operations had been left to Lord Kitchener.

He was wrong. By the time he had landed in Britain, Kitchener's dilemma in South Africa had been made plain by one commando strike after another. Beyond the narrow perimeters of the railroad route—patroled by new armored trains—the Boers owned the countryside and struck freely where they wished, lifting supplies, destroying British outposts, cutting the railway lines, and sniping at British columns on the march while suffering few casualties themselves. With every farmstead as a base of operations, the commando's reserve was the Afrikaner nation in arms, and it was that which Kitchener needed to defeat if he was to win the war. His tactics followed logically from this, and in December of 1901 Kitchener had extended the limited scorched-earth program, initiated by Roberts, to the entire theater of the war. In the year and a half of hostilities that remained, his soldiers were to destroy 30,000 Boer farms in the Free State and Transvaal, razing the houses, slaughtering the livestock, burning the croplands, and herding the human occupants—some 117,000 women and children and 100,000 native farm hands—into concentration camps where a quarter were to perish. By May of 1901, furthermore, he had also broken one of the fundamental taboos of the war by beginning to arm tribal blacks to hunt for the elusive Boer commandos. Already outraged by his tactics of devastation and the horrendous conditions in the concentration camps, the Boers regarded Kitchener's willingness to employ the "sons of Ham" against Christians as the final confirmation of British godlessness. Kitchener's tactics, rather than breaking their will to resist, confirmed it. And so the war went on, becoming each day more firmly equated with a struggle for spiritual as well as national survival in the minds of many Afrikaners and more of a demoralizing nuisance to the British public, who were finally being forced to confront the possibility that the Pax Britannica was not based on lofty ideals but on the brutal use of force.

Queen Victoria's death in January of 1901 had cast a pall of gloom across Britain. It grew deeper as the war dragged on and word of the mounting death toll among Afrikaner women and children in Kitchener's concentration camps began to circulate in the British press as the result of a crusading effort by a woman named Emily Hobhouse. One of those courageous ladies Britain regularly produced to right the wrongs of the world, Miss Hobhouse had betaken herself to the camps to launch a relief effort. As a result of her work, they had been transferred from Kitchener's administration to civilian control in October of 1901. But by then, some 20,000 Boer children were dead, Britain's sense of guilt was growing, and public confidence both in the morality of the war and the goals of the Empire in Africa had begun to falter. In Parliament, Lloyd George, the radical leader, had risen to prophesy that "a barrier of dead children's bodies will rise up between the British and Boer races in South Africa," and Campbell-Bannerman—leader of the Liberal opposition, had seconded him by complaining publicly of Kitchener's "barbarism."

Worried for his reputation, Kitchener by this time wanted only to bring the war to a close. Frustrated and baffled by the Boers' continued will to resist, he thought he glimpsed something primitive in it and in a letter to a friend characterized his enemy as "uncivilized Afrikaner savages with a thin white veneer. . . ." With disgust he described the "Boer woman in the refugee camp who slaps her great protruding belly at you and shouts, 'When all our men are gone these little khakis will fight you.' " She was, he continued, "a type of savage produced by generations of wild, lonely life." That she was also a fitting symbol for a nation whose defiance would outlast the war, whose furies had been handed on to its descendants, and whose struggle for independence would be continued for generations apparently did not occur to him.

By 1901, the war had become a struggle between force and spirit. Kitchener's methods were an extension of Roberts's. He divided and subdivided the countryside, built his lines of block houses and encased them in snarls of barbed wire. He poured matériel and men into the pursuit of the commandos and destroyed their bases of operation by devastating farms. In February, when Botha rejected an offer of peace, Kitchener became the more severe. By September, he demanded immediate surrender of the commandos. Failure to comply was to mean perpetual banishment for the commando leaders and fines and imprisonment for the ranks at war's end. The edict produced results. Some men, worn, weary, and worried for their missing families, began to turn themselves in. Disparagingly, those who remained in the field branded them "Hensoppers"—"Hand's Uppers"—and went on fighting. In the western Cape, half a dozen commandos under Jan Smuts roved freely over Namaqualand. In his war journal, *Commando,* Deneys Reitz records a day in which Smuts sent word to his units, asking for those men who had never seen the sea to be sent to him. "Some sixty or seventy arrived within the next forty-eight hours," writes Reitz, "and with these we set off for a small inlet on the coast called Fishwater. . . . Few of the men had ever seen a bigger stretch of water than the dam on their parents' farm. Mounted on their horses, they looked in wonder on the Atlantic. Then, like the Greek soldiers, rushed forward in a body crying, 'The sea! The sea!' each wanting to be first on the beach. . . ." For several days Smuts let them frolic like children, helping the local Colored fisherman, before turning them inland to resume the business of war.

Gallantry could not forever withstand superior force, however, and in the war's final phases Kitchener's tactics of total devastation began to take their toll. Food became scarce. The burnt-off veld provided little grazing for the commandos' famished horses, limiting their range. Some men returning home could barely identify the places where their houses had been, so thorough had been their destruction by the British.

In April of 1902, President Steyn and Vice President Burger rode to Pretoria under a flag of truce to discuss peace terms with Kitchener. They offered the British an "enduring treaty of friendship," a commercial union on the lines Rhodes had long pursued, enfranchisement of the "outlanders," mutual amnesty, and the use of English as well as Dutch in the schools and courts of the S.A.R. and Free State. "Must I understand from what you say that you wish to retain your independence?" the astonished Kitchener asked. "Yes," said Steyn. "The people must not lose their self-respect."

The war continued. More men died. The Boer forces were reduced to ragged, half-starved bands roving a wasteland. Of the original 70,000 who had volunteered for the commandos, only 15,000 remained in the field. Another 31,000 had been exiled to prison camps in Ceylon, India, the West Indies, and on St. Helena. Twenty thousand children, over four thousand women, and still more "native" and Colored farm hands had died in the concentration camps where thousands still languished. In the Free State and Transvaal, half the cattle and sheep on which the prewar Boer economy had depended had been destroyed and the work of generations lay in ruins. Riding through the blackened countryside in the final weeks of the war, Louis Botha counted a total of 36 goats alive in a region where fat cattle by the thousands had once grazed. Another peace offering was made to Milner. In return for their independence, the Boers signaled their willingness to cut the Rand out of the heart of the Transvaal and give it to Britain. When the offer was rejected, Botha called the 61 commando leaders remaining in the field to Vereeniging to talk peace anyway.

"I still see them gazing into emptiness," wrote their field predikant, Willem Kestell. "I still see the imponderable question engraved on their faces: Was this the bitter end of all our suffering, our struggle, of all our faith and strong appeal to God?" President Steyn of the Free State, drawn and sick, and the redoubtable Christiaan deWet with whom he had wandered the ravaged veld for months answered, "No," that "the war of religion must continue regardless of the facts." "Let us again renew our Covenant," deWet had pleaded. "If we fix our eyes on the past . . . we have ground to continue in faith. The entire war has been a miracle and without faith it would have been childish to commence. . . . It is still all faith and we know that a small people can by faith triumph over the most powerful enemy. . . ."

But in the small hours of the morning of May 31, 1902, Jan Smuts rose to speak in favor of peace. "We are not here as an army but as a people," he told his fellow commando leaders somberly. "We represent not only ourselves but the thousands who are dead and have made the last sacrifice for their people—the prisoners of war scattered over the world, the women and children who are dying by the thousands in the concentration camps. We represent the blood and tears of an entire nation. They call upon us . . . from the grave, from the field and from the womb of the future to . . . avoid all measures which may lead to the decline and extermination of the Afrikaner people and thus frustrate the objects for which they made all their sacrifice."

Salvation, survival in the face of threatened "decline and extermination," these had been the central issues of Afrikaner life, since the trek-boers had begun drifting away from the Cape in the 18th century and had taken refuge from their fears in a mystic acceptance of God's all directing will. In the 19th century, that mystic faith had been further reinforced when the Voortrekkers had faced the threat of potential annihilation by overwhelming numbers of blacks at Vegkop and Blood River and survived. Persuaded that God had marked them for some special destiny, they had begun to attach transcendent importance to the preservation of themselves as a "nation apart." Patriarchal, militantly certain of their own virtues, suspicious of all alien influences, passionately nationalistic and religiously conformist, the Afrikaners had risen to Britain's attempt to subvert their independence in 1899 as to a "holy cause" and their commandos had ridden out to war as a brotherhood of "True Believers" bound to the cause of God, Nation, and Volk by obligations that had their reasons in eternity and could not be abandoned even in defeat for fear of abandoning their own souls.

So it was imperative, at Vereeniging, that a new formulation of the old mystique be arrived at if the Afrikaners were not to lose faith in their special calling as a nation, and Jan Smuts was among those who provided it by suggesting that the simple survival of "Die Volk" ensured that the "objects for which they had made all their sacrifices" might yet be obtained in the future. It was a notion that future Afrikaner politicians would put to many uses, but at Vereeniging, Smuts's equation between "survival" and "salvation" permitted the defeated Boers to lay down their arms in the hope that their cause might live. It was inevitable, therefore, that Afrikaner nationalism would reemerge from the ashes of the war like the proverbial phoenix and that, reborn in defeat and nurtured on tales of martyrs and heroes in the bitter postwar years, it would prove more militant, more absolute, and more dangerous than ever before.

Shortly after Smuts's speech, fifty-five of the sixty-one delegates at Vereeniging had voted to surrender. By accepting Milner's peace treaty, they had accepted King Edward as their sovereign and for-sworn the independence of the Free State and Transvaal. In exchange, they were granted a general amnesty, allowed to bear arms, and assured that Dutch as well as English would remain a medium in their schools and courts. Milner furthermore had agreed that "as soon as circumstances permitted" both of Britain's new African colonies would be granted self-government, and until such time, no consideration would be given to enfranchising non-whites in either. When the peace of Vereeniging was signed, consequently the war had no real winners. The blacks who had been largely bystanders, but who had been promised a new political dispensation by the British after the war, had quietly had their hope of gaining a share in their own government betrayed. The British, who had lost five times as many men killed as the Boers, had also lost considerable prestige by being forced to field an army of 449,000 to subdue some 70,000 Afrikaner irregulars. And the Afrikaners, a small nation, had been badly bled and had seen the hopes of generations dashed.

42
MARTYRS AND MEMORIES

The war was over but there seemed no end to its griefs. Ruin lay across the veld. A host of martyrs had died for a lost cause, and from the Cape to the Limpopo barely an Afrikaner family was untouched by some tragedy. Returning home, every soldier, former prisoner of war and concentration camp internee would tell his own story of sacrifice and heroism, and in the war's aftermath, these tales—told and retold —were to become part of a folklore that would help the Afrikaners to preserve a sense of national pride in the face of defeat. Passed from one generation to the next, they became part of the living legacy of bitterness left by the war, and it is still possible to hear them told in South Africa today by those for whom memories of the war remain fresh after eighty years.

Past ninety, Mrs. Dippenaar—whose old-fashioned sense of propriety forbade her to reveal her first name to a stranger—had the quality of a living monument about her when we met. Sitting with a stiff erectness that spoke as much for her determined character as her advanced age, her eyes held something hawkish. Plainly not a woman to be trifled with, she wore her toughness like the corsets of her character, and her square, powerful hands were those of a farm woman. Yet when she spoke of her early childhood before the war, the incidents Mrs. Dippenaar recalled seemed bathed in luminosity and her mind skipped lightly from one remembered scene to the next.

"On my father's farm we had a dam so there was a great pond— big enough for us to have little boats," she began. "I had a little kaffir girl as a playmate . . . so clever! She could make little dolls of clay and horses and goats. Wonderful! . . . I remember going to church for Naagmaal. It was 28 miles away. We'd inspan our oxen and set out the night before. In the evening we'd vleis braai, and then on we'd go. Such happy times on that wagon! The rocking of it . . . Tappa tap tappa tap to the little dorp for church. . . . We had the Nederlands Church and old Mr. Pienaar was the predikant. He could talk for hours and we'd be sitting there, all straight and prim, my sister Cecile and I next to Mother and Father, in black, while Mr. Pienaar talked for an hour, an hour and a half, two hours, reading from the Bible. It was dark in church, cool and dark. I'd get sleepy and my Momma would thump me. 'Church is not a bedroom you know,' my father would say later. . . . We had a governess on our farm. A Miss von der Westhuizen as our teacher. My sister and I and two neighbors' girls were her pupils. We had the Nederlands, so she taught us English and arithmetic. . . . My Father was from Cape Town, you see. He said we must have both. Mother was a Miss Wessels, related to the late President Steyn of Bloemfontein —Oom Marthinus. . . . We were all related, Oom Marthinus, the Wessels, and so when we were in the concentration camps, we all stayed together. There is a photo of us—and there I am in a little dress Emily Hobhouse gave Mother. She had £300 Pappa had given her before he went off on commando. They were sewn into her corsets. Gold Krugerands. But you couldn't eat the gold." She paused, her fists doubling in their lace gloves. When she resumed her monologue, her voice had grown hard with anger.

"I remember when the English came for us. We had been warned they were coming and were burning the farms. Pappa got away.

He went off on commando. We were to trek in the wagons, but the English came before we could get away. We heard them riding in. We screamed so, and then they were there. 'Hurry up, hurry up, hurry up' they shouted. We screamed and cried—ran about grabbing what we could carry. And then they came into the house. We had a table and chairs and a sideboard of stinkwood. They took them out—they took the bedding from the beds, the chairs, tables, the cups, everything we had, and made a great fire. They threw everything on the fire. 'You can watch it burn,' they said. 'Then march!' . . . Everything we owned. Even the cups. Then we were put in the wagon. As we began driving away, they started killing our cattle. They bawled and bawled as their throats were cut. . . . Cutting, killing. The sounds were terrible. The smells. We were crying, shouting 'Our cattle, our cattle. Why kill our cattle?' . . . They were taking us to Tempi, the camp at Bloemfontein. Out on the veld, they caught my father and my two uncles. They tied them to the wagon, their arms bound behind them, and made them walk next to it over the veld. We could see them walking there, day after day. I said then, I hate the Engelsman. . . . They sent my father and his brothers away to India to prison. We never knew whether he was alive or dead. But my eldest brother, he fought the Engels right through the war till the bitter end. . . ."

"After they separated the men from the wagons," she continued, "my mother and my sister and I, my aunt and her children, were sent on to Tempi—the camp. It was terrible there. Rows of tents in the mud. The dying started almost right away and it was terrible, terrible. They would come each day to collect the corpses from outside the tents. The children were dying of enteric—in pain. You heard the crying all around you in the wind. We put the dead outside our tents to be collected. You'd look down the rows and see them lying there—big ones, small ones, big ones, small ones, lined up in front of the tents. And then the wagon would come and they'd stack the bodies on it, big ones, small ones, big ones, small ones. They would not bother to bury them until they had 100 or so to put in a common grave. Just put them all in a tent. It was winter. They were frozen. My aunt had a little girl. Her name was Cecilia, too. She had three children die at Tempi. She was lying on the floor of our tent with this lovely baby dead in her arms. My mother stood over her and then took the corpse away to go to the wagon. She put the baby on the wagon herself though. She wouldn't let the Engelsmen touch it then. That night there was a terrible storm and the tent where they kept the corpses blew away. The wind was so strong the bodies were rolling everywhere. My mother went out and found the baby, Cecilia, in the mud and rain. She let the rain wash her off and then took her back. The little corpse, to that place. I was eight then." She paused again, her hawk's eyes blazing, her fists clenched in their lace gloves. "I remember," she said, almost in a whisper as if talking to herself, "but we must forget. We can't walk backwards. . . . Yet you can't forget. It comes up again and again. It's in you and I'll remember it until I'm dead, that little corpse, rolling in the wind. . . ."

"Finally it was over. My aunt, Momma, my sister and I had one cousin—we were alive and it was over. My brother came for us. He was 20 years older than I and had never been caught by the Engels. He took us to our family farm, three days away, in Bultfontein. They had not burned it—only killed the cattle. And they'd missed the ducks on the dam. So we were lucky. We had something to eat at Bultfontein. For three months we lived on ducks' eggs and what my brother could find—mealies, flour, a little sugar. They had burnt this country to the ground you see. There was nothing left anywhere. When we went back to my father's farm, there were only ash heaps. And then, one of our Colored hands came from nowhere. 'I have one of the chairs!' she told my mother. 'It is burned, but I saved it for you.' That was all that was left—one chair. . . . I have it still. . . ."

"Some months after the war, my father came back. Momma collapsed. She'd thought he was dead in India. There'd been no word at all since that day they led him away from our wagon. My sister didn't know him. She ran away and hid and I thought, here's Pappa, but Momma's dead and Cecile is gone! He hugged me hard. I think he was crying. Later his family in the Karoo sent him some cows and sheep and we began again. . . . I wanted always to go back to the farm, to dig in the ash heaps to find mementos, but my husband Dr. Dippenaar refused to let me. 'Don't go looking for the past,' he said. 'It is burnt and dead and behind you.' But it isn't. It is in me. . . ."

*"Soweto brought a certain monotonous order
out of the noisome shanty towns it replaced . . ."
Soweto today (above).
Pimville (below), one of the black slums it replaced.*

*"A planner's dream . . . Soweto had become a nightmare . . .
its houses dilapidated . . . its neighborhoods crime-ridden . . .
its teachers ill-trained . . ."*

Sgt. Martin Hatting of Soweto police comforts the widow of a man murdered in political infighting among Soweto's Zulu (left above). Jaap Strydom (below) took over Soweto's schools after the 1976 riots. The Rev. Beyers Naudé (right above), was banned for his crusade against apartheid. Thys Lourens (below), one of the new generation of Afrikaner reformers, in his Soweto classroom.

*"Thinking South Africans know that we need the blacks
as much as they need us."*
A girl in Thys Lourens' class in the Soweto junior school.

"In the past, I could trust the families on my land completely . . .
I don't know anymore which . . . I can trust. It's changing, all changing,
and I don't know what the future holds for us white South Africans."
One of his Sotho herdsmen (above)
challenges Orange Free State rancher Jaap de Villiers (right).

"I think this must be God's country, truly. The Promised Land . . .
God gave it to us and we love it and will fight and die for it if we must."
Jaap deVilliers and his son Paul ride over land he was scheduled
to forfeit to the Sotho homeland of Qwa Qwa.

BOOK FIVE

—◆◆—

Yesterday, Today,
Tomorrow

43
OUT OF THE ASHES: UNION

Few afrikaners can forget the past. Their national pride and prejudices are rooted in it. Arches, effigies, sepulchers, and plinths marking places sacred to Afrikaner history dot the South African landscape, for the Afrikaners have transformed the saga of their own suffering into the hagiography of a civil religion every bit as reactionary as that of the original Calvinists, and their reverence for it is almost reflexive.

In a modern house of rectilinear light-filled spaces perched high on the shoulder of Table Mountain in Cape Town, Madelaine van Biljoen, a woman who travels in jet-set circles and makes her living writing gossipy features for one of the Cape's leading newspapers, offered an explanation of the "Afrikaner ethos" in terms that made it seem peculiarly as if she and Mrs. Dippenaar might be contemporaries.

"We are an essentially rural people," she insisted. "We value our traditions. We have respect for the authority of our elders, our teachers, our leaders. We value the land. 'I need a little place for the hollow of my foot,' we say in Afrikaans. The land is our root, but the church encircles us. It is our framework—it and that which *is* Afrikaans. We do not move outside of that framework, outside of the larger Afrikaner clan, and those who do are suspect. . . ." She paused to sip white wine from a long-stemmed crystal glass and then continued unselfconsciously. "And we are long on memory of 'the war.' They burnt our family farm, the Verdomde Engelse! Destroyed it. My father used to take the Union Jack, throw it on the floor and say, 'I spit on you! I stomp on you, your zebra rag!' Yet he insisted that we learn to speak the conqueror's language better than he. . . . My children don't feel quite this way, of course, yet the old resentments have died hard and we Afrikaners still believe that if another war comes, it is we who will stand and fight it while the Engelse will fly away home. . . ."

Johanne Kriegler, a Johannesburg attorney who has made his reputation defending those accused of offending South Africa's labyrinthine security and censorship laws, was another whose metaphors for the present were drawn from the past. "We Afrikaners aren't in the laager any more," he told us. "The present generation of Verligtes, in their weltanschauung, *want* a new vision for Africa. But they also keep themselves related to the mainstream of Afrikanerdom for fear of what happens to those who stray. We cannot place ourselves in opposition to our own beleaguered nation. We fear to, I believe, because we've always been a very small people and have faced a hostile world again and again. The blacks on trek. The Brits. Laissez-faire capitalism at its worst. We've been stomped and trodden, and no sooner had we raised our heads than we ran head on into a worldwide sense of post-imperial guilt for the white man's exploitation of the black! Now, we'll admit to some guilt. But we've also been caught in that other moral-political conflict between East and West, which has made our domestic situation much worse by exacerbating the conflicts in Africa and creating increased pressures for changes in this country that could destabilize it. . . . If the world's liberals could assure us of the maintenance of standards as we know them, of public administration and political integrity, of economic stability of the kind we need to continue black development, then you'd have the vast majority of whites in favor of majority rule. But the question is one of survival or *chaos,* simple as that, and we Afrikaners are out in the bloody wildernesses on trek again, earnestly searching for a Future!"

"We are on trek." "We are inspanned and on the move." "We are searching for a new Promised Land." Sometimes nostalgic, sometimes desperate, references to the past recurred in conversations with Afrikaners of all sorts during our travels, with a frequency which suggested that they still have as much need of their heroic myths today as when they first faced the full meaning of their defeat by the British.

Britain's victory in 1902 had given her control of territories that stretched from the Cape to the Zambezi and from thence northward through east Africa all the way to Cairo, with but one obstruction in German Tanganyika. Milner, whose faith in Britain's civilizing destiny was absolute, meant to consolidate the Empire's hold on the southern span of this giant land bridge by anglicizing South Africa from the ground up. "The ultimate end," he had written to an associate just prior to the Anglo-Boer War, "is a justly governed white community supported by well-treated black labor from Cape Town to the Zambezi." Determined to develop this "community" by forcing the backward Boers and blacks to accept the benefits of British "progress," Milner had used the years of postwar reconstruction to organize a British civil service to govern the region, to apply British methods to reorganizing its agriculture, industry, and mining, to encourage large-scale British immigration into the Boer republics, and to revamp South Africa's schools to promote the rapid anglicization of its youth.

Presented with a choice between accepting acculturation as British subjects or remaining second-class citizens in their own country, the Afrikaners had roused themselves to resist, and only a few months after Paul Kruger had sent them a final message, cautioning them "not [to] lose sight of the past" but to heed the "serious warning that lies in the saying 'divide and rule,'" they had begun to unite under the leadership of Jan Smuts and Louis Botha.

By 1905, Afrikaner political parties had been formed in the Transvaal, Free State, and the Cape; Church leaders in the north had begun to found Christian National schools, which used the vernacular Afrikaans, as an alternative to Milner's anglicized academies; and in the Cape, a resurgence of interest in Afrikaans had led to an outpouring of prose and poetry in the vernacular, which had quickly established it as a rich literary language and powerful political instrument. Finding the voice of their political passion in their own unique language, the Afrikaners had experienced a revival of spirit so potent that only three years after Vereeniging, Afrikaner nationalism had been re-established as a political force powerful enough to bring Milner's recall and to demand the immediate attention of the newly elected Liberal Prime Minister of Great Britain, Campbell-Bannerman.

Campbell-Bannerman's objectives in South Africa were identical to Milner's: to secure the region and the Rand against the ambitions of Britain's chief colonial rival in southern Africa, Germany, by forging a single "justly governed white community supported by

well-treated black labor from the Cape to the Zambezi." But unlike
Milner, he did not believe this could be achieved by force, and instead of condescending to them he chose to court the Afrikaners
through a policy of "conciliation." Immediately after a Zulu uprising
in Natal in 1906 warned Boer and Briton alike that the black majority
might also have its political ambitions for the future, Campbell-Bannerman had assented to a request from Smuts for immediate self-rule
for the Transvaal under an exclusively white, Afrikaner-dominated
government. The next year he had granted "home rule" to the
Orange colony on similar terms, thus opening the way for the creation of a single colonial dominion in South Africa.

There was, however, an ironic footnote to the events in Natal in
1906. Among those who had accompanied the British colonial troops,
which had bloodily put down the Zulu rebellion, was a bespectacled
Indian stretcher bearer named Mohandas Gandhi. Deeply disillu-
sioned in the "Pax Britannica" by the slaughter of the Zulu, who
had stood against Maxim guns armed only with assegais, Gandhi
would later date from the events in Zululand in 1906, the decision to
give his life to passive resistance to racial injustice, which eventually
brought the destruction of the British Raj in India.

When the Union of South Africa was brought into being in 1910,
white rule was enshrined in its Parliament. Only in the Cape and
Natal did non-whites retain a limited right to elect selected whites to
represent them in its counsels. Lord Selborne, representing the
British government in the final negotiations leading up to the Union,
had made its position on black enfranchisement clear from the outset.
"The black man," Selborne had written to Botha, "is absolutely
incapable of rivaling the white man. . . . No one can have any experience of the two races without feeling the intrinsic superiority of
the white."

Botha and Smuts had achieved near autonomy for the Union by
accepting "conciliation" with Campbell-Bannerman's government,
but the euphoria that had accompanied Botha's installation as Prime
Minister amid the ritual swank of Empire in 1910 was to be short-
lived. In the Free State and Transvaal, the war-ravaged economy of
the Boers had been further weakened by cycles of rinderpest and
drought, and poverty was becoming endemic. Marginal farmers were

leaving the land in ever-increasing numbers to search for work in the cities, only to find themselves exploited by their new British masters and competing with blacks for unskilled jobs. By 1913, there were race riots on the Rand, General Hertzog had broken with Botha to form a new "Purified National party," having declared that he would rather "live on a dung hill" with his own people than in the court of a British King, and more and more of his followers had begun to equate "conciliation" with "treason." Consequently, when Botha announced in 1914 that he meant to follow Britain into the war against Germany, and to launch an attack on the latter's South-West African territory from the Union, the decision triggered a political insurrection that had soon become a military one. Unable to reconcile fighting for their former enemies against the one nation that had given them support during the Anglo-Boer War, many of Botha's old comrades in arms had begun mounting commandos. And after the old "Lion of the West," Koos de la Rey, was accidentally shot on his way to confer with another Afrikaner dissident, what amounted to a civil war had erupted in the north. Proclaiming his intention to lead a new Boer army to Pretoria to bring down the Union Jack and raise a new republic, the always impetuous Christiaan de Wet rode into the field at the head of a commando army of 14,000. Botha met him with 30,000 Afrikaner "loyalist" troops at a place called Mushroom Valley. As he watched his old comrade's cavalry ride toward his own motorized lines, Botha is said to have turned to an aide and murmured, "Hier kom hulle. Hier kom die Engelse. . . ." ("Here they come. Here come the English. . . .")

Botha's army made quick work of deWet's commandos. The rebellion was scotched, and in 1915 South Africa entered the war with Germany by seizing its colony in South West Africa, the present Namibia. By 1916, Smuts had led a second expeditionary force into German East Africa and Tanganyika. A small affair when measured against the blood bath going on in Europe, where the British lost 400,000 men in a single campaign on the Somme, the implications of the Boer rebellion of 1914 were nevertheless enormous, not only for the future of South Africa but in geopolitical terms. Thousands had participated. Hundreds had been killed, and the political damage had been incalculable. One young rebel, Japie Fourie, who was executed by Smuts for his part in the rebellion, was elevated to the pantheon of Afrikaner martyrs in the tradition of those who had died at Slachters Nek. When de Wet and other surviving rebel leaders were tried for treason, Afrikaners throughout the country contributed to a fund, called "Helpmekaar" (Help One Another), organized by Daniel Malan, to pay their fines. Louis Botha, keenly aware of the disaffection of his old comrades, did not long survive the end of World War I, and when Smuts returned home to take his place as Prime Minister in 1918, he found Afrikanerdom ideologically divided between the moderates who were willing to let the past die and the new Nationalists who vowed never to forget it. And it was the latter's cause that would prosper among economically dispossessed Afrikaners in the uncertain era that followed World War I.

44

REVERBERATIONS OF
A WORLD WAR

Gunfire on the high veld in 1914 put an end to hopes of an easy reconciliation between Briton and Boer. Cannon fire in Europe over the next four years ended an age. Empires as well as men perished in the bloody slime of trenches along the Marne and Somme. The last remnants of the once powerful Austro-Hungarian and Ottomon Empires had been blown away by the war, and in Czarist Russia the fuse of revolution had been ignited by it. At Versailles, the German Empire—a kingdom of blood and iron welded from seventeen states—was dismembered and the German colonies distributed to the war's victors under a system of mandates devised for the newly formed League of Nations by General Smuts. As a reward for its efforts in 1915, the Union received the diamond-rich deserts of German South West Africa as its mandate, and Britain, not surprisingly, gained Tanganyika, Togoland, and the Cameroons, completing the long-sought land bridge that linked her African possessions from the Cape to Cairo. But the war had also exacted a terrible price of Britain and she would never have full advantage of its spoils. The "Grand Designs" of men like Rhodes, Milner, and Chamberlain in Africa had contributed directly to international rivalries which had plunged the great powers into a war so catastrophic that none had emerged from it whole. A generation had been slaughtered in the trenches, and though the old illusions would retain their luster for a while the future of the Empire had died with it. By 1920, what had been was no more. The old order was foundering, the old faiths were dying, and the world stood on the cusp of a new age of anxiety remarkably comparable to that in which the original Calvinism had flourished.

In the east, the Soviet Union had risen out of the ashes of Czarist Russia to preach a new secular creed of communism to a world that was losing faith in laissez-faire capitalism. Germany, paupered by the terms of the Treaty of Versailles, was declining into the economic chaos that would foster the growth of fanatic National Socialism. Britain, too exhausted by the war to resume the policing of her Empire, had quietly resigned her leadership to America and after 1926 had become dependent upon the newly formed British Commonwealth to maintain her imperial position. Where there had been widespread optimism and perfect faith in unending "Progress" at the turn of the century, there was now pessimism and insecurity, and when cyclic postwar recessions gave way to the Great Depression, deepening the gloom, uncertain men and women hungered for the lost security of the past. In a climate of fear, demagogues arose to preach aggressive nationalist creeds not only in the Communist east, where the state was to replace God as the object of worship, but in Nazi Germany and Fascist Italy, in Japan, and in the faraway Union of South Africa.

The progeny of a generation with bitter memories of a green world gone, of Kitchener's scorched earth and concentration camps, Afrikaner nationalism came of age in its problematic modern form in the decades between the two World Wars. An era of profound uncertainty everywhere in the world, it was marked in South Africa by accelerating change, deepening economic crisis and sporadic racial violence, which traced the weaknesses of the Union's flawed society as the earth's tremors follow its fire lines.

Rooted in Calvinism, Christian Nationalism was one of those pessimistic ideologies which speak to humanity's fundamental fears that its control over its own violent nature is at best tenuous. Like the original, it belonged to the family of reactionary political creeds that

always seem to thrive when men and nations feel themselves beginning to lose control over the ever incipient chaos of this world.

The ground had begun to shift under the Union as early as 1920
as the post-war economic downturn in Europe sent the price of gold
plummeting. In that season of sudden economic uncertainty, election
results showed a further erosion in the South Africa Party's majority,
and Smuts had hung onto power as Prime Minister only by forming
a coalition with the Cape's predominantly English Unionist party.
Hertzog's Afrikaner Nationalists and the left leaning Labor Party of
the Rand, on the other hand, had registered impressive gains in the
Free State and Transvaal, emphasizing the political division between
Afrikaners in the north and south, and there were also signs of deepening political discontent among the Union's non-whites.

In 1920, a Xhosa religious sect had openly defied the government's
reserve policies by seizing lands near Queenstown in the Cape where
their leader still held title to a piece of property and in 1921 a Colored
clan called the Bondelswarts, in the new Union mandate of South
West Africa, had rebelled against the imposition of a new tax. As if
to warn against any further political defiance from non-whites, Smuts
had struck at both with excessive violence, killing hundreds, but
within a few months of the Bondelswarts affair, he had faced a far
more complex and dangerous rebellion against his authority on the
Rand.

Between 1920 and 1922 no rain at all fell on the platteland. The
sun burnt the veld to whiteness. The animals and grasses died and
hope died with them. On hundreds of farms like that of Gerrit Visser,
near Richmond in the Free State, boys who are now men witnessed
the same sights. "As the wells began to go dry out on the range, our
animals came close and then closer to the house, smelling the water
in the deep well there. Finally as it began to go, our sheep were
packed all around the house, bleating for water. There was barely
enough left then to keep the humans alive and we could give them
none. . . . Their crying went on day and night until you almost
went mad with it. My father shot some of them to save their suffering, shot his livelihood, shot his hopes. And still they came and cried
until he could shoot no more and they simply dropped where they
stood and we had almost nothing. . . ."

As the plight of the platteland farmers worsened, the Union's

British-controlled banks had reacted to the general economic decline by shortening credit, and as rinderpest and drought took their toll, family farms that had formed the basis of Afrikaner life had begun to fall one by one, setting more and more Boers and their black farm-hands adrift on the land.

The Rand had drawn these dispossessed by the thousands, and in slums more squalid than Soweto, which began to grow up around the still prosperous English cities, Boer and black met as rivals for the same unskilled jobs. Soon, under the leadership of a brilliant African named Clements Kadalie, blacks had organized their own Industrial and Commercial Workers Union (I.C.U.) and had begun to agitate for an end to preferential hiring and wages for whites in the mines. When the mine owners, who saw a way of recouping their own fall-ing profits by putting blacks, who earned a pound a week, into jobs once reserved for whites, who earned a pound a day, appeared to comply with Kadalie's free labor proposals, the racial situation had be-come explosive. Persuaded that the mining barons, whom the Afri-kaans press had begun to refer to as "Hoggenheimer," meant to "plow them under" by forming a new alliance with the black ma-jority, 20,000 white workers, the majority of them Afrikaners, had struck the Rand, idling 180,000 blacks. As whites had taken their rage with the mine owners into the streets, looting, arson, and the murder of hapless blacks had spread.

By March of 1922 the Rand strike had also become a civil insur-rection. Commandos, proclaiming their intention to overthrow the Union government and replace it with an Afrikaner Socialist republic, were drilling in Johannesburg. Workers rallied to the slogan "Work-ers of the World Fight and Unite for a White South Africa," and the shadow of Bolshevism seemed to loom over the Rand. Smuts then prepared to retaliate. Martial law was proclaimed. Planes dropped leaflets over Johannesburg, warning the population to take cover, and as the Union militia moved into position around the city, guns began to pound the Reef towns and planes strafed workers crowding the main square in Johannesburg itself.

Panic spread as armored militia had stormed in. Three days after the onslaught had begun, the so-called "Red Revolt" of the Rand ended. Two hundred and thirty had been killed, 534 wounded, 5,000 were jailed, and new names had been added to the growing list of martyrs to the Afrikaner republican cause. By siding with the so-called "Kaffir Kings" of the Rand, Smuts had not only lost the trust of a vast segment of Afrikanerdom and helped to shape a political alliance between Hertzog's Nationalists and Labor, which would bring his defeat in 1924, but he had reinforced a shared sense of alienation from their British masters that bound the unhappy Afrikaners of the cities to their equally impoverished cousins on the platteland. And it was this rebonding of "Die Volk" that was to remake South African politics in the next decade.

The Rand Revolt had made it clear that the Afrikaners' dominant voice in Parliament was without any real force. In the final analysis, the British, who controlled the Union's economy, were its "power elite." The Afrikaners remained second-class citizens, occupying an uncertain middle ground between their British masters and the black majority, and the precariousness of this position had been brought home to them by the mine owners' willingness to exploit the latter's tragic predicament at the former's expense. On coming to power in 1924, therefore, Hertzog's new government had attempted to curb the power of the so-called "Kaffir Kings" and the ambitions of the new black proletariat by rescinding legal recognition of the black unions and creating "color bars" against hiring blacks for semi-skilled and skilled jobs. It also set out to frame a "New Deal" for the Afrikaners. Socialist, nationalist, and racist in nature, its policies were specifically aimed at countering the power of big British finance in South Africa by aggrandizing the power of the government through the nationalization of the railroads and the creation of a vast government-owned iron, coal, and steel industry called ISKOR, and by anchoring Afrikaner interests in a huge civil service and labor force hired to support these state enterprises. Understandable in the light of the fact that British interests then claimed just under 90 percent of the Union's business, Hertzog's brand of national socialism not only recast the old triangular rivalries of Boer, Briton, and black in a new form, by concentrating their economic interests in different spheres, but it did not meet the needs of the growing numbers of poor whites and blacks. Driven off the land by the protracted drought, they were the first to feel the effects of the worldwide Depression that began in 1929.

By 1931, one in five Afrikaners was classed as indigent. In the backveld dorps, as well as in the slums that grew up like cinctures of misery around the still prosperous English cities, poverty had become the Afrikaner way of life. With little else to sustain them in what amounted to yet another struggle against "decline and exermination," they had taken refuge from their growing feelings of inferiority to the British, and very real fears of being economically overwhelmed by the blacks, in a reassertion of pride in their own past. Under the tutelage of the newly formed Broederbond and its preacher-activists in the three Dutch Reformed Churches, they had become committed to a "reddingsdaad"—an act of national self-redemption, economically and spiritually. And while their predikants preached a return to purified Christian Nationalism, the Broederbond had guided the investment of an expanded "Helpmekaar" fund to develop Afrikaner enterprises in banking and business.

Trusting as always in the authority of their churches, whose pastors in turn trusted to the authority God had vested in them to lead His Chosen People, the Afrikaners had drawn into a kind of spiritual laager during the Depression. And they began to elevate their traditional values of kin, clan, hierarchical order, religious orthodoxy, and racial purity into cult values, all unaware that they were escaping from fear by a route that had carried their spiritual antecedents at Dort down the road to despotism long centuries before.

45
THE RISE OF
A SECULAR RELIGION:
AFRIKANER NATIONALISM

The Great Depression had produced a climate of reaction everywhere in the world. As the demagogues of the Ku Klux Klan preached a racist doctrine to dispossessed mobs in the American South, the Nazi Revolution, which was to carry Germany out of the shambles of its defeat in World War I to a dangerous new position of power in Europe, was under way. Mussolini strutted in Rome, and a shy Japanese botanist, the Emperor Hirohito, was worshipped as a nationalist god in Japan. The mood of reaction in South Africa was, therefore, no exception. The Afrikaners' defeat by the British, the prolonged drought and the Depression, had taken a toll of their spirit, entrenching their resentful sense of inferiority to the British and fears of being swamped by the blacks and increasing their susceptibility to zealots of the "new" nationalism like Daniel Malan.

A Broederbonder and ordained minister of the Dutch Reformed Church turned politician, Malan had broken with Hertzog to form his own "purified" Nationalist party in 1934 because he disagreed with the latter's decision to meet the exigencies of the Depression by fusing his party with Smuts's in a coalition government. Protesting that "fusion" meant an adulteration of the party's ethnic purity, Malan had thereafter emerged as the most important spokesman of the "new" nationalism, and during the Centenary of the Great Trek, he had delivered a speech at Blood River, redefining the meaning of the Trek and of the Broederbond's "reddingsdaad" in dangerous new terms.

"I scarcely need tell you that Afrikanerdom is on trek again," Malan had told his listeners. "It is not a trek away from the centers of civilization as it was one hundred years ago, but a trek back—back from the country to the city. . . .

"In that new Blood River, black and white meet together in much closer contact and much more binding struggle than when one hundred years ago the white-tented wagons protected the laager and muzzleloader clashed with assegai. . . . Where he too must stand in the breach for his People that Afrikaner of the new Great Trek meets the non-white beside his Blood River, partly or completely unarmed, without the defenses of a river bank or entrenchment, defenseless upon the open plain of economic equalization. . . . The groaning of the ox wagon evokes clearly again the star which held your forefathers on course through darkest night. Their star of freedom shines brighter on your path as well. But you know now that freedom meant more for them than simply the freedom to rule themselves and live out their nationhood fully. Their freedom was also and above all to preserve themselves as a white race. As you could never otherwise have realized you realize today that their task to make South Africa a white man's land is ten times more your task. . . . There is a power which is strong enough to lead us to our destination along the path of South Africa—the power Above which creates nations and fixes their lot. . . ."

Militant, messianic, and racist, Malan's neo-Calvinist Christian National creed was to gain rather than to lose strength as the world became embroiled in a Second World War that would finally shatter the old colonial order in Africa forever, and in 1942 he had pointed the Afrikaners down a perilous path toward the future. "It is through the Will of God that the Afrikaner people exists at all," Malan had declared that year on the anniversary of Blood River. "In His Wisdom He determined that on the southern point of Africa, the dark continent, a People should be born who would be the bearers of Christian culture and civilization. In His Wisdom, He surrounded this People by great dangers. He set the People down on unfruitful soil so that they had to toil and sweat to exist upon the soil. From time to time He visited them with droughts and other plagues. But this was only one of the problems. God also willed that the Afrikaans People should be continually threatened by other Peoples. There was the ferocious barbarian who resisted the intruding Christian civilization and caused the Afrikaners' blood to flow in streams. There were times as a result of this that the Afrikaner was deeply despairing, but God at the same time prevented the swamping of the young Afrikaner people in a sea of barbarism. . . ."

The notion that the Afrikaners were the "bearers of Christian culture and civilization," charged with an extraordinary mission in Africa, was to prove an exceedingly potent political doctrine in the years immediately after the war. By 1946, Russia was already pressing westward threateningly, as Suleiman had once done, spreading the influence of her potent ideology not only to the very gates of western Europe in Hungary but throughout the world. Concurrently, the Zionists in Palestine and the followers of Gandhi in India revived visions of their own glorified pasts to create new nationalisms, and by 1948, when the Malanites came to power in South Africa by preaching racial "apartheid," "blood purity," and "ethnic destiny," India had already cut its ties to Britain, heralding the end of Empire everywhere. Soon the cries of "Uhuru" were being heard in Africa, and as the world entered the tension-filled years of the Cold War, black nationalist movements gathered strength by glorifying that which was indigenously African and condemning that which was colonial and, by inference, white. But in too many states where black nationalism was primarily a negative force, based on hatred of colonialism rather than on positive policies, the visions of lost tribal glory supplied no workable answers to 20th century problems and "Uhuru" produced political and economic instability that in turn limited the tenure of "democracy" to "one man, one vote, one time."

As one after another of the new African nations became single-party states—ruled by strong men or military dictatorships—the failures of internal government were often masked by scapegoating an external enemy, and militant black nationalism found cohesion by turning its fury against South Africa. Looking north to black Marxist states, which openly declared their intent to destroy white rule in South Africa, the Afrikaners had acquired a modern "devil" to fear in "godless communism" whose cause prospered in the general disorder of the continent. Always in need of an adversary to lend cohesion to their cause and of commanding men to point their way in perilous times, the Afrikaners had found both when Hendrik Verwoerd set out to rescue South Africa from incipient "chaos" and "communism" by his radically reactionary programs of "separate development."

46
A MAN OF GRANITE:
VERWOERD

The Malanites had carried the election in 1948 on a resurgent wave of Afrikaner nationalism compounded of old resentment of the British, old dreams of re-creating an Afrikaner Republic, and new fears of the emergent "Black Peril" in Africa rather than on any positive policies. Jan Smuts, who had replaced Hertzog as Prime Minister when Parliament had narrowly rejected the latter's bid to keep the Union out of the war in 1939, had been vilified during the 1948 campaign for neglecting its affairs in favor of those of the Empire, and the Malanites had made much of the racial "mengelmoes" (mess) that had resulted from the continuing drift of blacks to South Africa's cities during the war years.

At the war's end, there were roughly 2.5 million blacks living in hundreds of squatter towns around every major city in South Africa, and the growth of these slums had been accompanied by intermittent race rioting and a steady increase in violent crime, committed by blacks, in cities like Johannesburg. The wartime economic boom furthermore had forced a breach in the color barriers of industry and brought roughly half a million blacks into skilled jobs once reserved for whites, not only spurring a resurgence of African trade unionism on the Rand but with it a new militancy among the emergent black proletariat of the cities.

Still insecure in the cities, the Afrikaners' old fears of being swamped in a "sea of blackness" had therefore been easily revived by the Malanites, and as white unemployment had begun to climb with the demobilization of Union troops at the end of the war, the Nationalists had been able to gain the support that won them the elections in 1948 by pandering to the Afrikaners' old anxieties and making much of the threat to their "Blood Purity" should the intermingling of the races be permitted to continue unchecked. Yet, by 1950, it was already apparent that the politics of fear that had won Malan the election and produced a string of negative "apartheid" laws had done nothing to answer South Africa's long-range racial dilemma. It was at this point that Malan had turned the task of giving some positive meaning to his policies over to Hendrik Verwoerd.

A giant of a man with blazing blue eyes and a thatch of white hair, Verwoerd has been described variously as a "Promethean Afrikaner," a "Man of Granite," the "Robespierre of the Afrikaner revolution," and a "paranoic fanatic." All four descriptions are apt, for from the moment he declared in his first speech to Parliament in 1948 that South Africa "must" and "would" remain a "white man's country" until his life was ended there eighteen years later by an assassin's knife, Verwoerd appears to have felt entrusted by destiny with the Promethean task of rescuing South Africa from the dark forces of history by restructuring its society entirely in accordance with his neo-Calvinist vision for "separate development." Ruthlessly inflexible in his dedication to this self-appointed task, Verwoerd, more than any other individual, shaped the milieu of modern South African life and to sketch his political career is to sketch a case study in the extremes of political reaction.

Dutch born, but reared in South Africa from the age of two, and educated at Stellenbosch in the years when it was the hot-bed of new Nationalist sentiment and neo-Calvinist philosophizing, Hendrik Verwoerd appears to have spent his life proving that he was a "Waar Afrikaner" in spirit if not by birth. A zealot in the cause of Afrikaner nationalism, he had disdained an Oxford scholarship to complete his post-graduate studies in Germany during the volatile years of Hitler's rise to power in Europe. At the University of Leipzig, he had been deeply influenced by the racist ideology of National Socialism and on his return to South Africa in the 1930's, Verwoerd had made no secret of his sympathy for the Nazi cause.

Politically, Verwoerd had risen to prominence as editor of the influential Nationalist newspaper, the *Transvaler,* and for fifteen years before he went to Parliament in 1948, had been writing passionately and at length on the ideology of Christian Nationalism. Invited to put his social theories into practice by Malan as Minister of Bantu Affairs in 1950, he had shaped his far-reaching "blueprint for the future" on the Christian National premise that God had set the races apart and meant for them to remain that way. It envisioned the eventual partition of South Africa into definitive racial domains in which each and all of its various populations would—by the unilateral decision of the Malanite Nationalists—be "free" to develop according to its own "ethnic destiny." Dogmatically certain that only thus could South Africa "avoid a blood bath and create order out of the chaos into which the Native Problem has been allowed to drift," Verwoerd had pursued this "Grand Design" for the "separate development" of South Africa's blacks, Coloreds, Indians, and whites in the same monomaniac manner as Rhodes had once pursued his own redemptive vision for Africa.

Under Verwoerd's leadership, the Nationalists had unfolded their ideas with the ruthless consistency that is often the mark of "True Believers" and, in the conviction that by forcing the races apart they were fulfilling Divine Will, had pushed one piece of "apartheid" legislation after another through Parliament. In 1950, the Group Areas Act was buttressed by a law that required the classification of the entire population racially and the registration and issuance of passes to black males according to their tribal origins. A year later, a Bantu Authorities Act established the first skeletal forms of black self-government in the tribal reserves, moves were initiated to strike

Coloreds in the Cape from the common voting rolls and the Cape's Xhosa lost the proxy representation in Parliament that had been theirs since 1936. By 1953, despite a constitutional crisis that shook the government, Coloreds had lost their political rights and the Nationalists had set in motion a far-reaching education act that was to create separate schools for Coloreds, Indians, and blacks, the latter organized along strictly tribal lines. In 1954 a Resettlement Act permitted the wholesale razing of the squatter towns, older mixed neighborhoods, and the forced relocation of their mixed populations in new government housing schemes like Soweto, which were duly subdivided on racial and tribal lines. And in 1956 the Industrial Conciliation Act created a cumbersome multi-tiered system for the regulation of industrial labor relations, which allowed for the organization of separate trade unions for the several races but prohibited blacks from striking and continued to reserve certain skilled jobs for whites.

"Create your own future," Verwoerd had commanded, preaching his gospel of "ethnic destiny" in speech after speech in which the name of God figured prominently. Yet like most reformers who would reorganize society in His name according to their own wills, Verwoerd and his followers became increasingly authoritarian and reckless in their uses of state force. Thus they not only forfeited the freedoms of the black majority to their Utopian vision for the future but began to subvert the rational legal order of South African society by substituting the Afrikaners' "duty" to the "national cause" and obedience to those in authority for the rule of law. And as their recklessness grew so also did black resistance. By 1958, when Verwoerd became Prime Minister, succeeding J. G. Strijdom who had died in office, the black nationalist movement in South Africa had been radicalized by the arrest of Albert Luthuli of the African National Congress and some 156 other leaders of the African resistance movement. The new and far more militant Pan African Congress had emerged to preach "Black Power" and "Africa for the Africans," and world opposition to "apartheid" had become strident as East and West courted favor among the emergent Afro-Asian states.

Verwoerd had answered his critics by declaring in his inaugural address that "the policy of separate development is designed for happiness, security, and stability provided by their home language and administration for the Bantu as well as the whites," and he had proved his sincerity by asking Parliament to approve the implementation of a program that was to result in the dismemberment of the Union and the creation in its stead of a plural Commonwealth of one white republic and ten black states; the latter to be organized on the extant tribal reserves and protectorates and their development guided and financed by the prosperous "core economy" of "White South Africa."

Though this final phase of Verwoerd's "Grand Design" represented the repackaging of some old ideas, originated by the British when they had chosen to deal with South Africa's "native problem" in the 19th century by sequestering its tribal Africans in special reserves, it was nevertheless philosophically consistent with the Calvinist cast of Afrikaner thought. Moreover, by granting South Africa's "black nations" precisely what the Afrikaners had always wanted for themselves—political independence and racial isolation—Verwoerd's scheme seemed to redefine the Afrikaners' mission and bring Christian Nationalism up to date by recognizing African political aspirations and providing an outlet for them. Furthermore, since much of black Africa was avowedly concerned with preserving that which was indigenously African, Verwoerd's notions of "separate development" seemed to be consistent with African nationalism as well and so to offer a reasonable answer to South Africa's racial dilemma. But it proved to have as little appeal for the newborn African states, formerly ruled by France, Belgium, and Britain, and their Third World allies in Asia as it had for the leaders of the black resistance movement inside South Africa. Rejected at the United Nations and by the Afro-Asian bloc within the Commonwealth as a cynical attempt to subvert the rights of South Africa's non-white majority by applying the dictum "Divide and Rule," "separate development" had reaped a harvest of hatred for South Africa. Stung, the stubborn Afrikaners had reacted by deciding to "go it alone," and in 1961 South Africa had declared itself an independent republic and withdrawn from the British Commonwealth.

Unwilling to recognize the sad reflection of their own kind of racially exclusive nationalism in the emergent Black Power Movement in South Africa, Verwoerd and his cohorts had plunged on with his "blueprint for the future" like a band of Calvinist saints reborn. Refusing to accept any culpability for a campaign of sabotage, which was undertaken by a radical interracial offshoot of the African National Congress, called "Spear of the Nation," they had chosen instead to blame the new black militancy on "Communist agitators" and had gone on a "witch hunt."

In 1962 Balthazar John Vorster, Verwoerd's Minister of Justice, was given extraordinary powers to arrest, detain, and ban anyone suspected of antigovernment activity. In the next two years several thousand dissidents were jailed or placed under house arrest in a police crackdown that virtually eliminated the leaders of the resistance movement inside South Africa.

The world reaction to the Nationalists' excesses had been predictable. The United Nations had called for an arms embargo against South Africa. The Organization of African Unity unleashed a cannonade of condemnation, and thousands of young black South Africans sought safety in exile or went into training as "freedom fighters" in Marxist guerrilla camps in Africa, many to lose their lives later in the vicious internecine struggles between warring black factions in Zimbabwe, Angola, and Mozambique. But none of this deterred Verwoerd. Lashing out at the republic's critics, he had cast himself in the role of the high priest of Christian Nationalism and by his defiance rallied the Afrikaners to their cause. "Perhaps it was intended that we should have been planted here in the crisis area," he had told them, "so that from this resistance may emanate the victory whereby all that has been built up since the days of Christ may be maintained for the good of all mankind. We are here to hold the fort so that they [the western nations] can regain their strength and start anew the battle for Christianity and Civilization. . . ."

47
A MAN OF CONSCIENCE: BEYERS NAUDÉ

Beyers Naudé, a man who once stood in the inner ring of church-state power in South Africa, is a "non-person." Convicted in 1973 of a technical offense against the terms of its Draconian Suppression of Communism Act, Naudé was subsequently made officially voiceless and forbidden to comment on public issues in South Africa by being banned. Kept under constant police surveillance by plainclothesmen who park their cars and vans opposite the modest house he shares with his wife in a middle-class Afrikaner suburb of Johannesburg, Naudé may not move outside of a prescribed area of the city and is forbidden to speak with more than two persons at a time, even in the privacy of his home. A man whose intellect and empathy for others are immediately evident, he is being punished for a crime that has never been legally described, under a sentence that has no temporal limits, and the anguish of his isolation is evident in his expression.

Naudé's credentials as an Afrikaner are impeccable. Of Voortrekker stock, he is the grandson of an important Transvaal leader in Kruger's era and the son of one of the founders of the Broederbond, of which he was himself once a member. Born to a patriotic tradition, Naudé distinguished himself in his own right among the Afrikaners by rising to moderator of the Transvaal Synod, one of the most prestigious posts in the hierarchy of the Nederduits Gereformeerde Kerk. But along the way to that powerful post, Beyers Naudé had become a doubter, deeply concerned by South Africa's drift toward despotism. In the early sixties his troubled conscience had led him to a break with his church, his government, and the Broederbond, which eventually resulted in his public condemnation for what amounted to heresy to the authoritarian ideology of Christian Nationalism.

Naudé's troubles began when he became chaplain at Pretoria University in 1949, one year after the Afrikaner Nationalist government of Daniel Malan had come to power, and they escalated as he rose in the hierarchy of his church. Pretoria was then a "hot bed" of religious nationalism, and most of its Afrikaans-speaking students were in complete agreement with the policies of "apartheid" being espoused by the new Nationalist government. But there were some among Naudé's youthful flock who became concerned as the spate of laws defining "separate development" were put into effect by Hendrik Verwoerd, then Minister of Bantu Affairs in Malan's cabinet. Their worries had in turn prompted Beyers Naudé to ponder the response of his own and the other Afrikaans churches to what he called "the unity and diversity of the human race."

Addressing the court during his 1973 trial on charges arising from his refusal to testify before a government commission investigating so-called "suspect organizations," Naudé said, "I found . . . that the truth of the Bible conveyed to us clearly that God created all the nations of the world in one blood, and therefore that the unity of the human race is fundamental to the calling of man on earth. . . ."

Naudé's "findings" had clashed with the most fundamental tenets of Christian National doctrine, which held that "apartheid" was in accordance with Scripture and that the Nationalist government, by acting to ensure the "ethnic purity" of South Africa's various tribes and races, was in fact acting as an instrument of divine will. But it was not until the sixties that events inside of South Africa had forced Naudé into a position of public apostasy to the "holy cause" of Afrikaner nationalism.

By 1960 the winds of change had been blowing across Africa for some time. The once mighty colonial powers were retreating from the continent in disarray, the old order was foundering, and black Africa was alive with the cry of "Uhuru!" Vying for Africa's treasure in resources, East and West both championed black nationalism by condemning white rule in South Africa. Britain, whose investments there were vast, had attempted to save face with the Afro-Asian members of the British Commonwealth by chastising the Afrikaners. Caught in the countercurrents of the time, the Afrikaners had believed they were once again being played as sacrificial pawns in a much larger game of power politics and had indicated their own reactionary mood by electing two Afrikaner extremists, Johannes Strijdom and Hendrik Verwoerd, as Prime Ministers after Malan.

"It was under Verwoerd that the impact of 'separate development' was first fully felt," remembers Beyers Naudé, pondering the events that led up to his "banning." "But by then the Afrikaners had been completely indoctrinated in the belief that 'separate development' was fully justified by Scripture. To think otherwise, in fact, had already become heresy. And given the beleaguered state of our nation just then, such heresy was doubly unthinkable to the Afrikaner majority because it also seemed like treason to God, Country, and Nation. . . . We are, after all, a people whose concepts of Nation, Race, and Destiny, of History itself, have always been interpreted to us by our ministers and therefore given as God's Truth. It has been thus ever since 1840 when our 'divine mission' as the lone tribe of white Christians among the heathen black tribes of Africa first became the central article of our faith, and rank-and-file Afrikaners have based their most fundamental concept of themselves—their very identity as a nation—on the idea of their Charge, their Destiny under God. Our own tribalism, furthermore, had been enhanced by the government's emphasis upon the tribal values of the Sotho, Zulu, Tswana, and so forth in those years, to the point that we had come to place enormous importance on our ethnic rituals—religious, social, and historic. Our monuments, therefore, had become more important than they ought to have been; our heroes became demideities, our simplest tribal custom—the braaivleis—gained an importance beyond itself, and in our favorite sport, rugby, we expressed a worship of prowess, physical fitness, and supremacy in action that in its own way gave outward expression to our concept of ourselves as the tribe that God had 'Chosen' in Africa for His own purposes. And all of this, of course, derived from our deep-seated fears as a small nation that had almost been overwhelmed time and again.

"When my father helped to found the Broederbond, we were under Britain's heel, impoverished and defeated. The Broederbond's aims, then, were noble and sincere: to save our people. But as the Afrikaners slowly began to grasp more and more influence, they too had tasted the sweet fruits of power, and as with other nations, this had yielded an appetite *for* power itself. But the change from noble aims to dubious ones occurred so slowly that it went all but unnoticed until it was too late. And then came Sharpeville . . ."

In the early fifties, Albert Luthuli, president of the African National Congress, had emulated Gandhi's earlier efforts by organizing a passive resistance movement to oppose the government's "apartheid" program. Incorporating blacks, Coloreds, Indians, and whites, it had culminated in 1955 in a Congress of the People at which a Freedom Charter, advocating a peaceful political revolution in South Africa, along the lines of those that had occurred in America and France in the 18th century, had been adopted. Seen as seditious by the government, the Congress had spurred police reaction. Soon afterwards, Luthuli was arrested. Released in 1957, he was rearrested in 1959 and placed under permanent house arrest after a rash of racial violence at Pretoria, Pietermaritzburg, and Durban. But his removal from the political scene had only created a vacuum that had quickly been filled by two less moderate black leaders: Robert Sobukwe of the Pan African Congress (PAC) and Nelson Mandela of the ANC had soon organized a black power movement with distinct leftist leanings. The racial violence, meanwhile, had continued. In January 1960 nine white policemen had been murdered by a black mob at a place called Cato Manor, near Durban, and in an atmosphere of growing tension, Sobukwe had ordered a mass protest for March against the hated "pass laws."

On March 21, at Sharpeville, a "black township" outside of Vereeniging in the Transvaal, ten thousand black workers had marched on the police station to burn their official identity cards as a protest against the "pass laws." Singing and shouting revolutionary slogans, they had converged on the station, where 75 white security police were on duty. Surrounded by the crowd, the police had opened fire, killing 67 and wounding 186 blacks, all of whom were shot in the back. Photographs of the dead, splashed across South Africa's newspapers the next day, suddenly superimposed a dreadful image on the Afrikaners' vision of "separate development" and set off a shock wave of black rioting, arson, and more killings, which suggested to some Afrikaners that a dangerous revolution was at hand in South Africa but to others that the country was becoming a police state in which murder was made possible by political policy.

"Few Afrikaners," said Naudé, "could reconcile that image from Sharpeville with their own idealized conceptions of 'separate development.' Most whites then lived secure, secluded, and in many ways closed lives, unaware of the pain and tension in the black communities, and so they found what was happening incomprehensible. But the image of the security policeman with the gun was the image the majority of blacks had of the government . . . and that image pointed to what was wrong. . . ."

A few months after the shootings at Sharpeville, the World Council of Churches called upon leaders of the eight Christian denominations represented in South Africa to meet at a place called Cottesloe, near Johannesburg, to consider the meaning of what had happened. Beyers Naudé, as moderator of the Transvaal Synod of the N.G.K., led one of the most powerful delegations to the conference. During its sessions, the Cottesloe group discussed and subsequently approved a series of resolutions, which were duly published with the approval of the majority of the delegates, including those of the N.G.K. Their effect on the public was electrifying because they represented a complete reversal of the traditional position of the N.G.K., not only rejecting the accepted wisdom that Scripture justified "apartheid" but taking issue point by point with the government's migrant labor system, the unfair wage differential between blacks and whites, and the prohibitions against non-white ownership of land outside of their "homelands." "The right to own land wherever he is domiciled and to participate in the government of the country is part of the dignity of the adult man," stated resolution sixteen, "and for this reason a policy which permanently denies to non-white people the right of collaboration in the government of the country of which they are citizens cannot be justified."

Quickly endorsed by the newspaper *Die Burger,* an important voice of moderate Afrikaner opinion in the Cape, the Cottesloe resolutions also warned against the "danger of nationalism" that can "make the nation an absolute value which takes the place of God." Politically explosive, they struck at the very foundations of Verwoerd's "grand design" for the "separate development" of the homelands. Stunned and infuriated by them, Verwoerd, who recognized that a breach between the Afrikaner moderates and conservatives could destroy his own power base, had swiftly marshaled the party and the Broederbond—which then claimed over 800 predikants from all three Dutch Reformed churches as its members—and had used their pulpits and the conservative Afrikaans press to demand that the "errant" churchmen recant.

After heated debates within the N.G.K. Synods, the Cottesloe resolutions were eventually repudiated, and most of the "guilty" churchmen shrived themselves further by approving the withdrawal of the N.G.K. from the World Council of Churches. But Beyers Naude refused to recant. "Are we," he asked publicly, "in these times of crisis prepared to listen again whether God perhaps has something to say to us? Or do we run the risk of our informing God that the route we are following is, in every detail beyond question, also His way for us? . . . Our church should be on guard not to create the impression that national existence as such has already become an end in itself. . . ."

But the times were out of joint. Even before Cottesloe, Verwoerd had reacted to increasing criticism of his policies within the British Commonwealth by scheduling a referendum on South Africa's "Union" status in that organization. The referendum, which took the measure not only of republican sentiment among the Afrikaners but of their reactionary mood at the moment, had indicated that the time was ripe to sever the ties that had bound South Africa to Britain since the Anglo-Boer War, and in 1961 South Africa had declared itself an independent republic. Moreover, in the aftermath of Sharpeville, black resistance had also taken a new and violent turn as extremists within the A.N.C., P.A.C., and the leftist white African Resistance Movement had cooperated in a campaign of organized sabotage, which had done nothing to advance the black cause but a great deal to strengthen the government's claims that the "godless Communists" were at work within South Africa and to make opposition to its policies even more hazardous.

"It became impossible to question them," Beyers Naudé remembers, "and the tragedy was that those of us who wanted to lead our people away from the evils of repression and racism then were scorned and cursed and branded as Communist traitors for pointing out that the A.N.C. had been a legitimate movement from 1912 until 1960, similar to our own Afrikaner movement in its objectives. And after 1960, the threat from blacks, inside and outside the country, brought a rugged determination out of the Afrikaners' past to resist *all* pressures and to draw together in a struggle for national survival, right or wrong. And so there was no place left for dissidence, no place to question our ordination by God to survive, no place for anything but uncritical obedience to the authority of the political and religious leaders, which took the place of individual conscience and compassion. To work for meaningful change, insofar as change might represent some betrayal of the orthodox position, became thereafter almost impossible within the Afrikaner establishment. . . ."

Unable to function within the limits imposed by this establishment, Beyers Naudé resigned his post as Moderator of the Transvaal Synod and his ministry in the N.G.K. in 1963 to become the leader of a new interdenominational, interracial organization called the Christian Institute, which continued to maintain that the "gospel" of "apartheid" was a false one. In 1973, however, as a result of his refusal to give evidence that might incriminate the Institute to a commission formed by the new conservative Prime Minister, John Vorster, Naudé was officially "banned" and placed under house arrest.

"I see the anguish of my people now," he said recently. "It is the anguish of a nation that truly does not know what direction is left to it, for of late, the Afrikaners have lost their sense of self certainty. The fundamental beliefs and assumptions that once were taken for granted have begun to crumble. Curiously, it is the present economic reality of the country that has forced them to conclude that the vision of Verwoerd may, after all, have deluded him. They have begun to see that economically, at least, our fate *is* intertwined with that of the black majority and that we must accept that the black man has a place in this country's society or see the country perish. But the problem for the present leadership remains one of risking too much change too quickly, for what is now required of the Afrikaner is that he abandon an ideology which has given him a sense of supremacy and security for self-doubt and self-examination at a time when he knows the survival of his nation is once again threatened. And as his very identity is linked with the ideology of national survival, his bonding, his history, his being are defined by it. *That* is humanly almost too much to ask of any people, especially one that has been politically and religiously indoctrinated for decades. . . ."

48
THE ACCOMPLISHMENTS
OF APARTHEID

Verwoerd had played upon the Afrikaners' old and new anxieties with infinite skill in the sixties by equating their defiance of black nationalism and international communism with the defense of civilization and Christianity in Africa. In language reminiscent of Malan, Kruger, and the Covenanters at Blood River in its messianism but of Rhodes in its megalomania, he had once more made it seem that the salvation of God's cause depended upon their national survival, and because they wanted to believe him, the Afrikaners had marched in lockstep behind the banners of Christian Nationalism like the despots of Dort reborn.

Isolated in Africa during the critical era, which had shaped the liberal philosophies of latter-day Europe and America, and persuaded by their bloody quarrels with the British that "liberalism" and all it represented was "corrupt," they had set out to reform South African society in accordance with their own radically reactionary notions that nations, not individuals, were God's chosen instruments and that He had given them a very special task to perform in Africa as the agents of His Order. Persuaded by their faith that "separate development" was "right, just, and in accordance with Scripture," they had willingly sacrificed some of the most cherished ideals of Western democracy in its name, and like their spiritual antecedents in Reformation Europe had, by diligent conformity to their "holy cause," created a climate of cold order in South Africa that proved conducive to its economic growth.

By the middle sixties, South Africa was a nation in transition. When the Nationalists had come to power in 1948, British interests, which represented a bare 8 percent of the population, had claimed just under half of South Africa's wealth, and most of the profits from the gold and diamond mines were being paid abroad. But by systematically taxing companies like Anglo-American to finance the expansion of parastatal enterprises in such vital areas of development as hydroelectric and nuclear power production, coal conversion and armaments manufacture, the Nationalists had not only set South Africa on the road to self-sufficiency but had laid the foundations of a new capitalist-socialist order that was to bring phenomenal prosperity to South Africa in the next decade.

"We never killed the goose that laid the golden egg," explained Piet Cillie, the former editor of *Die Burger*. "We simply stole its eggs and used them to build our independence. We thought of ourselves as a Third World people. We had, after all, had little more than the gun, the Bible, and the wheel until we began to accept the injection of British skills, capitalism, and political shrewdness into our lives. But we learned quickly from them that if ye would seek the political kingdom ye must also seek the economic, for therein lay the real sources of power. So we had learned a certain ruthlessness from our conquerors. We knew by then that, by letting capital pool in the hands of the upper classes, we were building the power that would fuel basic economic growth. We had no illusions about that or about the necessity to keep consumption down by keeping a large segment of the population poor. Developing countries can't afford democracy straightaway. They want to grow rch and competent first and that requires years of planning. . . ."

By the time John Vorster succeeded the slain Verwoerd in 1966, the Nationalists' ruthless management of South Africa's economy appeared to be paying dividends. The gross national product and the gross national income were growing at a real rate of better than 6 percent per annum. The national economic pie was being recut and redistributed, with roughly a third each going to British, Boer, and black. Though much of the country's new affluence could be attributed to the continuing exploitation of migrant black miners from the "homelands," Malawi, Lesotho, Mozambique, and other black states whose "real" wages—pegged to the price of gold then fixed in Washington at $35 an ounce—had not been increased since 1911, there had nevertheless been a steady improvement in the general standard of living among blacks in both the urban and rural areas.

Shortly after the spate of black demonstrations, which had culminated in the slaughter at Sharpeville, Pretoria had announced a new five-year building program, which called for the construction of 81,000 new township houses and an expansion of "hostel" housing for migrant black workers, contracted from the "homelands" to work in the expanding industrial centers. Black social services had also burgeoned under "separate development" and new schools, hospitals, clinics, and universities were being built at a rapid rate in the black townships and Colored and Indian Group Areas. Moreover, though Pretoria spent ten times less per capita on educating black school children than it did on whites, and extracted a sizable tax from their ill-paid parents in support of their separate but unequal schools, it had instituted the first system of general education for Africans in all of the continent and tripled black school enrollments in fifteen years. Nor had the basic development of the "homelands" been entirely neglected. Under Verwoerd, Pretoria had spent some 130 million rand on the enlargement and consolidation of these proposed black states, and Vorster had increased the basic budget for their development by about 50 million rand annually. Following an investment curve that roughly tracked the upward curve of the general economy, Pretoria had funded agricultural, reforestation, irrigation, and stock improvement projects in these backward areas; and in the seventies two more black states were to be cut away from the republic—the segmented Tswana republic of Bophutatswana and the subtropical enclave of Venda. But while such efforts, ironically, placed the land of "apartheid" in the van of black development in Africa, the overall improvement in the black standard of living within the republic had produced a surge in black population that had begun silently to wipe out their real economic impact. In 1952 South Africa's African population had been estimated at 7.5 million. By 1972, that number had more than doubled and projections indicated that this explosive growth would continue into the next century. Despite rigid "pass laws" and influx controls, more and more blacks, unable to subsist in the "homelands," had drifted into the prosperous urban-industrial areas. As the supply of unskilled labor had begun to outrun demand, a critical mass of unemployed and often desperate blacks had begun to build up in the overcrowded townships and in new squatter settlements, creating the potential for a racial explosion that would rock the republic to its foundations.

Carried halfway down the road to assimilation in the republic's expanding industrial economy, much as the Afrikaners before them had been, these blacks not only feared and resented the government's efforts to return them to the impoverished "homelands" but yearned for a better life. The most bitter, furthermore, were the best educated—the rising generation of young urban blacks who had been the chief beneficiaries of Verwoerd's extensive efforts in "Bantu Education." Literate, aware of the revolutionary trends in the rest of Africa, and a generation removed from the debilitating poverty and ignorance of the tribal areas where many of their parents had grown up, they expected and wanted more than to serve as the white man's dray. Their frustrated ambitions had already begun to fester into a political rage, not unlike that from which rampant Afrikaner nationalism had itself sprung, even before an economic downturn in the early seventies began to drive unemployment in cities like Soweto to extreme levels.

49
COMING TO TERMS
WITH TOMORROW

South Africa had prospered under Vorster. Still heavily reliant on exports of raw mineral and agricultural products to the Sterling markets when he succeeded Verwoerd, the republic had courted capital and trade in Europe and Japan under his aegis and by the seventies had emerged as a first-class Western industrial power on its own. From 1966 until 1972, its economy had grown at a rate topped only by that of Japan. White South Africans had become the single most affluent group in the world, surpassing Californians, and black South African wages were escalating at an average of 6.6 percent per year to push the black per capita income to one of the highest levels on the sub-continent. But "apartheid" and affluence made a volatile mix, and as the fires of black revolution had swept southward, consuming the last vestiges of white colonial rule in Africa, South Africa became the focal point of a profound economic and ideologic conflict that threatened the world itself with catastrophe: the conflict between its poor and its rich, between its often primitive and always numerous non-white nations, many of them recently roused to nationalism and revolution by the decay of colonialism, and its advanced, rich white minority in the industrialized West who still controlled most of the world's wealth and power. And at issue was not simply whether privileged white South Africa and the Afrikaners who ruled it could survive the onslaught of revolutionary black Africa, or whether capitalism would prevail over communism in this strategic region but whether the machinery of modernization would at last be put to work to rescue white and black Africans alike from a confrontation that held the potential to reduce the entire world to ruin.

By the mid-sixties, it had at last become evident that Verwoerd's reactionary vision of a world restored to some millennial tribal order through the enforcement of "apartheid" had delayed but not turned back the inevitable onslaught of the future. Drawn by dreams of bettering themselves, Africans had continued to flood to the cities, and under Vorster the acolytes of a new Verligte faith in economic growth had begun to preach that South Africa's only hope of salvation lay in immediate economic integration and gradual political reform.

Johan Liebenberg is a specialist in industrial labor relations and was among those chosen during the Prime Ministerships of John Vorster and his successor, Piet Botha, to advise their governments on labor reforms as a member of the influential "Wiehahn Commission." Liebenberg's offices at the Chamber of Mines are unpretentious to the point of being monastic and seem to suggest by their very barrenness that the men who hold the purse strings of South Africa's golden rand have little need to impress. Nor did his manner suggest anything less. In his stark presentation of the enormous economic problems confronting South Africa, Liebenberg left little doubt as to the importance of big business in its emergent alliance with South Africa's government or of the pivotal role capital had been assigned in the cause of Verligte reforms if South Africa was to survive.

"It takes a developing economy about sixty years to mature," he explained. "If we put the real beginnings of industrial development in South Africa in the decade between 1933 and 1943, that means we can expect to reach economic maturity in this country somewhere around 2000. In a mature economy, about 60 percent of the population is in so-called 'first class' jobs as entrepreneurs, professionals, and management and only 40 percent is in the 'second class' skilled and semiskilled laboring ranks. However, if you look at our population projections, you will find that in the year 2000, only 9 percent of South Africa's population will be white! And that means that 'separate development' is just not feasible, because you simply cannot expect 9 percent of the population to do 60 percent of the work while 91 percent of the population is compressed into 40 percent of the available work."

Laying figures before me like a man removing radioactive isotopes barehanded from their protective containers, Johan Liebenberg went on to document what he called the "frightening picture" that had emerged in South Africa over the last decade. Unchecked black population growth, he pointed out, had set a pattern that would require South Africa to build "another everything" in the next twenty years, simply to maintain its present standards for blacks as well as whites. Every subsidized house, every clinic, every beer hall, every hospital, every university, and every training center it had thus far erected for Africans would have to be duplicated. Most critical of all, however, was the creation of jobs. To keep black unemployment from soaring to catastrophic levels, the South African economy would have to be expanded by 300,000 new jobs a year every year between now and the year 2000, when it was expected that blacks would outnumber whites by ten to one. To manage such a colossal feat, South Africa would also have to build a school a day every day between now and then to educate its black masses, train 14,000 new teachers a year every year, and expend between 6,000 and 10,000 rand on every industrial job it created annually. "And since no country in the world, not even the richest, has that kind of capital available there must be some compromises," he said. "Now, we have to give first priority to the creation of a black middle class, both because we must have black middle management to draw upon simply to keep our productive capacity a step ahead of our population growth and because a black middle class would have a stake in the capitalist system that would make it immune to the appeals of communism. But even as we push to integrate our industry, we can't abandon 'homeland' development because our primary objective is to create jobs for Africans. And it is far cheaper to do that in agriculture than in industry. So we must carry on in two directions at once for a while —integrating our industry to develop a productive black middle class, but keeping the 'homelands' going separately so as to curb an influx of unskilled blacks into the cities. And this also means that for a while the wage gap between white and black workers will not disappear because it's far better to create more jobs for blacks at lower pay than it is to let the unemployment pressures in this country go on building and building until they explode—just to preserve what the liberals call a 'moral wage'. . . ."

Early in his career as Prime Minister, John Vorster had himself warned that a rise in urban black unemployment was potentially more threatening to South Africa than the possibility of invasion from the north. As early as 1967, therefore, he had moved to meet the problem by simultaneously soliciting increased foreign investment in South Africa to expand its industrial capacity and courting "detente" in Africa by offering to create a regional common market with its black neighbor states on terms that were economically advantageous to them. Abandoning the rhetoric of "apartheid" at home, Vorster had offered plump trade, aid, and development programs to black states stretching from the Portuguese Angolan enclave of Cabinda bordering Zaire in the west, to Zambia, Mozambique, and Malagasy in the east. By 1970 Pretoria was pouring millions into development and hydroelectric projects in Portuguese Cabinda, Angola, and Mozambique and had discreetly opened trade links with Malawi and Malagasy. But almost as quickly as they had brightened, the hopes of "detente" in Africa had begun to dim. Soon after Malagasy's conservative black government was toppled in a Marxist coup in 1972, terrorist activities had been stepped up in Rhodesia, Angola, and Mozambique. By 1974, when Portugal finally abandoned her quarrelsome colonies in Africa, factions representing Chinese, Soviet, and Western interests were hotly disputing each other for control of the region through surrogate guerrilla armies.

Faced with a wall of fire on the republic's northern borders, Vorster had sought to save something from the shambles by indicating to the leading Marxist contender in Mozambique, Samora Machel of "Frelimo," that, in exchange for racial peace, Pretoria would continue to subsidize his government to the sum of R100 million a year, just as it had that of his predecessors. Moreover, to underscore South Africa's "good intentions," Vorster had not only taken an active role in attempting to pressure Ian Smith of Rhodesia to acquiesce to a deal that would bring black rule there but had sent his representative, Pik Botha, to the United Nations to make an extraordinary speech.

"We *do* have discriminatory practices and we *do* have discriminatory laws," Pik Botha told that assemblage apologetically in what seemed an effort to forestall an effort by the radical left bloc of the Organization of African Unity to have South Africa expelled from the U.N. before Vorster's peace initiatives might prove effective. "If we have that discrimination, it is not because the whites in South Africa have any herrenvolk complex. We are not better than the black people. We are not cleverer than they. . . . We shall do everything in our power to move away from discrimination based on race or color. . . ." "Give South Africa six months," Vorster himself had pleaded four days later, "by not making our road harder than it is already . . . [and] you will be surprised where we will stand. . . ."

But the road *did* become harder because Vorster's search for "detente" had embroiled him in the Byzantine plots and counterplots of East and West to dominate southern Africa, and in Angola he had become party to a scheme, evidently masterminded by Henry Kissinger, which failed.

Situated in the heart of the region, Angola and the Cabinda enclave were not only rich in industrial diamonds and oil, claimed by Anglo-American and Gulf respectively but strategic to its control and had been much fought over, before and after the Portuguese pull-out, by factions representing French, American, Chinese, and Russian interests. By 1974, however, the East-West quarrel had been defined by a continuing war between the Western-backed forces of UNITA and the FNLA and the Soviet-assisted MPLA, which appeared to be winning with the help of Cuban advisors. The latter, moreover, had also begun to lend a hand to the Marxist guerrillas of the South-West African People's Organization (SWAPO), who were fighting for control of Namibia, still a South African mandate. There was consequently cause for alarm not only in Pretoria, but in Washington, Europe, and the pro-Western capitals of Zambia, Zaire, Ghana, and Nigeria, and it was apparently at Kissinger's suggestion that a covert agreement was made to "save" Angola by sending South African troops to the assistance of the beleaguered FNLA/UNITA forces.

Vorster, who may have recollected the fate of Jameson's raiders in a similar escapade, had resisted Kissinger's plan. But after SWAPO terrorists had attempted to sabotage a new South African-built hydro-electric dam at Cunene, which supplied irrigation waters to parched Namibia early in 1975, an S.A.R. column had crossed from Namibia into Angola. The timing of the move, however, was to prove disastrous. An upsurge of antiwar feelings in America, as a result of its debacle in Vietnam, had weakened the "hawks," and the support Kissinger had apparently assured Pretoria would be forthcoming from a CIA-supported army of mercenaries out of Zaire, did not materialize. Forced to temporize while Kissinger desperately attempted to force Gulf to finance the effort, the South African troops had fought a semisecret war against superior numbers of Soviet-armed MPLA troops for six costly months at the request of Washington and the pro-Western African states. But after the MPLA had been recognized as the government of the newest People's Republic in Africa by 25 of the OAU's 46 members, the S.A.R.'s so-called Zulu Column was withdrawn and Vorster's first major adventure in the world of "Realpolitik" had ended in a failure which was to have devastating consequences for South Africa.

With Cuban troops now entrenched in Angola, it had become the base of Soviet ambitions in the region and a safe haven not only for SWAPO but for Marxist forces then fighting in Rhodesia. Samora Machel, evidently wary of finding himself on the losing side, had used Pretoria's thrust into Angola as an excuse to repudiate his earlier promises of "non-intervention" in the ongoing wars of the region. France, seemingly for the same reason, had canceled its contracts to supply the Republic with further Mirage jets and other military hardware. The U.S. had begun to withdraw from overt and covert military activities in Africa and under Carter would attempt to win influence there by a "human rights" campaign, which seemed indirectly to indicate Washington's willingness to sacrifice the Pretoria regime's interests to its own. Worse still, South Africa had been made to seem militarily vulnerable, and as what had once been a buffer zone between herself and the radical "frontline states" farther north became a war zone where East had met West in a strategic contest that the former seemed to be winning, the threats of invasion from the north no longer seemed purely rhetorical. Isolated and under fire, as the African states, which had so recently courted its help in private supported a leftist line within the OAU and the U.N. in public, South Africa suddenly seemed more vulnerable than it had ever been. Western business interests, fearing the worst, had immediately begun to pull their capital out of the country, pushing it into an economic slide that simultaneously produced a devastating climb in urban black unemployment and a deepening mood of white reaction that rapidly strengthened the "Verkrampte" wing of the

National party. Under fire for the failures of his "Verligte" foreign policy, which had been fostered by the Cape moderates among his counselors, Vorster had been forced to retrench politically by courting the Verwoerdian conservatives of the Transvaal, and in January of 1976 he had appointed one of their most flamboyant representatives, Andries Treurnicht as Deputy Minister of Bantu Affairs.

Treurnicht, who prided himself on his pure Verwoerdian politics, announced upon taking office that he intended to invoke a rule his Verligte predecessor had wisely abandoned, which required that Afrikaans be used equally with English as a medium of instruction in all African schools in the Transvaal. As Afrikaans was regarded by most young blacks with much the same feelings as English had once been viewed by Afrikaners, the effect in already troubled Soweto— where soaring unemployment among the militant young had fueled the rise of a new leader in a young man named Stephen Bantu Biko— was tantamount to dropping a lighted match into gasoline. In June of 1976, while Vorster was in Geneva conferring yet again with Kissinger on Rhodesia, Soweto went up in smoke.

Six years later, the shock waves set off by that explosion were still rippling and ricocheting through South Africa and beyond. In the first wave of panic, capital had hemorrhaged out of the country, and many English-speaking professionals had soon followed their fortunes abroad. Staggering, the economy had faltered further, worsening conditions in the black townships. Fighting to save his political life, Vorster had reverted to the brutal tactics he had employed in the sixties to suppress the escalating unrest before it blossomed into a full-scale revolution while he also sought secretly to stanch the flow of capital from the republic by buying favorable publicity abroad. But when Biko was arrested and beaten to death by security police in 1977, South Africa's image abroad was damaged irreparably, and when it was also learned that Vorster's lieutenants in the Information Department had been misappropriating state funds, he was forced to resign. Ironically, however, it was the Transvaal traditionalists who lost the most politically in the fiasco, for by returning to the Verkrampte fold after Soweto, Vorster had taken the stigma of his administration's disgrace into its heart. When he fell, it was the Cape "Verligtes" led by Piet Botha, who profited from an Afrikaner backlash against the corruption revealed in the scandal.

50
ADAPT OR DIE

As the former Minister of Defense, Piet Botha had lived with the specter of a potential black insurrection coupled with invasion from the north long enough to be convinced that the Afrikaners' best hope of salvation lay in taming rather than antagonizing black nationalism in South Africa. True to the new Verligte faith, he seemed inclined to regard it as his duty not only to defend the Afrikaners' right to exist and manage their own affairs but to fulfill their "mission" by serving as the agents of civilization and economic growth in southern Africa. On coming to power in 1979, therefore, Botha had stumped the country warning the Afrikaners they must "Adapt or Die" and had signaled his intentions to replace Verwoerd's rigid schemes of "separate development" with his own programs for economic integration and gradual political reform by beginning to dismantle the basic structure of "apartheid."

First to go were many of the restrictions of "petty apartheid," which had prevented the races from mingling freely in public places and on South Africa's playing fields, and more substantive changes had followed in 1980 when his government had extended the right to strike to African trade unions and launched an expensive economic improvement program in the townships. But as Botha did not define his long-range goals and did not provide a timetable for change, neither these gestures nor his creation of a multiracial President's Council, made up of whites, Indians, and Coloreds—whose task it was to consider political schemes that would protect the rights of each of these minorities in any future confederal government that included blacks—served to defuse the racial rage of radicalized black and Colored youths in the urban townships. Sporadic rioting and strikes continued, and in June of 1981, as in each year subsequent to the original Soweto uprisings, marchers clashed bloodily with police in Johannesburg and Cape Town and an image of jackbooted men with dogs, facing phalanxes of shouting students was flashed across the world.

South Africa's economy, vulnerable to a worldwide recession that had enhanced its dependency on gold, had meanwhile ridden a roller coaster, booming as the price of the precious metal soared in 1980 and faltering again as it fell in 1981, despite gloomy predictions that by the year 2000, the Rand's riches would be exhausted. Exiled leaders of the rival A.N.C. and P.A.C., meanwhile, pleaded for an end to Western investment in hopes of enhancing the revolutionary potential in South Africa, and both were actively recruiting disaffected young blacks for guerrilla armies in Mozambique, Zimbabwe, and Angola. The P.A.C., which had openly identified itself with Marxism-Leninism and proclaimed itself to be the progenitor, through its militant arm, Poqo, of both the Black Consciousness Movement and Biko's South African Student Organization, began to advocate a "generalized assault on South African colonialism" from the townships and the "homelands." The Soviet-backed A.N.C., however, was apparently more successful in enlisting disaffected young blacks for its "national liberation army." In 1979 alone some three quarters of the 4,000 young men and women who slipped out of South Africa were said to have joined its revolutionary ranks. By 1980, many were back in South Africa to instigate a campaign of terror in the countryside much like that which had succeeded in polarizing blacks and whites in Zimbabwe and precipitated its revolution.

As the region rippled with shocks and countershocks in the first years of Botha's Prime Ministership, the political ground under the National party began to shift perceptibly. Polls showed deep divisions in the once united Afrikaner Volk between those who wished to pursue partition of the country and consolidation of the black "homelands" and those who wanted to retain the status quo and to deal with the country's racial dilemma by other means.

In 1977, surveys had shown little support among the Afrikaners of government proposals to extend voting rights to Coloreds and Indians or to explore the creation of a new legislative body that would incorporate some black representation; 80 percent of those Afrikaners polled indicated that they feared that any major revisions in the political order could destabilize South Africa and threaten its security. Three years later, 49 percent of the Afrikaners surveyed approved of

enfranchisement of Coloreds and Indians, and 56 percent indicated
that they would accept the creation of a new legislative body in which
urban and homeland black leaders would sit as equals with the Indian,
Colored, and white counterparts and be given a say in national affairs,
and the proposals had also gained backing from 82 and 78 percent of
the English-speaking voters polled. But the mood of moderation indicated by these polls did not give Botha a free hand with reforms. On
the contrary, his 1979 moves to abolish such fundamental apartheid
laws as those forbidding mixed marriages and miscegenation had contributed to a backlash among Afrikaner conservatives, particularly
in the Transvaal, that had manifested itself even within his own
government. Searching for a consensus, Botha had gone to the hus-
tings in an early election in April of 1980, and though he was returned
to office with a two-thirds majority and claimed a "mandate" from
the voters to proceed with his program, there had been spinoffs to
the left and to the right. Afrikaner reformers had bolted the party to
support the programs of the Progressive Federalists Party, under a
brilliant new Afrikaner leader, Van Zyl Slabbert, who endorsed a
qualified franchise for all, and Verkramptes had deserted the ranks
in droves to line up behind the hardliners of Herstige Nasionale Party
on the far right. More worrisome still was the continuing division
between Verligtes and Verkramptes in Nationalist ranks. More than
half of the party's political action group in Parliament, the caucus,
were considered to stand to the right of center, while Botha's own
cabinet was heavily weighted on the side of the Verligte reformers,
and the only arch-conservative of cabinet rank, Andreis Treurnicht,
then boss of the provincial party organization of the Transvaal, had
become a thorn in Botha's side. Despite the lessons of Soweto, Treurnicht still nurtured his own political hopes as a rival to Botha by
courting the support of right-wing extremists and those who had the
most to lose from reform: those among the six in every ten Afrikaners
whose civil service jobs would be threatened by dismantling apartheid's giant bureaucracy or by the open hiring of blacks in parastatal
industries. Stumping the country, preaching a return to Verwoerdian
verities, Treurnicht threatened to break with the party to form a new
coalition with H.N.P., raising a ghost from the past, and Botha,
mindful of the fact that every Afrikaner leader in history who
sought "fusion" with English interests had been toppled by a

resurgence of right-wing conservatism, had slackened the rhetorical pressures for reform within South Africa and focussed public attention instead on the threats it faced from without.

They were sizable. Though the new Reagan administration in Washington had announced its intention to "normalize" relations with Pretoria early in 1981, the UN still clamored for immediate elections in Namibia in spite of heightened SWAPO terror there. Inside Angola, new fighting had broken out between the Western-backed UNITA guerrillas and the Soviet-backed MPLA government and South African intelligence had also indicated a massive arms build up in SWAPO's camps there. As the rhetoric of the O.A.U. grew as warlike as that of the P.L.O., the Afrikaners—who once again found reason to claim the Israelis as spiritual kin—had launched a massive hit-and-run strike across the border into Angola in August of 1981. Successful this time, South African forces delivered a crippling blow against SWAPO and as their tanks and trucks rolled homeward they brought with them undeniable proof of direct Soviet involvement in SWAPO's war efforts in Namibia in the person of a captured Soviet military advisor and some 250 tons of Soviet material seized in SWAPO camps. Inextricably involved in a conflict of global dimensions, Botha and his supporters now found themselves attempting to bring a workable peace within South Africa through gradual reform while the entire region of southern Africa seemed to be drifting toward an East-West confrontation that could prove the prelude to Armageddon. Facing another time of testing, the mystics among the Afrikaners wondered whether they had not been brought full circle to stand as their ancestors at Blood River believed they had stood, with all the forces of chaos ranged against them while the realists searched for earthly solutions to a deadly dilemma.

51
PEACE OR WAR

Not long after the Soweto riots, two of the world's premier capitalists met in London. They were Anton Rupert of Rembrandt Tobacco, the quintessential "new" Afrikaner, and Sir Harry Oppenheimer, chairman of Anglo-American. They met to discuss how the power of big business in South Africa might be harnessed in the cause of reform, and as one result of their discussions, an elitist organization of Afrikaans- and English-speaking businessmen, called the Urban Foundation, was formed to lobby for improvements in the lot of urban blacks. Greeted with suspicion by Vorster, who feared such an organization might have political ambitions that could undermine the power base of the Nationalist party, the Urban Foundation nevertheless helped to promote a new alliance between business and government when Piet Botha replaced Vorster. Today one hears the same talk of "new dispensations," the "benefits of order," of "common markets," "foreign exchange," the "skills gap," and the new "politics of power" in government offices in Pretoria as well as in the glass and steel towers of Johannesburg.

"Our emphasis is twofold," Gerrit Viljoen, Minister of Education and the reputed chairman of the Broederbond and a spokesman for this new alliance, told a group of visiting American businessmen in South Africa. "Separate development will come closer to a real division of the land and wealth, leaving whites as one self-governing entity among several in a federal arrangement, which will have an open-ended future that could eventually bring political integration. And the urban blacks must be accepted as residents and receive political and physical concessions in the black municipalities, moving them toward self-government. . . . These changes," he assured, "would be evolutionary in nature but eventually the Afrikaners will remain as the Greek slaves did in the Roman Empire—as helots—the civilizing agents of a new order."

Viljoen was sincere. Pretoria had been pursuing a new Pax Afrikaner for several years. By 1982, four of the ten homelands were fully independent, four others were self-governing, and a joint secretariat had been organized to coordinate their relationships with the Republic. Using means similar to those espoused in Washington, D.C., to promote the "new federalism" and strengthen the regional authority of the states, the financial needs of these impoverished regions were increasingly being met by block grants, totaling almost R1,000 million annually, which their internal governments were expected to administer according to their own development objectives. In addition, Pretoria was sponsoring 130 direct-aid projects and had

offered fat tax incentives to would-be private investors in the homelands, not only within South Africa but abroad, and a new Small
Business Development Corporation had been formed in 1981 to make
low-cost loans to homeland business people. Though there were
mounting complaints of exploitation not only from low-paid homeland blacks but also from whites within the Republic who saw their
taxes being spent to help large corporations reap big profits, Pretoria
was clearly relying on something like "supply side economics" to
prime the pump of homeland development and bring its own long-
range hope of a viable new confederation of states closer.

But on the wider stage, it had met with less success. In 1980,
South Africa's trade with the north had exceeded a billion Rand, up
50 percent over 1979, the combative rhetoric of the OAU and Frontline States notwithstanding. Pointing to the hidden network of cooperation implied by this enormous trade volume, Botha had tried
to promote detente in the region by calling for a new "constellation
of states" and offering to sweeten the arrangement by sponsoring a
new regional Technical Center and development bank. Spurned, his
offer had been met by the formation of a "counter-constellation"
grouping that had joined Angola, Botswana, Lesotho, Malawi, Mozambique, Zambia, and Zimbabwe in economic accords aimed at
reducing their dependence on South Africa.

Botha's efforts to promote "political and physical concessions" for
urban blacks had also produced mixed results, and progress was
mingled with procrastination. Qualified blacks *had* been given the
right to buy 99-year leaseholds on their township houses, but not
on the land on which they stood. Restrictions against black businesses
inside the townships had been lifted, but by 1982—though a new
R34 million shopping center was planned for Soweto—only two
supermarkets had been opened in that most advanced of all the black
townships. A plan to electrify 100,000 of Soweto's houses was moving on schedule and a quarter had been "switched on" in January of
1982, but overruns on a cost estimate of R206 million to complete the
job made it questionable that full funding would remain available.
Moreover, despite a much-publicized plan to spend a billion Rand on
improving Soweto, Louis Rive, a city planner who had gone into that
township determined to transform it "from an undeveloped dormitory
into an economically viable self-run city" in 1980 had found his

hopes repeatedly frustrated by red tape. By 1982, though interim
funding of R10 million had been obtained to overhaul its sewage and
water systems and another R10 million was being spent to improve
its roads, very little had been done to meet its immediate need for
32,000 new houses. Bureaucratic constraints such as the requirement
that private companies, willing to capitalize new housing for their
own employees in townships like Soweto, obtain as many as fourteen
different approvals and permits before building could commence had
often stymied efforts to bring private funds to bear on the problem,
and though the government itself had announced its intention to
build ten new day hospitals, install 30,000 new phones, and stimulate
industrial development by creating three new industrial parks inside
Soweto, it too had often found its efforts stalled both by recalcitrant
Verkramptes in key Ministries and by the sheer inefficiency of its
bureaucracy. Thus, though the government had gained substantial
capital support in Europe and the United States, specifically to aid
in urban black development, and had raised its own expenditure for
African education by 37 percent in 1980, its plan to meet a critical
overall shortage of 500,000 housing units in the townships by a crash
building program remained hobbled in red tape in 1982. Moreover,
in February of 1982 something very close to a palace revolution occurred in the upper echelons of the Nationalist Party, when Andries
Treurnicht broke openly with Botha over the latter's continuing
efforts to bring a new political dispensation in South Africa.

   In the first two years of his prime ministership, Botha had attempted to circumvent the Verkramptes within his government by
streamlining the bureaucracy and strengthening the powers of the
executive while he had warily pushed his reform plans forward in
the face of growing resistance from the conservatives led by Treurnicht. Called into being in 1980, the President's Council made up of
whites, Coloreds, and Asians had been asked to make recommendations on the possible enfranchisement of the latter two groups, and
also to consider the eventual incorporation of representatives of both
the homeland and urban blacks in consultations aimed at the eventual
creation of a new multiracial confederal legislative body. By February
of 1982, amidst much tugging and pulling in the inner sanctums of
the government, it had begun to seem likely that Botha meant not
only to see that Coloreds and Asians were offered the vote but that

they would be directly represented in Parliament and would not, as the Verkramptes had wished, be shunted into a separate and unequal parliamentary body. "It is natural there can be only one government in the country," Botha had declared. "I have expressed myself against one man-one vote under the Westminster system . . . but in our view the terms deliberation, consultation, and co-responsibility [mean] a form of healthy power-sharing."

Rejecting any break in parliamentary apartheid and apparently fearful of Botha's hidden meanings regarding eventual power-sharing for the black majority, Treurnicht had led sixteen conservative members of the powerful parliamentary caucus in a bolt from the Nationalist Party that threatened to reduce the Prime Minister's majority in Parliament drastically and held the potential to derail his reform program altogether unless a new alliance with representatives of the minority New Republic party could be forged.

Buffeted politically, threatened militarily, and caught in a world-wide downturn that had made it increasingly difficult for South Africa to raise the capital it requires to proceed with promised crash efforts to bring massive physical improvements in the black town-ships, Botha entered a new winter of discontent in South Africa in 1982. Still searching for a resolution to the question of black power sharing, unable to make good on his promises of Progress through Capitalism at a pace sufficient to mollify alienated blacks, he faces a future in flux.

And the Pax Afrikaner, however sincere its objectives, remains sus-pect, tainted by its origins in "separate development" and by its re-semblance to the Pax Britannica as it was previously imposed by colonialists like Rhodes and Milner. The pilgrims from the platteland, like their Calvinist antecedents in Europe long ago, have been trans-formed and have emerged among the master capitalists of a Western world order that sees itself as a civilizing agent in Africa, dispensing its benefits to the continent's backward blacks in the cause of "en-lightened self-interest." The "conquered" Afrikaners, in short, have taken on the manners of their imperial conquerors, and what they once despised they have become: materialists who talk of "deals," "aid," "development," "cooperation," and "confrontation"—men of the real world concerned more with the powers on this earth than with those in Heaven. Nor do the ironies end there, for today's black radicals not only have as little wish to be "redeemed" by them in the cause of capitalism as the Afrikaners once had to be saved from backwardness by the British Empire, and the racially exclusive brand of national socialism advocated by the Black Power movement is a near copy of early Afrikaner nationalism with aims every bit as racially fanatic. Sam Nujoma of SWAPO, for instance, stated his objectives in Namibia with perfect clarity to a television interviewer. "I have no interest in power-sharing in Namibia," he said, "only power." Such sentiments are repeated regularly in Soweto.

Thus, even as the Afrikaners have begun trying to outrun the past, their old fears of annihilation continue to haunt them, and they are again preparing to fight, if need be, for their national survival. Though their incursions into Angola last year appear to have bought them time and opened a way to a "deal" in Namibia, where the American-backed Contact Group has assumed to guarantee a "bill of rights" to the white minority in any upcoming UN sponsored elections, the situation in the uranium-rich territory remains as tenuous as that in Angola and the quasi-Marxist states of Zimbabwe and Mozambique. And though the latter still remain economically tied to the republic, South African Defense Forces (SADF), reportedly on a par with the 25,000 stationed in Namibia, have been fighting a low-level guerrilla war along its northern borders for a number of years and the level of terrorism inside the republic has risen slowly. Threatened from within and without, the republic now spends in excess of R1,900,000,000 on defense annually, roughly 17 percent of its total budget. But the SADF has only 65,000 men on active duty, and though the South African Police, a force of 31,000, half of whom are blacks, and the Reserve Defense Forces could be called into action in any uprising or invasion, the Republic's declared enemies in the north have a combined standing army of 107,000 and its enemies within are unnumbered. Though to date no single radical group can claim the leadership of militant blacks and browns, the racial, tribal, generational, and ideological divisions that kept the nonwhite majority from unified action have been steadily eroded since 1976 by their shared rage with a system that has continued to rely on repression even as it offered "reforms" that do not touch their basic demand: power. Revolutionary violence, once abhorred by older blacks, is now regarded as a necessity by the majority who see it as an antidote

for their enforced political helplessness. "Fifty years of non-violence,"
Nelson Mandela declared fully twenty years ago, "brought the African people nothing but more and more repressive legislation." Still
imprisoned, Mandela is the extant martyr to the cause of black liberation, a cause which now subsumes the interests of young Coloreds as
well as Africans. "Which side of the gun are you on?" ask Soweto
youths who proudly identify themselves as "communists." Once in
eclipse, the fortunes of the ANC are on the rise since their successful
bombing of the main SASOL installations, 30 miles south of Johannesburg in June of 1980, and in addition to the 8,000 young blacks
said to be in training in Angola late in 1981, the ANC has 100 more
in leadership school in Cuba.

"We have used military force to buy us time," said Piet Cillie in a
pessimistic tone. "We have held back the terrorists of South West
Africa and pressed for a new political model of multiracial sharing
there. We have taken off some of the internal pressures by increasing
our investments in the homelands. But we still have not found a political answer to the urban black question and that may no longer
be left to ride. Economic accommodations will come first: there will
be increasing integration in the marketplace. But after that we will
have to come to political accommodations with the urban blacks that
many Afrikaners still insist are unthinkable. But 'never' is a word that
one must never use in politics and the unthinkable too will come. Because we have no choice. We are engaged in a crisis of existence here.
We can't shove it aside. We can't avoid thinking about it. It can't be
left unsaid. And we are all afraid—afraid we are going to be bloody
heroes."

Field Cornet Jacob Paul de Villiers is the leader of the Reserve
Defense Commando in the strategic southeastern corner of the
Orange Free State, where the Drakensberg mountains cleave off into
Natal and the borders of the republic abut the black state of Lesotho.
Through this region, the hydroelectric power grids and oil and water
pipelines, which supply the so-called "Golden Triangle" of industrialized Pretoria, Johannesburg, and Vereeniging, thread narrow cor-
ridors through lands held by another tribe, the populous and powerful Zulu, who have thus far refused "homeland" independence and

who by themselves outnumber South Africa's whites six million to
4.5 million. However strategic, it is also a majestic country of con-
centrated contrasts, a land of ochre mesas in the west, which suddenly
gives way to the sweeping sky-struck vistas of Natal and the towering
Drakensberg to the east, where one may stand, hawk high, to look
down on the valley of the Little Tugela and the beehive huts of the
Zulu as Piet Retief once did.

Jaap de Villiers has lived here all his life and loves the region with
the fierce, quiet love of a man tied to it by blood ties that go generations deep. Both he and his wife, Eunice, are descended from the
Voortrekkers who first opened it to white settlement. It was one of his
forefathers who directed Piet Retief to the passes that led down into
the "Promised Land" of Natal in 1838, and one of her ancestors rode
with Andries Pretorius to Blood River. Jaap's grandfather, Jacob
Paul de Villiers, died trying to take strategic Wagon Hill from the
British at Ladysmith in 1900; his father, Paul de Villiers, who was
captured shortly after that fatal battle, came of age in a prisoner of
war camp in Ceylon. Because Paul de Villiers refused to swear an
oath of loyalty to the British Crown, his repatriation to South Africa
was delayed at the war's end despite his failing health. When he
did finally return to Harrismith, he found his patrimony lost to him
by his mother's remarriage. He and his bride, Gertruida van Reenen,
started their lives together in a clay-and-wattle house they built
themselves in a remote untamed valley, south of Harrismith, and
their only son, Jaap, was born there in 1931. As a boy, he watched
his father grow prematurely old in a struggle to hold onto his lands,
which many of his fellow Free State Boers did not win, and one of
the brightest memories Jaap has of those difficult years revolves
around the trip he and his mother and father took to Pretoria in 1938
to see the torchlighted culmination of the Trek Centenary only a
year before Paul de Villiers died.

There is a fatalism about Jaap de Villiers today—as if all of that
personal history of struggle and sacrifice had prepared him for the
desperate role of a "bloody hero" in the war he believes must soon
come to South Africa. He goes about his daily business of cattle
ranching with the mesmerized quality of a man whose mind is on
other things, and though he is a superlatively skilled farmer, con-

servative of his land and stock and wise in the ways of the Sotho and Zulu who work for him, he carries his watchfulness with him like a knife.

"Look there," he will say suddenly as one rides with him over the rough country roads that tie his lands together. "Up there—a rooi-bolc. We saw the little buck up there the first time we used that koppie for maneuvers. The terrorists sometimes come that way out of Lesotho and so I set up our campsite there. I was training a local commando in guerrilla warfare, setting spring-up targets, human figures that pop up when you trip a hidden wire the way the terrorists do, when, suddenly, there was the little buck. . . ."

A big man, who moves with that unhurried grace one sees often in those who have spent their lives out of doors working among animals, Jaap took over the running of the farm from his widowed mother at eighteen and began building it into a complex of five farms. Some 13,000 acres, his holdings spread from the high veld of the Free State down over the Drakensberg's plummeting passes into Natal where the head waters of the Little Tugela feed his grazing lands on one side and those of the Zulu on the other. But for his use of four-wheel-drive vehicles and tractors instead of horses and oxen, de Villiers runs these ranches much as his Boer forebears did with the help of native farm hands, each of whom maintains a traditional tribal "kraal" on his lands. "Ou bass" to some 300 Sotho and Zulu, he supplies each family with food rations of 400 pounds of cornmeal a month, gave each household a basic herd of cattle, sheep, goats, and their grazing, provides veterinary services for their animals, medical care for their families, and schooling for their children and pays each hand a minimum of 30 rand a month—a wage in cash and kind that he reckons at roughly 200 rand.

"But it's not the same now as it once was," he reported unhappily as we headed for one of his Natal farms from which cattle rustlers had recently stolen more than a hundred unbranded heifers. "In the past, I could trust the families on my land completely. They were all settled and farming, running their own cattle and generally willing to work for what they had. One fellow had his own milling business —a truck, a car, a nice-sized herd of cattle, goats, money in the bank. He earned another 200 rand cash over what I paid him as a foreman. But he was an exception, because, traditionally, neither the

Zulu nor the Sotho will work unless they need to. A few years ago, there was a famine in Lesotho. We sent up a tractor and a team to show them how to improve their yields. We planted their mealies and harvested their crop and then left them the tractor to do the same the next year. Well, when we went back the next year, they'd done nothing. They told us they still had enough from the previous year and didn't need to plow and plant. Now, that's traditional. But not the rest. Not the guns. Not the terrorists who slip in and out of the country over the same paths the Sotho used last night to steal my cattle away to Lesotho. Not the fact that I don't know anymore which of my hands I can trust. It's changing, all changing, and I don't know what the future holds for we white South Africans any more. . . ."

The shape of Eunice and Jaap de Villiers' existence began to alter ten years ago when they were informed by the government that the "home farm," where Jaap's parent's lie buried and where they have raised their own three children, Paula, Paul, and Karen, would have to be forfeited to the Sotho "homeland" of Qwaqwa this year. At first resentful of a decision that he believed could only result in the ruination of lands his father had given a lifetime to rescue from the ravages of drought and misuse, Jaap eventually became convinced of the necessity of "separate development" as a compromise with black political ambitions in South Africa. But of late both he and his wife have begun to doubt whether any compromises will work. As the Afrikaners have become increasingly open to change, blacks generally have grown more militant, and have increasingly identified with the revolutionary positions of the radical leftist fronts in the north. In response, the Botha government has, therefore, steered a zigzag course, preaching the Pax Afrikaner while preparing for war; and in an atmosphere of pervasive menace. In the countryside, the pace of terrorism has been stepped up, and like thousands of other Afrikaners, Jaap and Eunice de Villiers have found themselves living in a spiritual wilderness. Surrounded by potential threats, the perpetual anxiety of their lives has inclined Eunice de Villiers toward mysticism and Jaap toward a stoic fatalism.

"I wonder sometimes how it will end," Eunice de Villiers said quietly as we drove together toward the Free State town of Bethlehem to watch her son Paul play a rugby match. "The last book of the Bible says a time will come when the East will overwhelm the West and reign over the world for three and a half years. It will be a time of false prophets in the East, a time of famine and plague, that will be followed by a time of fire when Christ will come again and the world will be destroyed. It is mad, perhaps, to think like this, but I wonder, as the world now stands, if that time isn't at hand and if Armageddon might not be here, in Africa. . . ."

Jaap de Villiers had restrained himself from religious speculations during most of our talks, but one evening, not long before we ended our visit with him, as we made our way back toward the "home-ranch" through a crimson light, he did put his feelings into words that seemed to summarize the Afrikaner tragedy.

"I think this must be God's country, truly," he said quietly, as we drove past fields rippling with blood-red sorghum, ready to harvest. "The Promised Land. And it is ours too. God gave it to us and we love it and will fight for it and die for it if we must. We have claimed it with our sweat and our blood. We will not just go away. And so, we will turn to Him, ask Him how to solve this puzzle, because it is His puzzle. The puzzle of this earth. But He means us to work for the answers. To keep our faith, to stand if we must against the forces of evil. There are Cubans and Russians in Angola and Mozambique and East Germans in the Transkei. Why? What is it they want here? To take from us what we have built up over the generations on the pretext of helping the black man? It is not the black man they care about. It is the gold. The diamonds. The minerals. The riches of the place. But our riches are these riches," he continued gesturing to the sweeping land whose contours are etched upon his heart, "This lovely land. This place. And we have been helping the black in good faith. And so we must go forward in good faith to whatever is there, waiting in the shadows. Then, whatever comes, we will know we have tried. Tried to be just. Tried to be fair. Because I *do* believe in my people. I *do* believe in my country. And I *do* believe in my God and with that I must go straight ahead. Yet, if it comes to a showdown and we find the whole might of the Communist world and the blacks who court favor with it ranged against us, I do not believe we Afrikaners can sustain ourselves indefinitely. And that is what is so painful," he added, his voice growing hoarse with emotion. "Because I do not know what to tell my children when they ask if a war comes what will become of us. . . . Yet I know that we *will* fight, even after all is lost, just as we did in the past. We will go to ground and fight from the land until the last man is gone. They shall not have this country of ours easily. . . ."

INDEX

247